365 Inspiring Verses
from the
New Testament

THE LORD IS MY Light

SHAUNA HUMPHREYS

Covenant Communications, Inc.

List of Abbreviations

CSB = *Children's Songbook*

DCBM = *Doctrinal Commentary on the Book of Mormon*

DNTC = *Doctrinal New Testament Commentary*

HC = *History of the Church*

TGBH = *Teachings of Gordon B. Hinckley*

TPJS = *Teachings of the Prophet Joseph Smith*

Acknowledgments

I express sincere appreciation to the staff at Covenant for their combined expertise, dedication, and support. And special thanks to my competent, compassionate, and patient editor, Samantha Millburn.

Published by Covenant Communications, Inc.
American Fork, Utah

Printed in China
First Printing: October 2014

20 19 18 17 16 15 14   10 9 8 7 6 5 4 3 2 1

ISBN 978-62108-805-9

Tell me the stories of Jesus I love to hear.
("Tell Me the Stories of Jesus," Children's Songbook, 57)

The New Testament of our Lord and Savior, Jesus Christ, tells us "the stories of Jesus": His miraculous birth; His mortal ministry, replete with breathtaking miracles, probing and thought-provoking parables, and eternally significant sermons; His infinite and intimate Atonement; and His glorious Resurrection. The sublime truths in these pages of scripture combine the Savior's eloquent and elegant words with the bold and beautiful testimonies of His beloved Apostles and disciples, who were privileged to enjoy His sacred companionship.

A beloved Primary song poignantly expresses our longing to experience the loving companionship of the Savior:

"I wish that his hands had been placed on my head,
That his arms had been thrown around me,
That I might have seen his kind look when he said,
'Let the little ones come unto me.'"
("I Think When I Read That Sweet Story," CSB, 56)

Throughout the New Testament, we will hear the Savior's voice tenderly entreating us—His little ones—to come unto Him. The sacred truths and testimonies contained therein will increase our desire to keep all these wondrous and magnificent "stories"—and ponder them in our hearts (see Luke 2:19).

May the Lord bless us with a desire to delight in this joyous, scriptural message of salvation through the merits and mercy of our Savior, Jesus Christ, and grow in our love for and testimony of God's Only Begotten Son, "Beloved and Chosen from the beginning" (Moses 4:2), whose work and glory is "to bring to pass [our] immortality and eternal life" (Moses 1:39).

JST 1 Jn. 1:1

Brethren, this is the testimony which we give of that which was from the beginning, which we have heard, which we have seen with our eyes, which we have looked upon, and our hands have handled, of the Word of life.

It all started, as do all of the very best stories, in the beginning—with a premortal Christ. Holy writ testifies that Jesus Christ stood gloriously by the Father's side before the world's creation. We read in the Pearl of Great Price, "But, behold, my Beloved Son . . . was my Beloved and Chosen from the beginning" (Moses 4:2). To the proud Jewish hierarchy who touted their lineal connection to Abraham, the Lord pointed out His premortal supremacy over that venerable patriarch: "Verily, verily, I say unto you, Before Abraham was, I am" (John 8:58). And in a dramatic revelation to the brother of Jared, the Savior reaffirmed His premortal status: "Behold, I am he who was prepared from the foundation of the world to redeem my people" (Ether 3:14).

"The testimony of scriptures written on both hemispheres, that of records both ancient and modern, the inspired utterances of prophets and apostles, and the words of the Lord Himself, are of one voice in proclaiming the preexistence of the Christ and His ordination as the chosen Savior and Redeemer of mankind—in the beginning, yea, even before the foundation of the world" (James E. Talmage, *Jesus the Christ* [Salt Lake City: Deseret Book, 1983], 13).

John 3:16

For God so loved the world, that he gave his only begotten Son, that whosoever believeth in him should not perish, but have everlasting life.

There is no greater evidence of God's love for His children than the gift of His Son to the world—the gift destined to bless everyone who has lived, who now lives, or who will ever live on this earth, because every spirit child of our Heavenly Father is a beloved child of God.

The babe born of Mary "was begotten of Elohim, the Eternal Father. . . . In His nature would be combined the powers of Godhood with the capacity and possibilities of mortality. . . . The Child Jesus was to inherit the physical, mental, and spiritual traits, tendencies, and powers that characterized His parents—one immortal and glorified—God, the other human—woman" (*Jesus the Christ*, 77). He came into the world "that through him all might be saved whom the Father had put into his power and made by him" (D&C 76:42).

Our willingness to receive and accept our Father's gift is signified by our faith in the Lord Jesus Christ—faith that motivates obedience to the principles of His gospel. The Savior entreats us to fully receive His gift: "If thou wilt do good, yea, and hold out faithful to the end, thou shalt be saved in the kingdom of God, which is the greatest of all the gifts of God; for there is no gift greater than the gift of salvation" (D&C 6:13).

Luke 1:28, 30–31

And the angel came in unto her, and said, Hail, thou that art highly favoured, the Lord is with thee: blessed art thou among women. . . . Fear not, Mary: for thou hast found favour with God. And, behold, thou shalt conceive . . . and bring forth a son, and shalt call his name JESUS.

From the Gospel of Luke, we receive our first picture of the magnificence of Mary, a noble daughter of God, the mother of our Savior, Jesus Christ. Long before the reality of her mortal life, Mary was the centerpiece of several prophetic visions. Nephi beheld her as a beautiful virgin: "And I beheld . . . a virgin, and she was exceedingly fair and white. . . . And I . . . beheld the virgin again, bearing a child in her arms" (1 Ne. 11:13, 20). The prophet Isaiah saw her in vision as well and testified of this beloved spirit daughter of heavenly parents (see Isa. 7:14).

Mary was also a beloved daughter of earthly parents and was betrothed to her dear Joseph, and it was during this period of betrothal that the angel Gabriel appeared to Mary. It is a tribute to her righteousness and resilience that fear did not overwhelm her. Indeed, she drew courage from the angel's reassuring words, "fear not," and upon learning that she was to be the mother of the Son of God, she simply and humbly replied, "Behold the handmaid of the Lord; be it unto me according to thy word" (Luke 1:30, 38). Truly, Mary is a remarkable and sacred example of unwavering faith, gracious humility, and steadfast obedience.

Luke 1:42, 45

*Blessed art thou among women, and blessed is the fruit of thy womb. . . .
And blessed is she that believed: for there shall be a performance of
those things which were told her from the Lord.*

These inspired words of salutation by Elisabeth, Mary's cousin, are a fitting tribute to the mother of the Son of God. And Mary's response is one of the greatest psalms of praise of all time. In true Israelite tradition, Mary demonstrates her knowledge of the sacred history of her people and pays high homage to God the Father, the Father of her Son: "My soul doth magnify the Lord, And my spirit hath rejoiced in God my Saviour. For he hath regarded the low estate of his handmaiden: for, behold, from henceforth all generations shall call me blessed. For he that is mighty hath done to me great things; and holy *is* his name" (Luke 1:46–49; see vv. 46–55 for full text).

The words of Elder Bruce R. McConkie provide a lovely tribute to this faithful, foreordained mother of the Son of God: "There is only one Mary, even as there is only one Christ. . . . Her mission was to bring the Son of God into the world . . . hers was a blessed privilege, being mortal, to bring into the world Him by whom immortality should come. And blessed is she forever!" (*The Promised Messiah* [Salt Lake City: Deseret Book, 1978], 466).

Luke 2:7, 18–19

And she brought forth her firstborn son. . . . And all they that heard it wondered at those things which were told them by the shepherds. But Mary kept all these things, and pondered them in her heart.

The wondrous message inherent in these verses is tender, powerful, and joyful. The circumstances of the Savior's birth are symbolic of His earthly ministry. He came as King of Kings; however, His mission and message were for all mankind, regardless of station or stature. How fitting, then, that His birth was first heralded by a heavenly host of angels singing praises to Him and to His Heavenly Father and next by a group of lowly shepherds who heard that glorious hymn, heeded the heavenly proclamation, and hastened to find the wondrous babe in a familiar setting. It was a joyous discovery they could hardly wait to share with anyone who would listen.

To a young, expectant mother far from home and far from the tender ministrations of her mother, this advent might have seemed overwhelming. Yet, months earlier, she demonstrated her confidence in God, evident in her response to the angel Gabriel. Mary's faith and obedience, coupled with the loving, protective care demonstrated by Joseph and reinforced by the humble adoration of the shepherds, made this a sacred experience never to be forgotten. Indeed, her heart was filled to overflowing with the miracle of this great blessing and all that subsequently transpired. It is no wonder that this glorious experience became so dear to this mother's heart.

Luke 2:15, 17

As the angels were gone away . . . the shepherds said one to another, Let us now go even unto Bethlehem, and see this thing which is come to pass. . . . And when they had seen it, they made known abroad the saying which was told them concerning this child.

"These were not ordinary shepherds nor ordinary flocks. The sheep . . . were destined for sacrifice on the great altar in the Lord's House, in similitude of the eternal sacrifice of Him who that wondrous night lay in a stable, perhaps among sheep of lesser destiny. And the shepherds . . . surely they were in spiritual stature like Simeon and Anna and Zacharias and Elisabeth and Joseph and the growing group of believing souls who were coming to know, by revelation, that the Lord's Christ was now on earth" (Bruce R. McConkie, *The Mortal Messiah*, 4 vols. [1979–81], 1:347).

The magnificent message the angel delivered was followed by a heavenly chorus sung by multitudes of a heavenly host. What was the message of their music? A glorious declaration of praise to God, who had sent His Son to bring peace on earth and goodwill to all men.

There was no debate, discussion, or equivocation; their eager footsteps took them in haste to the manger, and then they "commence[d] the infinitely great and eternally important work of taking the 'good tidings of great joy . . . to all people' . . . to their neighbors and friends, and even to strangers!" (Ibid., 348).

Luke 2:19

But Mary kept all these things, and pondered them in her heart.

This is an oft-repeated phrase in the Gospels regarding the Savior's mother and her feelings for her Son—the Son of God. She treasured these sacred events and miracles as events never to be forgotten. But more importantly, these were personal, testimony-building revelations.

As we ponder spiritual matters, we will also be blessed with personal revelation and a sure testimony of Jesus Christ. It has been said that pondering is the seedbed for personal revelation, and countless scriptural examples bear this out. Consider Nephi, who received personal knowledge of the Savior as he pondered his father's teachings in his heart, or the young Joseph Smith, who pondered on a scriptural passage until it entered into every feeling of his heart.

As children of God, we are all entitled to expanded spiritual understanding and personal confirmation of spiritual truths; however, pondering requires an investment of time and effort. A preoccupation with the mundane prevents pondering on matters of spiritual relevance. President Ezra Taft Benson taught us that we "must take time to meditate, to sweep the cobwebs from [our] mind[s] so that we may get a more firm grip on the truth," letting it take precedence over the "worries and cares of the world" (*The Teachings of Ezra Taft Benson*, [Salt Lake City: Bookcraft, 1988], 390).

Luke 2:34, 36–38

And Simeon blessed them, and said unto Mary his mother, Behold, this child is set for the fall and rising again of many in Israel. . . . And there was one Anna, a prophetess . . . And she . . . gave thanks likewise unto the Lord, and spake of him to all them that looked for redemption in Jerusalem.

Joseph and Mary presented their tiny infant, the mortal Messiah, in the temple at Jerusalem, as was the custom according to the Mosaic law. Also according to the law, they brought with them a temple offering of a pair of turtledoves or two pigeons.

Living in Jerusalem at this time was a righteous and devout elderly man named Simeon, who had been promised through inspiration by the Holy Ghost that before he died, he would see the mortal Christ. Through inspiration, Simeon attended the temple on the day when Jesus was presented, and he immediately recognized the promised Messiah. By the spirit of prophecy, Simeon testified of both the Child's mission and its attendant sorrow for Mary.

A second witness on this occasion was "a godly woman of great age [who] . . . recognized her Redeemer, and testified of Him. . . . Both Joseph and Mary marveled at the things which were spoken of the Child; seemingly they were not yet able to comprehend the majesty of Him who had come to them through so miraculous a conception and so marvelous a birth" (*Jesus the Christ*, 92).

Matt. 2:1, 11

Now when Jesus was born in Bethlehem of Judæa in the days of Herod the king, behold, there came wise men from the east. . . . And when they were come into the house, they saw the young child with Mary his mother, and fell down, and worshipped him.

"Much has been written, beyond all possible warrant of scriptural authority, concerning the visit of the magi, or wise men, who thus sought and found the infant Christ. . . . [W]e are left without information as to their country, nation, or tribal relationship; we are not even told how many there were . . . they are left unnamed in the scriptures . . . and may have numbered but two or many" (*Jesus the Christ*, 93–94).

"As to the men themselves, one thing is clear. They had prophetic insight. . . . The probability is they were themselves Jews who lived . . . in one of the nations to the East. It was the Jews . . . who were waiting with anxious expectation for the coming of a King. . . . [H]is first witnesses were to come from . . . the house of Israel, not from the Gentile nations, not from the nations . . . who knew not God and who cared nothing for the spirit of prophecy and revelation found among the Lord's people" (*The Mortal Messiah*, 1:358).

Guided by the Spirit, "they returned to their homeland, still guided from beyond the veil and basking in the light of Him in whose presence they had knelt" (Ibid., 361).

Luke 2:40, 52

And the child grew, and waxed strong in spirit, filled with wisdom: and the grace of God was upon him. . . . And Jesus increased in wisdom and stature, and in favour with God and man.

Although the scriptural accounts of Jesus's boyhood and growth to manhood are brief, there is a wealth of information and insight in these few words. We know He experienced mortality just as others do. He was born with the veil of forgetfulness over His mind—thus He *increased* in wisdom. John, His beloved Apostle, testifies of this: "And he received not of the fulness at first, but continued from grace to grace, until he received a fulness; And thus he was called the Son of God, because he received not of the fulness at the first" (D&C 93:13–14).

The Joseph Smith Translation of Matthew provides added insight regarding the development and expansion of Jesus's mind and spirit: "And . . . he spake not as other men, neither could he be taught; for he needed not that any man should teach him" (JST Matt. 3:25). Clearly, this does not mean Jesus ignored or disrespected the tutoring in the law and scriptures that He would have received just like any other Jewish boy. Rather, it means that in addition to those earthly educational observances, He was taught from on high and received additional wisdom and light from the Holy Ghost.

As Jesus grew in favor with God and man, He brought opportunity to the downtrodden, freedom to the oppressed, light to those in darkness, forgiveness to the repentant, and hope to those in despair.

Luke 2:46, 48

After three days they found him in the temple, sitting in the midst of the doctors, both hearing them, and asking them questions. . . . and his mother said unto him, Son, why hast thou thus dealt with us?

Study, prayer, and meditation made Jesus spiritually remarkable at an early age. This is evidenced at the Feast of the Passover, which Jesus attended with Mary and Joseph when He was twelve years old, this being when Jewish boys "came of age" and were expected to be present at the temple ceremonies that were an integral part of the feast. Not only did Jesus ask questions of the learned doctors, but He also gave astonishing answers to their questions (see Luke 2:47). It is here that we also note Jesus's comprehension of His divine sonship as He reminds His mother that He "must be about . . . [His] Father's business" (Luke 2:49), meaning His Heavenly Father's business. His words are a gentle but firm reminder to Mary of His paternity: that His literal Father was not Joseph of Nazareth but the Almighty God.

Nevertheless, Jesus showed deference and obedience to parental authority: "And he went down with them, and came to Nazareth, and was subject unto them: but his mother kept all these sayings in her heart" (Luke 2:51). "What marvelous and sacred secrets were treasured in that mother's heart; and what new surprises and grave problems were added day after day in the manifestations of unfolding wisdom displayed by her more than mortal Son!" (*Jesus the Christ*, 109).

Matt. 3:13–15 (JST Matt. 3:43–44)

*Then cometh Jesus . . . unto John, to be baptized . . . John forbad him, saying,
I have need to be baptized of thee . . . Jesus answering said unto him, Suffer
me to be baptized of thee, for thus it becometh us to fulfill all righteousness.*

John the Baptist preached a bold and unequivocal message: faith in the Lord Jesus Christ, of whom he was the foreordained forerunner; repentance; baptism by immersion; and the promise of baptism by fire or the Holy Ghost by One who was mightier than he (see Matt. 3:11). Regarding this devoted and righteous champion of the Son of God, Jesus would later proclaim, "Among those that are born of women there is not a greater prophet than John the Baptist" (Luke 7:28).

We may wonder why the Son of God would desire or need to be baptized. "He, being holy, had no need for the remission of sins, no need to come forth in a newness of life, no need to become clean so as to be sanctified . . . Jesus was baptized as a token of humility, *and in his baptism he made a covenant with his Father to love and serve him . . . He was baptized in order to gain salvation in the celestial kingdom of God, thereby setting the perfect example for all men*" (Bruce R. McConkie, *A New Witness for the Articles of Faith* [Salt Lake City: Deseret Book, 1985], 247–248; emphasis added).

"And now, if the Lamb of God, he being holy, should have need to be baptized by water, to fulfill all righteousness, O then, how much more need have we, being unholy, to be baptized, yea, even by water!" (2 Ne. 31:5).

Matt. 3:16–17

And Jesus, when he was baptized, went up straightway out of the water: and, lo, the heavens were opened unto him, and he saw the Spirit of God descending like a dove . . . And lo a voice from heaven, saying, This is my beloved Son, in whom I am well pleased.

This was a solemn and spiritually splendid occasion for both John the Baptist and the Savior as the Father testified of His relationship to Jesus and expressed His deep and divine approval of His Only Begotten Son. Additionally, "the descent of the Holy Ghost upon the baptized Jesus" was a sign that "had been indicated to John as the foreappointed means by which the Messiah should be made known to him" (*Jesus the Christ*, 119).

In this covenant, as in all things spiritual, the Savior "marked the path and led the way" ("How Great the Wisdom and the Love," *Hymns*, no. 195), granting all mankind the privilege of receiving the Holy Ghost—a gift freely given to all who enter the waters of baptism. "The gift of the Holy Ghost is the greatest of all the gifts of God in this life" (*Discourses of Wilford Woodruff*, sel. G. Homer Durham [Salt Lake City: Bookcraft, 1946], 5). By the power of the Holy Ghost we are able to confess that Jesus is the Christ (see Moro. 7:44). We are also promised that "if [we] will enter in by the way, and receive the Holy Ghost, it will show unto [us] all things what [we] should do" (2 Ne. 32:5). These are magnificent promises and blessings inherent with receiving the gift of the Holy Ghost.

JST Matt. 4:1–2

Then was Jesus led up of the Spirit into the wilderness to be with God. And when he had fasted forty days and forty nights, and had communed with God, he was afterwards an hungered, and was left to be tempted of the devil.

As He was about to formally begin His mortal ministry, Jesus sought the companionship and private tutoring of His Father far away from the distractions of everyday life. It was a time of intense meditation and sacred communion and communication, a time of final preparation for a mission of mercy and redemption that would pave the way for the potential salvation of the souls of all of God's children.

As Jesus returned from His lengthy sojourn in the wilderness, Lucifer considered Him fair game and preyed on what he considered the Savior's vulnerabilities, including acute hunger and thirst following an arduous fast. Satan taunted Jesus, prefacing the first of his temptations with the words, "If thou be the Son of God," a blasphemous insult, considering the Father's recent and powerful witness of Christ's paternity on the occasion of His baptism. And then, heaping insult upon insult, Satan dared the Savior to use His God-given powers for personal gratification by turning stones into bread.

The Savior's firm rebuff reminds us that while our physical needs are often urgent, our spiritual needs are equally compelling, and it is the word of God that provides the lasting nourishment our hungering and thirsting spirits so desperately need (see Matt. 4:4).

JST Matt. 4:5–6

Then Jesus was taken up into the holy city, and the Spirit setteth him on the pinnacle of the temple. Then the devil came unto him and said, If thou be the Son of God, cast thyself down: for it is written, He shall give his angels charge concerning thee: and in their hands they shall bear thee up.

Once again, we witness the devil's effrontery as he appeals to the Savior's mortal side with the same insulting insinuations of the word *if*. Being mortal, Jesus was subject to temptation as are the rest of us. He "was in all points tempted like as *we are*, *yet* without sin" (Heb. 4:15). Being Deity, He had no *desire* to sin and was able to see through Satan's insidious appeal to a quick claim to fame that would thrust Him immediately into the headlines of the time. His godly powers would certainly have enabled Him to do just that, but He had no intention of exploiting His Father's love or of misusing the time and powers of angels. Nor was He interested in a flashy shortcut that would appeal to men's shallow cravings for a flash-in-the-pan superhero rather than an eternal role model.

While Satan had cleverly couched this temptation in a counterfeit context of scripture, the Savior's comeback was a wise and worthy appeal to the sacred written word: "It is written again, Thou shalt not tempt the Lord thy God" (Matt. 4:7). He was not interested in personal worldly acclaim. He had already made it clear that His "work and [his] glory [was] to bring to pass the immortality and eternal life of man" (Moses 1:39).

JST Matt. 4:8–9

Jesus was in the Spirit, and it taketh him up into an exceeding high mountain, and sheweth him all the kingdoms of the world, and the glory of them; And the devil came unto him again, and said, All these things will I give thee, if thou wilt fall down and worship me.

In a third temptation, Satan sought to buy off the Savior's soul with the promise of vast wealth, including every kingdom in the world, when, in actuality, the devil owned not a single square inch of real estate: "The effrontery . . . was of itself diabolical. . . . Satan, an unembodied spirit . . . seeking to tempt the Being through whom the world was created by promising Him part of what was wholly His . . . asked the embodied Jehovah to worship him" (*Jesus the Christ*, 124–25), an unembodied outcast banished forever from the realms of His Father's glory. It was an offer as empty as the brightly wrapped boxes under artificial Christmas trees in department stores.

In a similar situation, when Satan challenged Moses to worship him, "Moses looked upon Satan and said: . . . "I am a son of God, in the similitude of His Only Begotten; and where is thy glory, that I should worship thee?" (Moses 1:12–13). Likewise, the Savior's response to Satan's counterfeit offer is simply magnificent and magnificently simple: "Get thee hence, Satan: for it is written, Thou shalt worship the Lord thy God, and him only shalt thou serve" (Matt. 4:10)— the supreme reminder of His divine and undivided loyalty.

JST Matt. 4:18–19

And Jesus, walking by the sea of Galilee, saw . . . Simon called Peter, and Andrew his brother, casting a net . . . And he saith unto them, I am he of whom it is written by the prophets; follow me, and I will make you fishers of men.

In this inspiring call to follow the Savior and embark in His service, the Lord introduces Himself, making sure those humble fishermen are unmistakably aware of who He is—the Son of God, the perfect Exemplar with the perfect plan for saving the souls of His Father's children.

The Savior was a master of metaphor, and His use of it on this occasion was both remarkable and spiritually meaningful. In a parallel account of the Savior's call to these disciples, who would later be numbered among His Apostles, Luke records that when the Savior instructed Peter and his fellow fishermen to let down their nets one more time following an unsuccessful night of fishing, they were astonished when their nets filled to capacity and beyond. Jesus then said, "From henceforth thou shalt catch men" (Luke 5:10) and promised that their "catch" would be no less spectacular.

The Savior knew how important it was for these men to catch fish but was symbolically offering them an even greater vocation. Elder James E. Talmage explains it beautifully: "Theretofore they had caught fish, and the fate of the fish was death; thereafter they were to draw men—to a life eternal" (*Jesus the Christ*, 186). "And they straightway left *their* nets, and followed him" (Matt. 4:20), thus beginning their sacred labor for the souls of men.

JST Matt. 4:19

And he saith unto them, I am he of whom it is written by the prophets; follow me.

The Savior graciously invites us to become His followers, and it is through faithful adherence to gospel principles that we learn *how* to follow Him. Alma lists the qualities that define disciples of Christ: "And now I would that ye should be humble . . . submissive and gentle . . . full of patience and long-suffering . . . temperate . . . diligent in keeping the commandments of God at all times; asking for whatsoever things ye stand in need, both spiritual and temporal; always returning thanks unto God for whatsoever things ye do receive" (Alma 7:23).

True discipleship means sacrificing an old way of life for a new to accept the ultimate atoning sacrifice of our Savior. It is an exercise in obedience and personal commitment. Sacrifice in obedience requires inner changes that enable us to honestly perform the outward gestures of discipleship, to be "*doers* of the word, and not *hearers* only" (James 1:22; emphasis added).

President Dieter F. Uchtdorf reminds us that discipleship is a process—a refining and purifying process. It is an inviting pilgrimage of personal progress that we can begin here and now, without any prerequisites. It is our privilege to become Christ's disciples (see "The Way of the Disciple," *Ensign*, May 2009, 75–77).

Matt. 5:1–2

And seeing the multitudes, he went up into a mountain: and when he was set, his disciples came unto him: And he opened his mouth, and taught them.

The Savior's teachings often seemed to be in direct conflict with the law of Moses, to which the scribes and Pharisees adhered with fanatic devotion. They had long since lost a compassionate connection to their fellowmen, being more obsessed with the letter than the spirit of the law. For many who followed the Savior, however, His words offered a breath of hope and renewal in a time of stagnant spirituality.

The Sermon on the Mount is rich in specific blessings that come from right living and in the eternal happiness that attends the efforts of those who choose to live the law of love, which is the basis of the perfect gospel the Son of God proclaimed. To present this discourse, the Savior ascended a mountain, which would allow Him to address a sizable audience; it may also have been symbolic of the higher law He was about to share.

The Beatitudes might well be called the Savior's autobiography. Every attribute He espouses in this masterful sermon is embodied in His own personality and life, and each is an invitation to align our lives with Him and the saving principles of His gospel.

Matt. 5:3 (see also 3 Ne. 12:3)

Blessed are the poor in spirit (who come unto me): for theirs is the kingdom of heaven.

"Those who are poor in spirit—who are broken in spirit, sad of spirit or depressed, or those who are so sin-laden and thereby spiritually bankrupt—cannot be saved on their own. The words 'who come unto me' . . . complete the intended message. There is no virtue in being broken or in being a spiritual beggar, except to the degree that we come unto the Lord. That is, whenever we look to the Lord, thereby acknowledging our inability to gain happiness and the abundant life without his saving grace, we are blessed. The supernal invitation is forever the same: 'Yea, come unto Christ, and be perfected in him'" (Joseph Fielding McConkie and others, *Doctrinal Commentary on the Book of Mormon*, Vol. 4 [Salt Lake City: Bookcraft, 1992], 65; see also Moro. 10:32).

If we are truly poor in spirit, we *desire* to draw near to Christ, receive His gospel, repent of our sins, enter the waters of baptism, and enjoy the companionship of the Holy Ghost, thereby becoming heirs to His celestial kingdom.

"Come unto Jesus, ye heavy laden, / Careworn and fainting, by sin oppressed. / He'll safely guide you unto that haven / Where all who trust him may rest" ("Come unto Jesus," *Hymns*, no. 117).

Matt. 5:4

Blessed are they that mourn: for they shall be comforted.

Mourning wears a variety of cloaks. Some type of personal loss, such as death, divorce, or unemployment, may cause our sorrow. We may also sorrow because of personal sins and shortcomings we are struggling to overcome, which weigh heavily on our spirits.

We are blessed by the comfort and empathy of family and friends who reach out to us in our times of need, when our hearts and spirits seem about to break. The most blessed and complete source of comfort, however, is the Savior. The Savior's healing power is infinite and complete, and His compassion for those who suffer or sorrow in any way is incomparable.

We gratefully anticipate the time when there will be no more tears, pain, sorrow, or death. But in the meantime—here and now when we struggle to cope and find comfort—we need only to reach out to our Savior in faith, and we will figuratively feel His comforting hand wiping away our tears. As we kneel in humble petition for comfort, as we earnestly study His pleasing word, and as we cry out to Him, our souls can be "pained no more" (Mosiah 27:29). We can know that "with his stripes we are healed" (Isa. 53:5).

Matt. 5:6 (see also 3 Ne. 12:6)

Blessed are they who do hunger and thirst after righteousness: for they shall be filled (with the Holy Ghost).

We have all experienced hunger and thirst in varying degrees, and we are willing to put forth whatever effort or expense might be necessary to acquire or prepare a pleasing meal so our bodies will feel satisfied and replete.

To hunger and thirst after righteousness is to experience that same intense desire for *spiritual* food, and there is never a shortage when it comes to spiritual nutrition. However, a casual approach to the spiritual nutrients of prayer, scripture study, and service will net less than the desired reward the Savior promised: that we can be filled with the Holy Ghost. This is a twofold blessing. He heals and cleanses our spirits, thus making room for our spirits to be filled with light and truth, the special attributes of this third member of the Godhead. And He bears witness to our spirits that Jesus is the Christ and that the saving ordinances of His gospel are checkpoints in our progression toward salvation.

The Prophet Joseph Smith tells us that the ultimate reward for "hungering and thirsting after righteousness" is exaltation (*Teachings of the Prophet Joseph Smith* [Salt Lake City: Deseret Book, 1976], 150). Thus, the Beatitudes point us toward a heavenly reward.

Matt. 5:7

Blessed are the merciful: for they shall obtain mercy.

Forgiveness is inextricably intertwined with mercy. The whole world has need of these two cleansing and refreshing attributes, and while we cannot individually hope to solve the world's problems, we can make a start—one home, one neighborhood, and one place of employment at a time. We can refuse to let molehills become mountains of misunderstanding between us and those we care about. We can instead develop and exercise the quality of mercy that leads to unconditional forgiveness.

It is our obligation to show mercy through forgiveness so that "old grievances [will be] forgiven and forgotten," enemies will become friends again, skeletons will be buried, and "the closet of dry bones [will be] locked and the key . . . thrown away" (Spencer W. Kimball, *The Miracle of Forgiveness* [Salt Lake City: Bookcraft, 1969], 282).

Shakespeare's Portia in *The Merchant of Venice* describes it beautifully:

The quality of mercy is not strain'd,
It droppeth as the gentle rain from heaven
Upon the place beneath: it is twice bless'd;
It blesseth him that gives and him that takes: . . .
It is an attribute of God himself.
(IV, i)

Matt. 5:8

Blessed are the pure in heart: for they shall see God.

The Lord uses the heart as the criteria by which He will judge us. Those who are pure in heart have a firm commitment to and trust in God. Simply stated, the pure in heart are obedient.

Our lives are filled with encounters of the most sacred kind, and as we become ever more pure in heart (obedient), we *see* God as He enriches our lives in countless ways. We *see* Him as He comforts and protects us. We *see* Him when He is mindful of our needs and requests, whether they be as mundane as helping us find our lost keys or as urgent as finding a lost child (in every sense of the word *lost*). We *see* Him when He soothes our wounded hearts and lifts our discouraged spirits. He manifests Himself to us through the pages of scripture, the teachings of living prophets, the thoughtful charity of others, and the ministrations of the Holy Ghost.

Our Redeemer's love continually purifies our hearts. His outstretched hands, which bear the scars of His Crucifixion, are visible reminders that He is the ultimate purifying agent. It is through His Atonement—and *only* through His Atonement—that we will receive the cherished eternal blessing of seeing God face-to-face.

Matt. 5:9

Blessed are the peacemakers: for they shall be called the children of God.

Our Savior is the founder of peace because He brought into the world and preached a brand of peace that eluded the understanding of many who heard His message. "For O how beautiful upon the mountains are the feet of . . . the founder of peace, yea, even the Lord, who has redeemed his people; . . . who has granted salvation unto his people" (Mosiah 15:18).

"In the full sense, only those who believe and spread the fullness of the gospel are peacemakers within the perfect meaning of this Beatitude" (Bruce R. McConkie, *Doctrinal New Testament Commentary*, Vol. I [Salt Lake City: Deseret Book, 1972], 216). Isaiah understood this perfectly when he said, "How beautiful upon the mountains are the feet of him that bringeth good tidings, that publisheth peace . . . that publisheth salvation" (Isa. 52:7). There are no greater tidings than the message of the gospel of Jesus Christ and no greater privilege than being His messengers.

Like Nephi of old, our mandate is to talk of Christ, rejoice in Christ, and prophesy of Christ so that our families and friends "may know to what source they may look for a remission of their sins" (2 Ne. 25:26) because that is the ultimate key to becoming heirs of God and joint-heirs with Christ.

Matt. 5:13

Ye are the salt of the earth: but if the salt have lost his savour, wherewith shall it be salted? it is thenceforth good for nothing, but to be cast out, and to be trodden under foot of men.

Salt is a staple seasoning, purifier, and preservative that adds flavor, purity, and longevity to many of the foods we eat. Sometimes the absence of salt in our food is simply an oversight, and sometimes it is a deliberate omission. In both instances, however, we quickly and easily notice its absence when we bite into a bland and flavorless disappointment instead of the tasty morsel we had anticipated.

In referring to His Saints as salt, the Savior graciously invites us to participate with Him in the work of saving souls—purifying them by inviting them to partake of the rich and flavorful and pure message of the gospel of Jesus Christ, thereby preserving their status as beloved children of our Heavenly Father.

Our failure to invite others carries with it significant eternal consequences whereby we simply become spiritual underachievers, whose lukewarm efforts fall far short of the Savior's expectations. On the other hand, "when men are called unto mine everlasting gospel, and covenant with an everlasting covenant, they are accounted as the salt of the earth and the savor of men" (D&C 101:39)—a title and status well worth claiming.

Matt. 5:16

Let your light so shine before men, that they may see your good works, and glorify your Father which is in heaven.

The Savior exhorts us to wholeheartedly and enthusiastically dedicate ourselves to good causes. Moroni gives us the criterion for recognizing that which is good: "For every thing which inviteth to do good, and to persuade to believe in Christ, is sent forth by the power and gift of Christ; wherefore ye may know with a perfect knowledge it is of God" (Moro. 7:16).

The Savior also makes it clear that our good works should be acts born out of a loving desire to serve and not from compulsion. Each of us can make a difference in reflecting our love for the Savior and draw others nearer to Him by doing our home or visiting teaching and truly keeping the welfare of those families uppermost in our hearts and minds. We also make a difference by reaching out to a neighbor who has a heavy heart, daring to share the gospel with a friend, attending the temple as often as possible (and maybe even when it seems impossible), and performing random and quiet acts of kindness that spring spontaneously from our hearts.

Our opportunities for service are numerous, and the Savior's response is breathtaking: "Inasmuch as ye have done *it* unto one of the least of these my brethren, ye have done *it* unto me" (Matt. 25:40).

Matt. 5:22

But I say unto you, That whosoever is angry with his brother without a cause shall be in danger of the judgment.

When we are ill-used, it is unfortunately a natural—might we say *a knee-jerk*—reaction to retaliate in anger, which may take the form of hot and hateful words. It may even escalate into physical actions that inflict harm on another person. But heated words and hurtful actions can only result in regrets and spiritual injuries.

As always, we look to the Savior's life for the perfect example of anger management. He was reviled, slandered, falsely accused, taunted, ignored, abused, kissed by a traitorous Apostle, spit upon, cruelly beaten, humiliated by a torturous crown of thorns, and put to an ignominious death, in full sight of a jeering crowd, by indifferent Roman soldiers. At any of those times and in any of those situations, He could have reacted in kind, using His God-given powers to extract justice for Himself; He could have allowed His close friends and Apostles to defend Him, and He could have even summoned legions of angels to His defense. But He showed divine and dignified restraint. As our hymn says, "Once all things He meekly bore" ("Jesus, Once of Humble Birth," *Hymns*, no. 196).

"Letting off steam always produces more heat than light" (*The Neal A. Maxwell Quote Book* [Salt Lake City: Bookcraft, 1997], 13). Jesus Christ is the light of the world; His is the example we desire to emulate as we douse the fires of anger.

Matt. 5: 23–24

Therefore if thou bring thy gift to the altar, and there rememberest that thy brother hath ought against thee; Leave there thy gift before the altar, and go thy way; first be reconciled to thy brother, and then come and offer thy gift.

The Lord cautions us that the spirit of contention is "of the devil, who is the father of contention, and he stirreth up the hearts of men to contend with anger, one with another" (3 Ne. 11:29). And Satan doesn't particularly care what the source of our contention is; it can be something as small and petty as the way a person dresses or as deep as doctrinal disputes.

Contention results in feelings that impede the spiritual progress of both the instigator and the target of barbed remarks and actions. We are sometimes lulled into thinking that as long as what we say stays away from the other person, there is no harm. The Lord has a different opinion about this: "And see that there is no iniquity *in the church*, neither hardness with each other, neither lying, backbiting, nor evil speaking" (D&C 20:54; emphasis added). He is addressing His remarks squarely to members of the Church.

Unchecked, contention can become so spiritually corrosive that it crowds out the Spirit of the Lord and cankers our souls. It is good to remember that the Lord created us with two cheeks so that we can always turn one or the other.

JST Matt. 5:33–34

And now this I speak, a parable concerning your sins; wherefore, cast them from you, that ye may not be hewn down and cast into the fire.

When we discover a frayed seam or an unsightly rip in a piece of clothing we are fond of wearing, our immediate reaction is not to throw it away, thinking it has no further value. Instead, we do our best to repair it, often enlisting the aid of someone with the expertise to make it look and feel as good as new.

Likewise, when some part of our home falls into disrepair, we don't simply torch the place or bring in the wrecking ball. Instead, we carefully assess what might be needed and go to work using all the proper materials and resources to fix it.

The same principle applies to spiritual repairs. We don't give up on ourselves—and neither does the Savior. Instead, we roll up our sleeves and delve conscientiously into the renovative process of repentance, all the while knowing that our efforts require the expertise of our only reliable resource, our Savior Jesus Christ. "The purging out of sin would be impossible but for the total repentance of the individual and the kind mercy of the Lord Jesus Christ in his atoning sacrifice. Only by these means can [we] . . . be healed . . . and still be eligible for the glories of eternity" (*The Miracle of Forgiveness*, 339).

Matt. 5:44

Love your enemies, bless them that curse you, do good to them that hate you, and pray for them which despitefully use you.

The Savior's love set Him apart and endeared Him to those who had eyes to really see Him. Those who would not see and hear the Son of God denied themselves the blessing of basking in the warmth of His gracious love.

Like the Savior's, our circle of love should include those who are not necessarily easy to love, those who might not even appreciate our love. This application of the Lord's law of love sets a new standard, as it goes beyond what we should not do (bear grudges, avenge wrongs, hate our enemies) and suggests that love is a catalyst for positive actions. We should remember that love given is never wasted.

Edwin Markham penned these insightful words:

He drew a circle that shut me out—

Heretic, rebel, a thing to flout.

But Love and I had the wit to win:

We drew a circle that took him in! (Sarah Anne Stuart, *A Treasury of Poems: A Collection of the World's Most Famous and Familiar Verse* [New York: Galahad Books, 1996], 32).

Gratefully we acknowledge that the Savior's circle of love takes us in—no matter what. Can the circle of our love do anything less?

"Without love of God and love of neighbor there is little else to commend the gospel to us as a way of life" (*Teachings of Gordon B. Hinckley* [Salt Lake City: Deseret Book, 1997], 317).

JST Matt. 5:48

Ye are therefore commanded to be perfect, even as your Father which is in heaven is perfect.

Our loving Heavenly Father and Savior never ask us to do anything unless They know we are perfectly capable of doing it. The Lord, in His omniscience and perfect patience, knows that we achieve our goal of perfection one obedient step at a time and only through His merits, mercy, and grace. Just like any other work of art, we do not become perfect (whole, finished, or complete) without a great deal of polishing, touching up, or even starting over.

"Our perfect Father does not expect us to be perfect children yet. He had only one such Child. Meanwhile, therefore, sometimes with smudges on our cheeks, dirt on our hands, and shoes untied . . . we present God with a dandelion—as if it were an orchid or rose! If for now the dandelion is the best we have to offer, He receives it, knowing what we may later place on the altar" (*The Neal A. Maxwell Quote Book*, 243).

It is good to remember the Savior's divine admonition: "The things which are impossible with men are possible with God" (Luke 18:27). His saving grace and infinite Atonement, coupled with our very best efforts, enable Him to pick us up, dust us off, and point us toward our potential for perfection.

Matt. 6:9

After this manner therefore pray ye: Our Father which art in heaven, Hallowed be thy name.

The Savior gave us the perfect pattern for prayer in what we call the Lord's Prayer. It teaches us that we should express reverence and gratitude to our Heavenly Father, pray for our temporal and spiritual needs, pray for forgiveness and the ability to forgive others, and pray in the name of Jesus Christ, who is our Advocate with the Father. He cautions us against repetitious, self-congratulatory, and vain prayers, "to be heard of men, and to be praised for [our] wisdom" (Alma 38:13). "For every one that exalteth himself shall be abased; and he that humbleth himself shall be exalted" (Luke 18:14).

President Hinckley's words are wise and timely on this topic: "Be prayerful. . . . You cannot make it alone and do your best. You need the help of the Lord. . . . Ask the Lord to forgive your sins. Ask the Lord for help. Ask the Lord to bless you. Ask the Lord to help you realize your righteous ambitions. . . . Ask the Lord for all of the important things that mean so much to you in your lives. He stands ready to help" (*TGBH*, 468).

Matt. 6:16

Moreover when ye fast, be not, as the hypocrites, of a sad countenance: for they disfigure their faces, that they may appear unto men to fast. Verily I say unto you, They have their reward.

The Savior often referred to the false piety of the Jewish hierarchy in ancient Israel to teach valuable lessons regarding correct spiritual conduct. It is interesting to note that He often referred to these so-called religious role models as hypocrites—persons who put on a false appearance of virtue or religion. The Pharisees were highly skilled in such ostentatious behaviors, which were most often designed to elevate themselves by reminding others how far short they fell by comparison.

But true fasting encourages a deeper sense of reliance on God, increased spirituality and faith, and a greater desire to share our bounties with those in need. The fast is designed not for instant praise of men but for future divine approbation. Consider the Prophet Joseph Smith's forthright statement regarding improper piety when fasting: "I love that man better who swears a stream as long as my arm yet deals justice to his neighbors and mercifully deals his substance to the poor, than the long, smooth-faced hypocrite" (*TPJS*, 303). It should be obvious only to the Lord when we are engaged in a fast; He neither desires nor approves of a public show of piety.

Matt. 6:20–21

But lay up for yourselves treasures in heaven, where neither moth nor rust doth corrupt, and where thieves do not break through nor steal. For where your treasure is, there will your heart be also.

On the television, we hear persuasive advertisements for sophisticated home security systems guaranteed to protect our property and precious earthly treasures from unwanted invasion day and night. We provide the money required for such a service, then we can set the proper controls on the alarm system, sit back, and trust that all will be well. Good-bye, break-ins!

Unfortunately, we hear all too often of incidents where the best-laid security plans have gone awry, outsmarted by thieves who, intent on breaking in, have devised ways of disarming them. Or we've heard of something as simple and unpredictable as a power outage that has rendered the expensive equipment impotent in providing the promised protection. The loss is heartbreaking!

The Savior offers a far more secure system of protection—a spiritual security system that never fails, with a "code" that can never be broken. If we are more intent on accumulating spiritual treasures than things that have a transitory earthly shelf life, we will not only be spiritually wealthy, but we can also rest assured that nothing and no one can rob us of our rich abundance.

JST Matt. 6:22

The light of the body is the eye: if therefore thine eye be single to the glory of God, thy whole body shall be full of light.

Jesus often proclaims that He is the light of the world (see John 8:12), and He generously shares His light with all who are desirous to receive it. As we accept His glorious light, we are expected to use it wisely: "As long as the natural eyes are unimpaired, [we] can see and be guided by the light of day; and as long as [our] spiritual eyes are single to the glory of God—that is, as long as they are undimmed by sin and are focused solely on righteousness—[we] can view and understand the things of the Spirit. But if apostasy enters and the spiritual light turns to darkness, 'how great is that darkness!'" (*DNTC*, Vol. I, 240).

This scripture also wisely warns us about the spiritual dangers of serving with motives other than being on the Lord's errand, of serving with one eye on the goal of being a fit and well-tuned instrument in God's hands while our other eye is looking around to make sure others know about all of our good deeds. The light of God's approval far outshines the flickering beam of worldly praise.

Matt. 6:24

No man can serve two masters: for either he will hate the one, and love the other; or else he will hold to the one, and despise the other. Ye cannot serve God and mammon.

In His powerful Sermon on the Mount, the Savior addressed numerous principles for correct and righteous living. In speaking to the Jews, He was acutely aware of their past idolatrous practices and the disastrous consequences. Their false physical gods of the past were gone, but other "masters" had taken their places and divided the people's hearts—the amassing of worldly wealth and treasures, love of the praise of men, and lack of compassion for those less wealthy, less popular, or supposedly less righteous.

His words provide a solemn warning to all of us, and the choice is clear. Whom will we choose as our shepherd? To whose voice will we hearken? Whom will we choose to trust? The Savior unequivocally states that we cannot have it both ways.

In a modern-day revelation, the Lord reiterates the dangers of divided loyalties: "They seek not the Lord to establish his righteousness, but every man walketh in his own way, and after the image of his own god, whose image is in the likeness of the world, and whose substance is that of an idol, which waxeth old and shall perish in Babylon, even Babylon the great, which shall fall" (D&C 1:16).

JST Matt. 6:38

Wherefore, seek not the things of this world but seek ye first to build up the kingdom of God, and to establish his righteousness; and all these things shall be added unto you.

The Lord respects and honors steadfastness, strength, and dedication in those who choose to serve and follow Him. These are qualities prophets and leaders in all dispensations have demonstrated and that faithful members of The Church of Jesus Christ of Latter-day Saints throughout the world act on as they prove their willingness to serve faithfully in whatever callings they are given.

The Savior's words remind us that what we eat or drink or wear is not nearly as important as the service we render in His behalf (see Matt. 6:31). It all comes down to our priorities and our willingness to lose ourselves in His service and focus outward instead of inward. "Instead of visiting Babylon frequently and eventually perishing there, true sons and daughters of God seek to . . . establish the righteousness of the Righteous One on earth" (Robert L. Millet, *Coming to Know Christ* [Salt Lake City: Deseret Book, 2012], 8).

Each small act of obedience is rewarded with an outpouring of God's blessings and approval. As we do His will, it will be our privilege to hear His words of approval: "Blessed *art* thou" (Luke 1:42) and "Well done, *thou* good and faithful servant" (Matt. 25:21). His blessings will be abundant in our lives.

John 21:17

He saith unto him the third time, Simon, son of Jonas, lovest thou me? . . .
And he said unto him, Lord . . . thou knowest that I love thee.
Jesus saith unto him, Feed my sheep.

Anyone who prepares food or enjoys fine dishes someone else has prepared knows a satisfying meal must be well planned and attractively presented. Caloric content as well as nutritional value must be taken into consideration, and the special dietary needs of those who will be eating the meal must also be carefully assessed. And no matter how elaborate the preparations or how attractive the presentation, if the food is served indifferently, it promises to be a disappointing culinary experience.

When the Savior thrice exhorted Peter to *feed* His sheep, He was obviously very serious about careful preparation and presentation in the service we render in His name. Our service must be substantive and filling—not a "fast-food" effort filled with empty spiritual calories. Putting our best foot forward in the Lord's work means just that—making every effort to serve with all our might, mind, and strength. So when we feed His sheep, they will know they are not being served lukewarm leftovers thoughtlessly tossed to a faceless flock, whose individual needs have not been considered.

The Savior's directive requires our personal dedication and consecration: "Take heed therefore . . . to feed the church of God, which he hath purchased with his own blood" (Acts 20:28).

Matt. 7:7

*Ask, and it shall be given you; seek, and ye shall find;
knock, and it shall be opened unto you.*

The Savior wisely recommends that we do not *tell* God what we want but rather that we wisely *ask* for what we need. Our Heavenly Father knows what we really need and what will be good for us. Our vain repetitions are not a successful way to get His attention, nor will they convince Him to fill our orders, "for your Father knoweth what things ye have need of, before ye ask him" (see Matt. 6:7–8). Rather, He counsels us to "ask in faith, nothing wavering" (James 1:6), and to be contrite and obedient: "Wherefore he that prayeth, whose spirit is contrite, the same is accepted of me if he obey mine ordinances" (D&C 52:15).

The key to effective prayer is faith—faith that we will receive an answer from a God who knows our needs and how those needs will best be met. President Gordon B. Hinckley counsels us that instead of just placing our orders with the Lord, like a grocery list, we need to think carefully about what we are praying for and to whom we are speaking. Then we must listen prayerfully and respectfully for His answer (see *TGBH*, 469).

Matt. 7:24–25

Therefore whosoever heareth these sayings of mine, and doeth them, I will liken him unto a wise man, which built his house upon a rock: And the rain descended, and the floods came, and the winds blew, and beat upon that house; and it fell not: for it was founded upon a rock.

The Savior used the metaphor of sand, rocks, and water to impress upon us how critical it is to hear and act upon His words. Hearing without doing is like the house of sand a child builds that gets washed away by the tide because it has no true substance or foundation. The onset of tribulation and adversity can easily erase a shaky testimony.

Our sure foundation consists of the principles of truth and righteousness found in the restored gospel, the first of which is faith in the Lord Jesus Christ. Helaman's powerful testimony leaves no doubt as to the identity of that sure foundation. "It is upon the rock of our Redeemer, who is Christ, the Son of God, that ye must build your foundation . . . whereon if men build they cannot fall" (Hel. 5:12).

We rejoice in the Savior's promise to those who build their lives on His sure foundation: "Therefore, fear not, little flock; do good; let earth and hell combine against you, for if ye are built upon my rock, they cannot prevail" (D&C 6:34). The Savior is our sure protection against the tides of evil that seek to wash away our convictions and testimonies.

John 4:14

Whosoever drinketh of the water that I shall give him shall never thirst; but the water that I shall give him shall be in him a well of water springing up into everlasting life.

As the Savior conversed with the Samaritan woman at the well, He taught her that while our bodies need regular nourishment, our spirits need the blessed nourishment of the bread and water of life. We are all children at the well, needing that water of which the Savior speaks. And what is that water? It is the word of God that refreshes, revitalizes, and renews our drooping spirits. It is the gospel of Jesus Christ, the iron rod of saving principles and ordinances—pure and clear and eternal, free from the contamination of deceit and fleeting pleasures. And like the life-sustaining manna given to the children of Israel as they wandered in the wilderness, so He promises us spiritual nourishment that will sustain us regardless of the wildernesses we may be called to traverse.

In His sermon to the Nephites, the Savior issued a benevolent invitation with the words "blessed are all they who do hunger and thirst after righteousness" (3 Ne. 12:6). All those who accept this invitation and gather at His well of righteousness will be filled with the Holy Ghost, through whose ministrations we will be taught, enlightened, comforted, and led to a greater love for our Savior.

Luke 18:42–43

And Jesus said unto him, Receive thy sight: thy faith hath saved thee. And immediately he received his sight, and followed him, glorifying God: and all the people, when they saw it, gave praise unto God.

Perceiving the noise of the multitude, a blind man inquired as to its source and was told that "Jesus of Nazareth passeth by" (Luke 18:37). Upon hearing this, the man begged for Jesus's mercy. Obviously this man knew Jesus, at least by reputation, and knew that "unto many *that were* blind [Christ] gave sight" (Luke 7:21). Four significant events then occurred: the blind man received his sight, he followed Jesus, he glorified God, and those who witnessed the miracle also praised God. As with all instances of the Savior's healing hand, we know that faith preceded the miracle here.

It is important to note that the healed man expressed open and public gratitude for the magnificent gift he had received. He did not procrastinate, thinking perhaps to send a thank-you note at a later time. We sense his deep acknowledgment of God's goodness, and the man's outpouring of appreciation was contagious.

An even greater miracle of spiritual healing eclipsed this restoration of sight, and the Savior desires to bestow this greater miracle on all true disciples. It is the miracle of having eyes that see what is worth seeing, ears that hear what is worth hearing, and hearts that understand His words and are converted. "But blessed *are* your eyes, for they see: and your ears, for they hear" (Matt. 13:16).

Mark 4:39

And he arose, and rebuked the wind, and said unto the sea, Peace, be still.
And the wind ceased, and there was a great calm.

When the winds are still and the sun is bright, no body of water is more peaceful and beautiful than the Sea of Galilee. Yet, in a matter of minutes, violent storms can whip these tranquil waters into a fury of raging billows.

It was just such a storm that battered the small ship on which the Savior and His disciples had set sail across this lake. The immensity of the tempest brought wild water cascading over the ship's sides, and the Apostles clearly feared for their lives. Through all this turmoil, the exhausted Savior slept soundly. Finally, awakened by His fearful companions, He arose and rebuked the raging elements. He overrode nature's rage and His disciples' fears with a calm, decisive, and dignified command: "Be still." Then He gently chided His disciples: "Why are ye so fearful?" (Mark 4:40).

The Savior also cares about us enough to calm our personal storms and rebuke our demons. Can we possibly doubt that He who can control the forces of nature can also bring peace to our troubled souls? We need only to summon that particle of faith that enables us to cry out, "Lord, save us: we perish" (Matt. 8:25). His calm voice will answer our petitions as He quietly bids us to "be still, and know that I *am* God" (Ps. 46:10).

Luke 21:36

Watch ye therefore, and pray always, that ye may be accounted worthy to . . .
stand before the Son of man.

Perfect and sinless as He was, the Savior communed regularly with His Father. He spent forty prayer-filled days in the wilderness; He often went up into a mountain to pray; He offered marvelous intercessory prayers; He prayed and wept over little children; He spent His last night as a mortal man in prayer in a garden, pouring out His heart in tender submission to His Father's will. His perfect example is the perfect definition of *always*.

Perhaps we tell ourselves that to pray *always* means it's good to pray when we are not too tired or busy. Maybe we think *always* means we need to pray only when we are in trouble. We might even rationalize that we should *always* pray only if we really feel worthy to talk to God. But *always* in the Lord's vocabulary means just that.

Alma knew exactly what the Lord meant by *always*: "Counsel with the Lord in *all* thy doings, and he will direct thee for good" (Alma 37:37; emphasis added). To His Saints in the latter days, the Savior gives this commandment: "Pray *always*, lest you enter into temptation and lose your reward" (D&C 31:12; emphasis added). And the Psalmist reminds us: "Evening, and morning, and at noon, will I pray, and cry aloud: and he shall hear my voice" (Ps. 55:17).

Luke 7:13

And when the Lord saw her, he had compassion on her, and said unto her, Weep not.

One of the Savior's most spectacular miracles occurred in a little Galilean village called Nain. This is the first recorded instance of Jesus raising someone from the dead, and it is rendered on behalf of a sorrowing widow who has lost her only son. In a culture where a woman's status depended solely on the males in her household, the death of this woman's only son is the final assault on her social image.

As Jesus and His entourage enter the village, they witness the funeral procession on its way to the burial site. The mother's grief is evident, and in a tone of utter compassion, the Savior singles her out with two words: "Weep not." These compassionate words, spoken by One whose divinity is again about to be manifested, will serve as the perfect antidote for this bereaved and God-fearing woman's tears. The Savior simply touches the bier and says, "Young man, I say unto thee, Arise" (Luke 7:14), and it was so! Then, in a final gracious gesture, the Savior delivers the young man to his mother, who is a righteous woman and a precious daughter of God, a God whose love and mercy have no respect for gender—not then and not now.

Matt. 18:3–4

Verily I say unto you, Except ye be converted, and become as little children, ye shall not enter into the kingdom of heaven. Whosoever therefore shall humble himself as this little child, the same is greatest in the kingdom of heaven.

On a certain occasion, dispute arose among the Apostles regarding their status in the Lord's earthly kingdom. Who would deserve the greatest status in the kingdom of God? Upon arrival at Peter's home, the Savior settled the matter when He took a little child upon His knee and rehearsed the necessary qualifications for citizenship in both His earthly and heavenly kingdoms.

According to the Savior, we must become as little children—meek and submissive, contrite in heart and spirit. To achieve this status, we must first embrace the Atonement and then apply the principle of repentance in our lives. In so doing, we become pure like little children. This is the same doctrine revealed to King Benjamin, who taught his people that it is only through the Atonement of Jesus Christ that we can achieve the childlike traits of submissiveness, meekness, humility, patience, and love (see Mosiah 3:19).

"True greatness in the Lord's earthly kingdom is measured . . . by intrinsic merit and goodness. Those who become as little children and acquire the attributes of godliness for themselves, regardless of the capacity in which they may be called to serve, are the 'greatest in the kingdom of heaven'" (*DNTC*, Vol. I, 415).

Luke 15:7

I say unto you, that likewise joy shall be in heaven over one sinner that repenteth, more than over ninety and nine just persons, which need no repentance.

The Savior frequently used parables to share gospel principles and teach eternal truths. The parable of the lost sheep reminds us that the Lord knows and loves each one of us and greatly misses us when we stray into spiritually dangerous and damaging paths.

In this parable, we might be inclined to feel a bit unappreciated or neglected if we perceive ourselves as part of the ninety and nine. It is important to remember that at no time does the Savior value the souls of sinners more than the ones who remain faithfully in the fold. Rather, He reminds us that if even one of us is lost—and there are times when we all fall into this category—it is cause for heavenly sorrow.

In the Lord's ledgers, there is a balance between justice and mercy. Through the Atonement of Christ, debts can be forgiven and sins erased. The repentant sinners are joyful additions to God's kingdom, and their newly acquired spiritual status in no way diminishes the worth of those who remain constant and true. God's love and grace are sufficient for *all* of His children. How joyfully we should embrace the tender ministrations and watchful care of the Good Shepherd for both Saint and sinner alike.

John 16:33

These things I have spoken unto you, that in me ye might have peace. In the world ye shall have tribulation: but be of good cheer; I have overcome the world.

The long reach of adversity's arm touches all, regardless of age, gender, social status, or degree of personal righteousness. Our only real defense against adversity lies in our tenacity in clinging faithfully to the principles of truth and righteousness found in the restored gospel, with the first principle being faith in the Lord Jesus Christ.

"Our afflictions often become our greatest blessings. It is in our extremities that most often we meet God, not in our comfort. Thus any time conditions come to pass . . . that lead us toward the truth or contribute to our eventual well-being, we have indeed been blessed" (*DCBM*, Vol. 3, 224).

The rewards for faithfully enduring tribulation are not always realized in this life. The Savior specifies that blessings come both in life and death, meaning that often the very best rewards await us in the next life. That is not to say that we do not reap earthly rewards as well. In the midst of affliction, the Lord's generosity and tender mercies in our everyday lives continually amaze and humble us. And when well and truly examined, our "cup runneth over" (Ps. 23:5).

Mark 10:17

And when he was gone forth into the way, there came one running, and kneeled to him, and asked him, Good Master, what shall I do that I may inherit eternal life?

We sense sincerity in this young man's earnest inquiry. Note his use of the word *inherit*, as if the gift of eternal life requires no effort on our part; it will just naturally be ours when the Father's will is read. The Savior ascertained that the man, who was a strict observer of the law of Moses, lacked only one thing: "Sell whatsoever thou hast, and give to the poor . . . and come . . . follow me" (Mark 10:21).

The Savior knew this man's Achilles' heel was his attachment to material possessions. He had come looking for a simple, prescriptive action he could fulfill without moving too far out of his comfort zone. But what the Savior asked him to do was too much, and both the Savior and the young man were sorrowful as this seeker turned away (see Mark 10:17–22).

The Savior knows we all have attachments that must be relinquished if we are to qualify for the gift of eternal life. Changing our attitudes is the catalyst for our obedience to God's commandments, and this change enables us to claim the blessings of the Atonement, through which we then become *legal heirs* to the gift of eternal life (see Romans 8:17).

Mark 10:13–14

And they brought young children . . . and his disciples rebuked those
that brought them. But when Jesus saw it, he was much displeased, and said
unto them, Suffer the little children to come unto me, and forbid them
not: for of such is the kingdom of God.

The disciples' actions may seem a bit harsh, but taken in its historical and social context, this incident is not so surprising. Women and children were perceived as second-class citizens at best, and the disciples had not yet caught the full vision of the Savior's love for *everyone*, so it seemed to them very presumptive of these mothers to bother the Son of God. But Jesus taught His disciples and all of us a significant lesson.

In the ensuing scene of infinite tenderness, the Savior gathered these little ones into His arms and blessed them; each one felt the warmth of His loving embrace. This was not a hasty group hug after which the Savior moved on to more pressing matters. There was *nothing* more pressing or urgent, *nothing* more important than this precious interchange. It was a personal experience that neither the children nor their mothers would ever forget. We can only imagine that the touch of the Master's hand would linger long after less significant events faded from memory.

And there is never a time when the Savior is too busy to take His children into His arms and His heart and seek Heavenly Father's most tender blessings for them.

Luke 15:8

Either what woman having ten pieces of silver, if she lose one piece, doth not light a candle, and sweep the house, and seek diligently till she find it?

As with all the Savior's teachings and parables, we must look for the unspoken layers of spiritual significance tucked away in His metaphors. Even though the woman had several more equally valuable coins, she could not afford to casually ignore the one she had lost.

This lesson reminds us that our lost treasure might be family members or friends who are temporarily wandering in strange roads (see 1 Ne. 8:32) and that we can never afford to lose one of them. It is both our responsibility and privilege to search diligently for ways to bring these souls back into the light of the gospel.

The Savior talks about lighting a candle, and very often, we must share our light with those who have lost theirs and lovingly coax them away from the dark and dingy places of spiritual inertia. Our search may not produce immediate results, but in the Lord's merciful timetable, we will find the precious coins, and we, like the good woman in the parable, will have reason to rejoice with those we love—and most especially with the Lord, whose personal search for His lost sheep is an eternal quest.

John 10:14

I am the good shepherd, and know my sheep, and am known of mine.

The scriptures abound in symbolism, and the shepherd motif is rich in metaphoric meaning. In ancient Israel, shepherds kept close personal watch over their flocks both day and night: "And there were in the same country shepherds . . . keeping watch over their flock by night" (Luke 2:8). The shepherds called their sheep by name, and each sheep knew the voice of its shepherd and would respond only to that voice.

The shepherd was never behind the flock pushing and shouting, neither was he in the midst of the flock, where confusion might arise. He was clearly visible in the lead position, anticipating any pitfalls and charting safe paths.

This relationship of the shepherd to his sheep is symbolic of the Savior's relationship with us. He guides our footsteps in the sure and safe path that leads to eternal life. He is our friend who will never turn His back on us or betray us; He will never be ashamed to be seen in our company. His love and care are constant and unconditional. His goodness and mercy are expansive enough to fill the universe and personal enough to tenderly guide, guard, and comfort us until we are safely back in His eternal fold.

John 8:10–11

When Jesus had lifted up himself, and saw none but the woman, he said unto her, Woman, where are those thine accusers? Hath no man condemned thee? She said, No man, Lord. And Jesus said unto her, Neither do I condemn thee: go, and sin no more.

We can only imagine the terror and shame this woman felt as the scribes and Pharisees dragged her before the Savior, demanding that He pronounce upon her a judgment of death by stoning. However, the Savior teaches us valuable lessons about mercy and repentance in this familiar and powerful incident. His response was astonishing to both the accuser and the accused as He invited only those who were without sin to cast the first stone. One by one, the woman's accusers quietly slipped away.

What followed was breathtaking. As Jesus spoke personally and quietly to the trembling woman, His gentle admonition packed an eternal punch: "Sin no more." Here is a clear invitation to repent and thereby merit the Lord's forgiveness.

What He says to one, He says to all. He holds out His hands to us, beckoning us to abandon sin's ways and follow Him. And His scarred palms remind us that He has graven us—sorrows, sins, flaws, failures, and all—on the palms of His hands (see Isa. 49:16). His scars are a gracious guarantee of His forgiveness as we truly and sincerely repent; they are signs of an immeasurable mercy from One who is all about second chances.

Luke 18:22

Come, follow me.

When the Savior says, "Come, follow me," we know we can trust His perfect example of friendship. During His earthly ministry, He was a friend to the poor and rich alike, to those who were easy to love and those who were not, to those touched by sin as well as the exemplary, to those afflicted by every imaginable infirmity and those who were whole and strong. He also offered friendship to those with questionable occupations and those with solid social standings, to those of differing racial and cultural groups as well as those whose heritage was like His own.

The Savior said, "I will call you friends, for you are my friends, and ye shall have an inheritance with me" (D&C 93:45). To be the Lord's friend and have an inheritance with Him—can there be a greater gift bestowed upon us? We read in Proverbs 17:17 that "a friend loveth at all times," not just when it is easy or convenient. This is the measure of the Lord's friendship and sets the standard for our own.

John 8:12

I am the light of the world: he that followeth me shall not walk in darkness, but shall have the light of life.

As children of God, we are commanded to walk in the light of the gospel. The Son of God is the source of that light, and He is available to everyone. His light can be ignored or left behind or rejected, but it can never be extinguished. Its energy source is eternal. Those who avail themselves of this light find their pathway is always illuminated when they need it.

John knew and bore witness that the Savior is the light of the world: "In him was life; and the life was the light of men. And the light shineth in darkness" (John 1:4–5). We look to light as a guide and comfort when darkness falls. It provides illumination for our tasks and protects us from physical dangers that might otherwise go undetected. In a more deeply significant sense, the Savior—He who is the light of the world—comforts, protects, and guides us when we experience spiritual darkness. There is no spiritual abyss the Savior's light cannot penetrate, illuminate, and dispel.

Like the Psalmist, we too can rejoice in that light: "For thou *art* my lamp, O Lord: and the Lord will lighten my darkness" (2 Sam. 22:29).

Matt. 17:20

If ye have faith as a grain of mustard seed, ye shall say unto this mountain, Remove hence to yonder place; and it shall remove; and nothing shall be impossible unto you.

Faith in the Lord Jesus Christ is the first principle of the gospel—a powerful principle with a powerful promise. Faith can produce physical miracles, such as the moving of mountains, the calming of storms, and the healing of physical infirmities, but the fruits of our faith are often more quiet and less spectacular.

The Lord's highest priority for us is the miracle of our broken hearts—our sure and abiding faith in Christ and in the power of His Atonement. We must focus our faith not in *our* good intentions and desires but in the Savior's intentions for us. He sees a broader picture, knows what we do not know, and knows our needs far better than we do. Faith involves a shift from what we know in our heads to what we feel in our hearts.

Faith moves us past our fears and personal storms and prompts us to focus on our Savior's love and promise of eternal life. "Fear thou not; for I *am* with thee: be not dismayed; for I *am* thy God: I will strengthen thee; yea, I will help thee; yea, I will uphold thee with the right hand of my righteousness" (Isa. 41:10).

Matt. 14:27

But straightway Jesus spake unto them, saying, Be of good cheer; it is I; be not afraid.

In the very early hours of the morning, after privately communing with His Father in prayer, the Savior saw that the ship on which His disciples were sailing was tossed with waves and that the "wind was contrary" (Mark 6:48). His immediate reaction to their dilemma was to set out toward them, walking on the water. But the disciples' immediate reaction was fear as they failed to recognize their Master.

At some point in our lives, we have all felt fear. Some feel it more often than others, and some to a greater degree than others. There are many kinds of fear—fear of failure, fear of losing friends or loved ones either through death or betrayal, and fear of darkness, which can be either temporal or spiritual.

The Savior is aware of our fears and can perfectly assuage them. His wounds remind us that He has borne all our sorrows, felt all our grief, and known every doubt and fear that will ever assail our troubled minds. As we look to Him for solace, His promise is as sure now as the one He gave to His fearful disciples. His comforting words bid us not only to abandon our fears but to find joy in recognizing our Master.

Matt. 14:29–30

And when Peter was come down out of the ship, he walked on the water, to go to Jesus. But when he saw the wind boisterous, he was afraid; and beginning to sink, he cried, saying, Lord, save me.

When Peter eagerly accepted the Savior's invitation to walk on the water, so great was his faith that he confidently set out across the waves. When he kept his eyes on the Savior, all was well, but when he looked down at the billowing, tempest-tossed water beneath his feet, he momentarily forgot the object of his confidence and began to sink.

The wondrous lesson we learn from Peter's experience and from our own such faltering footsteps when we look downward instead of upward is that "*immediately* Jesus stretched forth *his* hand, and caught him" (Matt. 14:31; emphasis added). He did not let Peter experience a near drowning and then reach out in a grandiose, last-minute, lifesaving gesture. As the Savior drew a frightened Peter to His loving bosom, He gently chided the fearful Apostle: "Wherefore didst thou doubt?" (v. 31).

In modern scripture, we read the Savior's comforting words: "Look unto me in every thought; doubt not, fear not" (D&C 6:36). He reassures us that He is always there for us—especially when our footsteps falter. Each time the Savior reaches out to steady us, we learn to look past the dangers beneath our fearful feet and upward toward His outstretched healed and healing hands.

John 10:10

*I am come that they might have life, and that
they might have it more abundantly.*

The abundant life the Lord promised is a richly rewarding "here and now" experience based on obedience to His commandments: "Verily I say, that inasmuch as ye do this, the fulness of the earth is yours . . . Yea, all things . . . are made for the benefit and use of man, both to please the eye and to gladden the heart" (D&C 59:16, 18).

The abundant life is also rich with promises for the hereafter. However, there are no shortcuts to an eternally abundant life. There was no quick and easy way for the Savior to accomplish His atoning mission of salvation, nor is there a way for us to bypass the steps that make us worthy recipients of that sacrifice. We cannot afford to mortgage our eternal happiness in order to gratify fleeting earthly pleasures, "for a man's life consisteth not in the abundance of the things which he possesseth" (Luke 12:15).

As we divest ourselves of all ungodliness, we are filled with the Lord's eternally abundant bounties. "And the LORD shall . . . satisfy thy soul in drought . . . and thou shalt be like a watered garden, and like a spring of water, whose waters fail not" (Isa. 58:11).

Luke 15:20

And he arose, and came to his father. But when he was yet a great way off, his father saw him, and had compassion, and ran, and fell on his neck, and kissed him.

In this parable, we learn of a son who has squandered his inheritance in unsavory activities. He has known the ultimate Jewish disgrace of feeding and dining with pigs and has seen and bitterly regretted the error of his ways as he turns homeward.

We can only imagine his slow and faltering footsteps as he approaches his home, perhaps wondering whether he will be asked to turn around and go back to wherever his errant ways had previously taken him. Instead, we see the love of a tender parent as the father of this wayward young man runs to meet him and welcomes him back into the family fold with a warm and tearful parental embrace.

The father's response is richly symbolic of the Savior's embrace of mercy for a repentant sinner. It is the arm of mercy the Savior extends to all of God's children who repent. He never gives up on us, even when we are "a great way off" and even when we might give up on ourselves: "Behold, he sendeth an invitation to all men, for the arms of mercy are extended towards them, and he saith: Repent, and I will receive you" (Alma 5:33).

Luke 14:33

So likewise, whosoever he be of you that forsaketh not all that he hath, he cannot be my disciple.

For the rich young man who found it impossible to sell his vast possessions, there were limits to what he was willing to do to be Christ's disciple. In contrast, when the Savior invited Peter and Andrew to follow Him, their responses were positive and immediate. There were no limits to what they were willing to do to become disciples of Christ.

The Savior invites each of us to follow Him: "And whoso layeth down his life in my cause, for my name's sake, shall find it again, *even life eternal*" (D&C 98:13; emphasis added). Laying down our lives means that we are willing to *live* for Him, to follow Him. We are willing to lay down less-than-pleasing habits that have taken up comfortable residence within us and replace them with pleasing and positive Christlike behaviors. As we sacrifice our old ways of life for a new way, we accept and receive the blessings of the atoning sacrifice of the Savior.

Ultimately, the Lord's word is clear regarding true discipleship: "He that receiveth my law and doeth it, the same is my disciple; and he that saith he receiveth it and doeth it not, the same is not my disciple" (D&C 41:5).

Matt. 16:15–16

He saith unto them, But whom say ye that I am? And Simon Peter answered and said, Thou art the Christ, the Son of the living God.

Peter's declaration was and is a powerful testimony—one forged in Peter's soul as he walked and talked with the Savior. His was a testimony gained through personal revelation, a testimony strengthened by the Savior's personal ministrations. The scriptures are replete with similar testimonies borne by other prophets of old.

In a personal declaration of His identity, the Savior reminds us that He is the literal Son of God, God's only Begotten in the flesh: "Behold, I am Jesus Christ the Son of God. . . . In me hath the Father glorified his name" (3 Ne. 9:15). The Father Himself bore witness of this fact to the Nephites: "Behold my Beloved Son . . . in whom I have glorified my name" (3 Ne. 11:7).

Our own beloved prophet Thomas S. Monson also bears witness to the Savior's divine sonship, His great atoning sacrifice, and His glorious Resurrection (see "He Is Not Here, but Is Risen," *Ensign*, Apr. 2011, 5). This is the most important thing members of The Church of Jesus Christ of Latter-day Saints can know—that Jesus Christ is indeed the Son of God, our benevolent Savior, who offers us the gift of eternal life.

Mark 5:34

And he said unto her, Daughter, thy faith hath made thee whole; go in peace, and be whole of thy plague.

There are several unique aspects of the miraculous healing of the woman with the "issue of blood" (Mark 5:25; see also v. 25–34). This was a woman who was considered unclean and socially unacceptable because of a twelve-year disease. She had heard of the Savior's healing powers, and she knew He could heal her if she could just unobtrusively touch His robe.

What happened next was truly marvelous—she was immediately healed. The Savior, "knowing in himself that virtue [or power] had gone out of him" (v. 30), inquired as to who had touched Him. There must have been some trepidation in the woman's heart as she came forward, but the Savior immediately put her at ease with His affirmation that her faith, more than His touch, had made the miracle possible. Addressing her as "daughter" and commending her for her faith made her feel honored and respected—something she may have never known or hoped for. His admonition to "go in peace" was an assurance that through her faith God had saved her and that she could confidently pursue the pathway to eternal life.

Our Savior's love and grace are miracles that can touch and heal each of us, but it is our faith that makes it possible for us to reach out to Him and be made whole.

Luke 22:32

But I have prayed for thee, that thy faith fail not: and when thou art converted, strengthen thy brethren.

The Savior spoke these wise and tender words to His beloved Apostle Peter, and it is a message that reminds each of us that ours is a lifelong, ongoing, and sacred process of individual conversion. The Savior entreats us to live so that our examples invite instead of repel others, so others will believe us, instead of despising us. But the message of the gospel will fall on deaf ears if our behavior belies our words. Elder Jeffrey R. Holland made the observation that in order to be effective missionaries, we must first be exemplary members of The Church of Jesus Christ of Latter-day Saints (see "Witnesses unto Me," *Ensign*, May 2001).

The Apostle Paul admonishes, "Be thou an example of the believers, in word, in conversation, in charity, in spirit, in faith, in purity" (1 Tim. 4:12). We strengthen our brethren by learning, living, and then sharing the joyful message of the gospel as found in the holy scriptures. As we do so, we will experience the literal fulfillment of the Savior's promise: "Lift up your heart and rejoice, for the hour of your mission is come; and your tongue shall be loosed, and you shall declare glad tidings of great joy unto this generation" (D&C 31:3).

John 1:12

But as many as received him, to them gave he power to become the sons of God, even to them that believe on his name.

"The gaining of a strong and secure testimony is the privilege and opportunity of every member of the Church. . . . It becomes each of us to acquire such a testimony. This is the very foundation of our faith. This is the thing upon which we build all else, the testimony which we carry in our hearts concerning our Eternal Father and His Beloved Son" (*TGBH*, 647–48).

Notice that President Gordon B. Hinckley uses the words *gaining* and *acquire* when speaking of testimony, both of which denote action. A testimony is not something that arrives suddenly and unexpectedly like little promotional gifts we sometimes receive in the mail. It comes only through great personal effort and the whisperings of the Spirit's still, small voice as we earnestly seek this precious gift.

Job bore witness of the sacred process: "But *there is* a spirit in man: and the inspiration of the Almighty giveth them understanding" (Job 32:8). As we study, pray, and seek the affirming witness of the Holy Ghost, our personal testimony of the Savior can be as sure, sweet, and sacred as that borne by Job: "I know *that* my Redeemer liveth" (Job 19:25).

John 6:35

I am the bread of life: he that cometh to me shall never hunger; and he that believeth on me shall never thirst.

We have all experienced the loss of something that has special significance or value, and we spare neither time nor effort in our search for those lost items, often enlisting the aid of friends or family members or heavenly powers.

It is this same kind of effort the Savior expects us to expend in searching the scriptures. He is not talking about a casual perusal, a daily prescriptive dose, or a Sunday stroll through a few pages of sacred truths as we attend our meetings. He invites us to get to know Him intimately, and there is no other venue that provides this same opportunity. The scriptures bear testimony of Him through the mouths of apostles and prophets and through the words of the Savior Himself.

And there is no substitute for the real thing. Lessons or commentaries are intended only to supplement what we have already found in our search. "It has been wisely said that the greatest commentary on scripture is scripture" (*Coming to Know Christ*, 129).

The Savior promises that we will be happy and blessed if we hunger and thirst after a testimony of Him. And because of His infinite love for us, He will provide the living water and perpetual manna that will be eternally refreshing, filling, and satisfying.

Matt. 13:24–26

Another parable put he forth unto them, saying, The kingdom of heaven is likened unto a man which sowed good seed in his field: But while men slept, his enemy came and sowed tares among the wheat, and went his way. But when the blade was sprung up, and brought forth fruit, then appeared the tares also.

"In giving the parable of the wheat and the tares, Jesus was actually summarizing the doctrines of the apostasy, the restoration of the gospel in the latter-days, the growth and development of the latter-day kingdom, the millennial cleansing of the earth, the glorious advent of the Son of Man, and the ultimate celestial exaltation of the faithful" (*DNTC*, Vol. I, 297).

In this dispensation, the Lord again explained the important lesson contained in this parable of the latter days: "In the last days, even now while . . . the blade is springing up and is yet tender—Behold, verily I say unto you, the angels . . . are ready and waiting to be sent forth to reap down the fields; But the Lord saith unto them, pluck not up the tares while the blade is yet tender (for verily your faith is weak), lest you destroy the wheat also. Therefore, let the wheat and the tares grow together until the harvest . . . then ye shall first gather out the wheat from among the tares, and after the gathering of the wheat, . . . the tares are bound in bundles, and the field remaineth to be burned" (D&C 86:4–7).

John 1:3

*All things were made by him; and without him was
not any thing made that was made.*

The account of the Creation is a testament of God's love for His children. The Creation could have simply been a utilitarian exercise, giving us just the basics needed to live and survive, but the Savior, under the direction of our Heavenly Father, created a masterpiece of unsurpassed beauty and variety. There are infinite varieties of foliage, flowers, fruits, vegetables, birds, animals, fishes, and insects. And each variety is suited to its particular environment.

There are also innumerable types of geographical variations that make the earth a tribute not only to God's creative powers but also to His desire to please our eyes and gladden our hearts. Who has not thrilled to see the miracle of a bud unfold into a gorgeous flower, a tree laden with delicious fruit, a forest heavy with foliage that provides both shade and beauty, or a bird with bright feathers and a beautiful voice? Wherever we choose to live, there is a special and unique beauty attached to all living things.

In Moses chapter 2, we read that after each creative period, the Lord "saw that all things which [He] had made were good" (v. 18), and this was pleasing to God because He knew it would please His children.

Matt. 22:37

Thou shalt love the Lord thy God with all thy heart, and with all thy soul, and with all thy mind.

It is significant to note that the word *all* is prominent in this great commandment. We are admonished to love God with *all* of our heart, with *all* of our soul, and with *all* of our mind, not just with portions that will leave us free to divide our loyalties with less worthy recipients or pursuits. Also, the words *heart, soul,* and *mind* indicate a perfect unity of personal effort and commitment.

Surely, then, this commandment is a blessing rather than a burden because it is designed to draw us ever closer to claiming the divine promise of exaltation. Note that this is not merely a *suggestion*—it is the Lord's *command*, one He desires for us to take into our hearts; in other words, He expects us to completely internalize it. This command goes beyond lip service and becomes the impetus for obedience in all things, which is proof positive that we love the Lord.

Each week as we partake of the sacrament, we promise to remember our Savior in order to better keep this first and great commandment. This remembrance demands the *utmost* loyalty, but we can love and remember someone always only when we truly know them.

Matt. 22:39

Thou shalt love thy neighbor as thyself.

The second great commandment is to "love thy neighbor as thyself," and this begins at home. It is the next logical step to the first and great commandment. And where better to keep it than within our own families—in our relationships with our spouses, our children, and our siblings? Do we remember to honor our promises to love and care for one another? Do we always conduct ourselves in a way that we would be pleased to have our families remember?

Our heartfelt and pure love of God initiates a ripple effect that reaches outward and touches others' lives. When we diligently heed His first and great commandment, God's love is poured out upon us ever more abundantly. In turn, we feel a desire to share that love with our fellowmen.

We must be keenly aware of our brothers' and sisters' needs, be they physical, emotional, or spiritual, and be willing to nurture them. "This principle of love is the basic essence of the gospel of Jesus Christ. Without love of God and love of neighbor there is little else to commend the gospel to us as a way of life" (*TGBH*, 317).

Luke 10:29

And who is my neighbour?

We read that a certain lawyer engaged in dialogue with the Savior, most probably with the express purpose of demonstrating the lawyer's superior intelligence and knowledge of the law. But the lawyer's question provided the impetus for the Savior to share one of His marvelous parables, that of the Good Samaritan.

We are familiar with the circumstances of the story and its characters: the man left robbed and bleeding (most likely a Jew); the priest (an ordained religious leader), who, after a quick and cursory glance, hurriedly passed by on the other side of the road; the Levite (possibly a temple worker), who took a little longer to assess the situation and then crossed over to the other side of the road; and the Samaritan (a despised heretic), who not only stopped and looked but also quickly administered first aid and then took the injured man to an inn and arranged for convalescent care.

The Savior's follow-up question to the learned lawyer was concise and cogent: "Which now of these three . . . was neighbour unto him that fell among the thieves?" (Luke 10:36). The lawyer's answer was, of course, the only correct one: "He that shewed mercy" (v. 37).

What the Savior said next to the lawyer He says to all of us at all times: "Go, and do thou likewise" (Ibid.).

Matt. 25:40

Verily I say unto you, Inasmuch as ye have done it unto one of the least of these my brethren, ye have done it unto me.

These powerful words regarding service to our fellowmen and to our God are echoed in the words of one of our beloved hymns: "Then in a moment to my view / The stranger started from disguise. / The tokens in his hands I knew; / The Savior stood before mine eyes. / He spake, and my poor name he named, / 'Of me thou hast not been ashamed. / These deeds shall thy memorial be; / Fear not, thou didst them unto me'" ("A Poor Wayfaring Man of Grief," *Hymns*, no. 29).

Opportunities for service abound, whether they be in our families, our Church, our neighborhoods, or our communities. True service is selfless and is rendered with a glad heart and a willing spirit rather than out of a sense of duty. Service is not something to cross off our "how-to-get-into-heaven" checklists. It is done without fanfare, occasionally anonymously, and often without recognition.

As parents, we serve our families daily and in countless ways. Does it make a difference? Does anyone notice? The impact may not be immediate, but in days and years to come, our children will feel touched and blessed by what we have done and will have this pattern in place for their own selfless acts of service.

Luke 11:39

Now do ye Pharisees make clean the outside of the cup and the platter; but your inward part is full of ravening and wickedness.

The Savior often referred to the need for inner integrity, especially when He was dealing with the Pharisees of His day. In fact, He likened their lack of inner cleanliness to a "whited sepulcher," a phrase denoting an outward appearance that belies the corruption within.

In Joseph Smith's day, the Savior illustrated just such a dichotomy when speaking of those whose professions of godliness were nothing but empty rhetoric: "They draw near to me with their lips, but their hearts are far from me" (JS—H 1:19). These words carry a timely caution for all of us. It is possible, but not admirable, for us to be pennies passing ourselves off as silver dollars.

The Savior desires that we be clean inside and out. Our thoughts, words, and actions must mesh perfectly and consistently. When we are on weekdays what we profess to be on Sundays, our every action can withstand the closest scrutiny, and we can gladly and confidently walk in the light. Then, there is no fear of exposure that would bring shame or embarrassment to our families and friends. And more importantly, there is no hypocrisy that would disappoint the Lord and jeopardize our right to an inheritance in our Father's kingdom.

John 3:14–15

And as Moses lifted up the serpent in the wilderness, even so must the Son of man be lifted up: That whosoever believeth in him should not perish, but have eternal life.

When the children of Israel were afflicted with poisonous serpents, the Lord directed Moses to make a brass serpent and raise it on a pole so that anyone who was bitten could simply look and be physically healed (see Num. 21:6–9). This, of course, was a type or symbol of the Savior being lifted on the cross in His climactic act of Atonement. The scriptures also offer us the opportunity to look and live, to become intimately acquainted with the Savior.

We are always far more comfortable associating with friends than with mere acquaintances. The Lord desires to be our friend: "I will call you friends, for you are my friends, and ye shall have an inheritance with me" (D&C 93:45). Notice that He did not say we are His *acquaintances*. Let us cultivate that intimate friendship by knowing Him and deserving His gracious compliment. When we look to God, our spirits are strengthened and healed; thus we are infused with spiritual power.

The way is easy, and the directions are clear: "Behold, I am the law, and the light. Look unto me, and endure to the end, and ye shall live; for unto him that endureth to the end will I give eternal life" (3 Ne. 15:9).

John 3:3

Jesus answered and said unto him, Verily, verily, I say unto thee, Except a man be born again, he cannot see the kingdom of God.

We are born again through baptism, a sacred covenant or agreement between ourselves and God in which we promise to honor the terms He has set. Thus, our baptismal covenant is an ongoing process, not just an event. Each Sunday we have the privilege of renewing this sacred covenant as we take the sacrament.

We promise to help each other with difficulties, not to be too busy with our own burdens, assuming and hoping someone else will pick up the slack. We promise to be compassionate and comforting to those who have cause to mourn for as long as we are needed in that capacity. We also promise that we will stand as witnesses of Christ "in all places that [we] may be in" (Mosiah 18:9). There is no room for living a double standard—one for Sundays and Church and another for other days and places.

If we are faithful to our baptismal covenant, the Lord promises us that we will come forth in the First Resurrection, or the Resurrection of the just: "I, the Lord, am merciful and gracious . . . and delight to honor those who serve me in righteousness and in truth unto the end. Great shall be their reward and eternal shall be their glory" (D&C 76:5–6).

Mark 7:21

For from within, out of the heart of men, proceed evil thoughts.

This scripture makes it obvious that there is a reciprocal agreement among our thoughts, words, and deeds. Each one produces a chain reaction. The Savior taught that every action, whether good or bad, begins with a thought. For example, we first contemplate dishonesty in any form before it becomes a done deal.

More importantly, however, our inner integrity is reflected in our virtuous thoughts, words, and actions. The Greek philosopher Plato penned these words: "Beauty depends on simplicity—I mean the true simplicity of a rightly and nobly ordered mind and character. He is a fool who seriously inclines to weigh the beautiful by any other standard than that of the good. The good is the beautiful. Grant me to be beautiful in the inner man" (*The Republic*).

If we truly remember at all times to whom we look as our Exemplar—if our thoughts are Christ centered—we achieve an inner beauty that produces a chain reaction in word and deed with pleasing eternal consequences.

Luke 9:24

For whosoever will save his life shall lose it: but whosoever will lose his life for my sake, the same shall save it.

The admonition in this scripture has direct application to losing ourselves in the service of others. We do this in good works quietly and sincerely rendered without any expectations of a public pat on the back. "There are so many times when genuine human service means giving graciously our little grain of sand, placing it reverently to build the beach of brotherhood. We get no receipt, and our little grain of sand carries no brand; its identity is lost, except to the Lord" (*The Neal A. Maxwell Quote Book*, 315).

Mother Teresa of Calcutta devoted her life to the selfless service that reflected the Savior's example. Words she lived by remind us that our service must be motivated solely by our desire to give and not receive: "People are unreasonable, illogical, and self-centered. Love them anyway. If you do good, people may accuse you of selfish motives. Do good anyway. . . . The good you do today may be forgotten tomorrow. Do good anyway. . . . People who really want help may attack you if you help them. Help them anyway. Give the world the best you have and you may get hurt. Give the world your best anyway" (Paradoxical Commandments).

Luke 16:15

And he said unto them, Ye are they which justify yourselves before men; but God knoweth your hearts: for that which is highly esteemed among men is abomination in the sight of God.

The Savior spoke these bold words to the Pharisees of His time; however, we would all do well to heed this advice.

The Lord admonishes us to be a learned and educated people, regardless of our chosen vocation or profession: "Seek ye out of the best books words of wisdom; seek learning, even by study and also by faith" (D&C 88:118). The Prophet Joseph Smith reiterated the Lord's counsel regarding learning, emphasizing that there are two crucial elements in the learning process: *study* and *faith* (see D&C 109:7).

In Satan's plan of pride, he would have us believe that once we are well educated, we can certainly teach the Lord a thing or two. Another falsehood of Satan's is that once we are learned, we should realize that the scriptures are out-of-date and out of fashion. Nephi knew well the dangers of these two trains of thought when he wrote, "And they shall contend one with another . . . and they shall teach with their learning, and deny the Holy Ghost, which giveth utterance" (2 Ne. 28:4).

Coupled with faith in God and our knowledge that He is the source of all light and truth, we should eagerly seek and love learning in all ways that will enlighten us and give us *true* wisdom.

Luke 7:48

And he said unto her, Thy sins are forgiven.

During Christ's earthly ministry, many people flocked to Him to receive His healing powers: "And great multitudes came unto him, having with them *those that were* lame, blind, dumb, maimed, and many others, and cast them down at Jesus' feet; and he healed them" (Matt. 15:30).

We marvel at those wondrous miracles; however, the greatest miracle for those Jesus healed and helped was the healing of their spiritual infirmities—the miracle of forgiveness. The scriptures tell us that the people were made whole, which implies a completeness of body and spirit.

The miracle of spiritual healing is available to all of God's children as we turn toward His healing wings. We are reminded of the words of a beautiful hymn: "Come, O thou King of Kings! / We've waited long for thee, / With healing in thy wings / To set thy people free [from the burden of sin]" ("Come, O Thou King of Kings," *Hymns*, no. 59). The Lord's healing and forgiving wings are ready to receive us as we truly repent and desire to be made whole.

And when we receive the cleansing forgiveness that only our Savior can bestow upon us, we can rest assured that He files the offenses under "Everlastingly Forgotten."

Matt. 25:1–2

Then shall the kingdom of heaven be likened unto ten virgins, which took their lamps, and went forth to meet the bridegroom.

In this parable, the Savior is speaking to members of the Church, sadly predicting that a certain percentage of us will miss His feast (His Second Coming) due to our poorly planned or delayed spiritual preparations. Sometimes we are caught up in looking for signs when our focus should be on personal preparation, so His Second Coming will be a great rather than a dreadful day for us (see Mal. 4:5).

The parable of the ten virgins has special significance in this respect. President Spencer W. Kimball explains the relevance and application of the parable in our preparations: "In our lives the oil of preparation is accumulated drop by drop in righteous living. Attendance at sacrament meetings adds oil to our lamps. . . . Fasting, family prayer, home teaching, control of bodily appetites, preaching the gospel, studying the scriptures—each act of dedication and obedience is a drop added to our store. Deeds of kindness, payment of offerings and tithes, chaste thoughts and actions, marriage in the covenant for eternity—these, too, contribute importantly to the oil with which we can at midnight refuel our exhausted lamps" (*Faith Precedes the Miracle* [Salt Lake City: Deseret Book, 1972], 256).

Mark 9:24

And straightway the father of the child cried out, and said with tears, Lord, I believe; help thou mine unbelief.

We are familiar with the tender story of this family, who brought their son, whose body was wracked by a terrible spirit, to be healed by the Savior, who tells the father of the boy, "If thou canst believe, all things *are* possible to him that believeth" (Mark 9:23).

According to one young woman's wise words, we can relate to this family too: "They know what they are asking for is possible . . . and they want so much to believe. But because they are human, they have that little lapse in their faith. Yet Christ saw what they brought to the table and accepted it, 'unbelief' and all.

"Sometimes I am like that family. I know the enabling power of Christ. I've seen it work in my life every day. Yet sometimes . . . I experience that momentary doubt, and echo those poignant words, 'Help thou my unbelief.' Then I feel Christ's smile. He does not give me a look that makes me feel ashamed, but simply says, 'I'll show you the way and we'll work this out. I'll help you through it'" (Aislynn Beckstrand Collier).

There is nothing that cannot be healed through faith in the Lord Jesus Christ, who graciously helps our unbelief. Even faith the size of a minuscule mustard seed has wondrous potential from which a large and lovely plant can grow.

Luke 5:31

And Jesus answering said unto them, They that are whole need not a physician; but they that are sick.

The Savior is referring here to spiritual illnesses, or sins, to which we are all susceptible at one time or another and in one way or another. The Apostle Paul reminds us, "For *all* have sinned, and come short of the glory of God" (Rom. 3:23; emphasis added).

Thankfully, there is one Physician on whom we can fearlessly rely. His reputation is without blemish. He is a specialist for all maladies, and He always accepts new patients. But His greatest specialty lies in His desire and power to heal our spiritual infirmities. However, He can only accomplish this if we are willing to repent and change our actions and the intents of our hearts. Then He can heal us and guide us back to His straight and narrow path to walk in His ways.

His prognosis is the same for all of us and is filled with love and encouragement: "Behold, mine arm of mercy is extended towards you, and whosoever will come, him will I receive; and blessed are those who come unto me" (3 Ne. 9:14). There is no spiritual infirmity beyond His healing powers. Truly, He is *the* most competent, thorough, and caring Physician.

Luke 11:28

Blessed are they that hear the word of God, and keep it.

God's laws are eternal and were in effect in our premortal life. The very fact of our mortality bears this out: our obedience *there* ensured our eligibility to receive an earthly body *here*. Obedience is a law with a past, present, and future. The Lord reminds us that He is bound when we do what He says, but when we choose not to do so, we have no promise, either in this world or in the world to come (see D&C 82:10). There must be consequences for both obedience and disobedience. And obedience to one law or commandment does not compensate for disobedience to another.

For every obedient step we are willing to take toward our Savior, He gladly meets us more than halfway. We find this reassurance time and again in the holy scriptures: "Be faithful and diligent in keeping the commandments of God, and I will encircle thee in the arms of my love" (D&C 6:20).

Our strength comes through humbly *learning and doing* the will of the Lord, relying always upon His grace. Obedience to God's laws makes of our hearts the fertile soil that can nurture a bumper crop of sacred truths and eternal blessings.

Matt. 10:32

Whosoever therefore shall confess me before men, him will I confess also before my Father which is in heaven.

An ambassador is a diplomatic envoy, one who is a representative of a cause or person. Through the saving power of Christ's Resurrection and Atonement, we are all privileged—even authorized—to become His ambassadors. Even as He intercedes for all of His children, so must we make intercession for Him in all of our relationships and interactions. Our spiritual lives depend on our courage and commitment to His cause.

Paul's life and labors in the cause of Christ provide an example for all members of The Church of Jesus Christ of Latter-day Saints. We are all enlisted, so those around us should be able to recognize that we are unabashed ambassadors of Jesus Christ, but first and foremost, we must recognize that status for ourselves. We must know and understand that "he shall make intercession for all the children of men; and they that believe in him [and champion Him] shall be saved" (2 Ne. 2:9).

The gospel of Jesus Christ ensures that we are all candidates for salvation. The Savior's grace enables us to become bold ambassadors of His gospel and fit candidates for salvation.

Luke 17:15–17

And one of them, when he saw that he was healed, turned back, and with a loud voice glorified God, And fell down on his face at his feet, giving him thanks: and he was a Samaritan. And Jesus answering said, Were there not ten cleansed? but where are the nine?

Ten men stood afar off and cried out for the Savior's mercy, and the Savior miraculously healed them from the dreaded and socially repulsive disease of leprosy. So swiftly was their boon granted that they noted their healed condition almost immediately. Yet only one of them turned back to offer his thanks.

We can almost hear our collective "tsk-tsk" as we marvel at the nine men's failure to acknowledge the source of their miracle. Surely *we* would never lack gratitude for the Lord's myriad blessings. Yet the Lord tells us He is deeply offended when we show our ingratitude by failing to keep His commandments: "And in nothing doth man offend God, or against none is his wrath kindled, save those who confess not his hand in all things, and obey not his commandments" (D&C 59:21). Because the Lord purchased us through His Atonement, "it is his right to expect [us] to keep His commandments. By failing to do so [we] manifest gross ingratitude for all that has been done for [us]" (Bruce R. McConkie, *Mormon Doctrine* [Salt Lake City: Bookcraft, 1979], 380).

"The arithmetic of appreciation is far less practiced and known than the multiplication tables" (*The Neal A. Maxwell Quote Book*, 147).

John 1:29

Behold the Lamb of God, which taketh away the sin of the world.

The scriptures testify of the Savior's role as both Lamb and Shepherd. John the Baptist unequivocally identified the Savior as God's Lamb, prophetically designating the sacrificial role of the Savior on behalf of all mankind. He then boldly proclaimed in the presence of Jesus, "And I saw, and bare record that this [Lamb] is the Son of God" (John 1:34).

As our Redeemer, Jesus also became the Shepherd for all mankind. Ezekiel testifies of the Savior's messianic role as Shepherd: "So will I seek out my sheep, and will deliver them out of all places where they have been scattered in the cloudy and dark day" (Ezek. 34:12), "for there is one God and one Shepherd over all the earth" (1 Ne. 13:41).

Our Savior thinks of us as His lambs, and we marvel at His circle of love that includes large and small, young and old, male and female. The words of Isaiah tenderly remind us that our Good Shepherd nourishes us—His lambs—with His word and gathers us to His bosom with the arms of His redeeming love: "He shall feed his flock like a shepherd: he shall gather the lambs with his arm, and carry *them* in his bosom" (Isa. 40:11).

John 13:15

For I have given you an example, that ye should do as I have done unto you.

The world is teeming with people who beckon us toward their crowds, hoping for our admiration and emulation. All too often, however, the disparity between their words and their actions leaves us confused and reluctant to set our feet on their poorly lit paths, which are often treacherous. But when the Savior says, "Come, follow me" (Luke 18:22), we know that heeding His words will lead us in the paths of righteousness because of His perfect example.

He sets for us the perfect example of love and compassion for one another. He loved the woman at the well and the woman taken in adultery; the lepers, the blind, the crippled, and the otherwise unfortunate ones He so graciously healed; the multitudes He compassionately fed after a long and exhausting day of teaching and healing them; and the children He blessed and wept over and prayed for. We read of His desire to gather and protect His children "even as a hen gathereth her chickens under *her* wings" (Matt 23:37) and of His desire to find even the one lost and straying lamb.

The Savior's example is indeed the "light [that] shineth in the darkness" (John 1:5), the light that sets the perfect and safe example of balancing the letter and spirit of His laws judiciously.

Mark 16:15

And he said unto them, Go ye into all the world, and preach the gospel to every creature.

Before His final ascension to His Father, the Savior's last words to His eleven Apostles as they stood atop the Mount of Olives were, "And ye shall be witnesses unto me both in Jerusalem, and in all Judæa, and in Samaria, and *unto the uttermost part* of the earth" (Acts 1:8; emphasis added). Those ancient Apostles took their call literally and seriously and "went forth, and preached every where, the Lord working with *them*" (Mark 16:20).

The Lord promises that "in whatsoever place ye shall proclaim my name an effectual door shall be opened unto you" (D&C 112:19). In the early days of the Restoration, missionaries went wherever they were called, regardless of their great poverty and sometimes poor health. In Great Britain alone, in a little over one year (1840–1841), nearly 8,000 converts were baptized. Talk about effectual doors being opened!

And the miracle of worldwide missionary work continues as men and women of all ages and in an amazing variety of circumstances demonstrate their desire to stand as witnesses of the Savior, who clearly defines "all the world"— including our homes, families, friends, and neighbors—as the circumference and embrace of our service.

Matt. 18:21–22

Then came Peter to him, and said, Lord, how oft shall my brother sin against me, and I forgive him? till seven times? Jesus saith unto him, I say not unto thee, Until seven times: but, Until seventy times seven.

We often have high expectations of those with whom we share our closest relationships. When that closeness or trust is violated, we may often be tempted to nurse a grudge and let our wounds fester and grow. It is not always easy to forgive those who have wronged or injured us, and all too often, we immerse ourselves in these grievances, rehearsing and rehashing them both privately and publicly until we are physically and spiritually exhausted.

So, Peter's question is one we have probably all asked at one time or another. The Savior's answer is certainly not intended to give us a formula whereby we keep a tally sheet, and when we have crossed off 490 offenses, we can cross off the sinner as well. He is not telling us to do the math and then be done with the sinner!

It is fortunate, indeed, that this is not the way the Savior works when it comes to His patient and ongoing forgiveness for our manifold mistakes. And it is His desire that we follow His loving example. The Apostle Paul understood this principle of forgiveness well when he said, "And be ye kind to one another, tenderhearted, forgiving one another, even as God for Christ's sake hath forgiven you" (Eph. 4:32).

John 14:6

Jesus saith unto him, I am the way, the truth, and the life: no man cometh unto the Father, but by me.

We are surrounded by voices that entice us to walk in ungodly paths, voices that attempt to distract and intimidate us as we cling to the iron rod. These voices would have us believe that society's approval far outweighs the Savior's approbation. Amidst an increasing crescendo of natural disasters, financial instability, and media that is often fascinated and fixated on that which is sensational as opposed to that which is rational, we might be tempted to ask ourselves, "What or whom can we truly trust?"

In response to a concerned disciple's query, as well as our own, "How can we know the way?" (John 14:5), the Savior reassures not only His beloved Thomas but all of us. He answers that question in this simply stated yet grandly profound scripture. Tenderly, the Savior tells us, "Fear not, little children, for you are mine" (D&C 50:41). Like Nephi of old, we can talk of Christ and rejoice in Him (see 2 Ne. 25:26) because He is our spiritual lifeline, our loving Shepherd who "leadeth [us] in paths of righteousness" (Ps. 23:3) until we return safely back to our Heavenly Father's presence. It is Christ in whom we put our trust. How blessed we are to know His way, His truth, and His life.

Matt. 11:28–30

Come unto me, all ye that labour and are heavy laden, and I will give you rest. Take my yoke upon you, and learn of me. . . . For my yoke is easy, and my burden is light.

The Prophet Joseph Smith taught that in order to have faith in the Savior's promise to give rest to our souls, it is imperative that we become familiar with the attributes of His divine character. We must know that He is "merciful and gracious, slow to anger, long-suffering and full of goodness" and that He is "of a forgiving disposition, and does forgive iniquity, transgression, and sin . . . that he is a God who changes not" (*Lectures on Faith*, 42).

The Savior's offer to share our difficulties is inseparably connected to His Atonement. He suffered in Gethsemane, bled at every pore, and endured the agonies of Calvary because He wanted to make everyone's burdens light. All He requires of us in this sacred offer of friendship is our obedience. He tenderly entreats us to repent and come unto Him. His is an invitation issued in the first person by the very Author of our Salvation.

"It is a call . . . to forsake the world, to come unto Christ . . . to conform to his teachings—with the sure promise that in such a course will be found spiritual rest and peace" (*DNTC*, Vol. I, 469).

Matt. 20:13–14

But he answered one of them, and said, Friend, I do thee no wrong. . . . Take that thine is, and go thy way: I will give unto this last, even as unto thee.

As with all of Christ's parables, He is speaking symbolically, not literally, as He tells the story of the laborers in the vineyard. This parable is a particularly beautiful explication of the Atonement and of the Savior's mercy and saving grace. It is a reminder to all of us that what He *says* to one—what He *gives* to one—He is willing to say and give to *all*.

It is also a timely reminder that it matters not at what hour of the day we begin our labors in the Lord's vineyard. At the end of the day, what matters most is what we have done or become.

The Savior does not dispense His mercy like merchants who advertise a sale and then run out of the product before satisfying all those who have waited in line. His offer is good for *everyone* who labors faithfully, and He graciously encourages us even when we falter in our labors, demonstrating that it is by His grace rather than our works that we are saved. Our efforts are blessed only through His divine pardon: "Pardon faults, O Lord, we pray; / Bless our efforts day by day," and might we even say, "hour by hour" and "minute by minute" ("God, Our Father, Hear Us Pray," *Hymns*, no. 170).

Mark 12:42–43

*And there came a certain poor widow, and she threw in two mites, which make a
farthing. And he called unto him his disciples, and saith unto them,
Verily I say unto you, That this poor widow hath cast more in,
than all they which have cast into the treasury.*

Joseph Smith's translation of this scripture adds further insight and meaning to this incident: "For all the rich did cast in of their *abundance*; but she, *notwithstanding her want, did cast in all that she had; yea, even all her living*" (JST Mark 12:50; emphasis added). We sense a certain amount of fanfare and clanking as we imagine how the rich noisily tossed their large contributions into the coffers, and we even sense how they cast a few furtive glances around to ensure that their generosity was well noted. By contrast, we intuit the quiet and even apologetic offering of the widow, who probably hoped no one noticed or compared her minuscule mites to those large offerings, though the Savior deemed her offering mighty in comparison.

The Savior called special attention to this incident so His followers—and that includes all of us who take upon us His name—might learn "that the giver is greater than the gift; that sacrifice of all, though such be small in amount, is greater than the largess of kings who neither miss nor need that which they give away; and that it is the intent of the heart, not the value of the gift, which counts on the eternal ledgers" (*DNTC*, Vol. I, 628).

Luke 7:9

I say unto you, I have not found so great faith, no, not in Israel.

The familiar account of this Roman centurion, whose beloved servant was critically ill and not expected to live, is a study in faith, irrespective of ethnicity or religious persuasion. It seems logical to suggest that this centurion was also a man possessed of great humility. For example, he didn't deem himself worthy to have the Savior enter his home, nor did he even consider approaching the Savior personally but sent Jewish envoys to deliver his urgent request. He also possessed a reverent respect for and faith in Jesus's healing power and authority. He believed Christ needed but to say the word and the servant would be healed. And not least of all, he was a man concerned for the welfare of an underling in a time and culture where such were often abused or neglected.

There was no question in the centurion's mind that his petition would not fall on deaf or disinterested ears; and his forthright faith was immediately rewarded. The Savior's regard for this man's faith reminds us that our membership in His Church does not guarantee us a front-row seat in His kingdom, especially if our faith and works lack the steadfast stamina others sometimes demonstrate.

John 10:16

And other sheep I have, which are not of this fold: them also I must bring, and they shall hear my voice; and there shall be one fold, and one shepherd.

It was during the Savior's ministry among the Nephites that He clarified the full meaning of His words regarding His other sheep: "And now, because of stiffneckedness and unbelief they understood not my word; therefore I was commanded to say no more of the Father concerning this thing unto them. . . . And verily I say unto you, that ye are they of whom I [spake]" (3 Ne. 15:18, 21). In addition, He shared with the Nephites that there were yet other sheep to be gathered, meaning the lost tribes of Israel. All of the sheep to which he referred were of the house of Israel and were not the Gentiles.

At no time did the Savior manifest Himself personally to the Gentile nations, nor would he: "Great, however, will be the Lord's . . . blessings to the Gentiles who accept the truth, for unto them the Holy Ghost shall bear witness of the Father and of the Son; and all of them who comply with the laws and ordinances of the gospel . . . [as taught by those commissioned to minister to them] shall be numbered in the house of Israel" (*Jesus the Christ*, 677), and shall become a valued part of the Lord's covenant fold.

Matt. 25:13

Watch therefore, for ye know neither the day nor the hour wherein the Son of man cometh.

We are all familiar with the saying "There's no time like the present," a saying that applies in multiple ways to our physical *and* spiritual lives. We are continually being reminded to have adequate supplies on hand for times of need. These may be occasioned by natural disasters, illnesses, unemployment, or other unexpected emergencies. When these needs arise, it is too late to heed that reminder; the time for preparation has passed.

That same philosophy governs our spiritual preparations for the time when we will meet our Savior, either at our going or at His Coming. In either event, we usually have no way of knowing just when this will happen, so there can be no last-minute scrambling to replenish our spiritual pantries and no cramming for our final examination. The Lord tells us that "if [we] are prepared [we] shall not fear" (D&C 38:30). One of our well-known hymns also reminds us that now is the time to watch and carefully prepare:

"Improve the shining moments; / Don't let them pass you by. / Work while the sun is radiant; / Work, for the night draws nigh. / We cannot bid the sunbeams / To lengthen out their stay, / Nor can we ask the shadow / To ever stay away" ("Improve the Shining Moments," *Hymns*, no. 226).

Luke 9:23

And he said to them all, If any man will come after me, let him deny himself, and take up his cross daily, and follow me.

The Savior entreats us to become all that lies within our spiritual potential. The development of this potential lies in our day-to-day acts, thoughts, and deeds. It is a cumulative effort in *becoming* who and what our Heavenly Father and Savior desire us to be. They assure us that the seeds of spiritual greatness lie within all of us, but these seeds must find fertile soil in order to take root and blossom.

The word *daily* in this scripture is crucial. It is a call to move forward, not just once in a while but each and every day: "Life is not really a constant *vertical* climb. The process of spiritual growth . . . seems to be one of climbing, *pausing* for rest and refreshment and reassurance, *and then resuming* the climb, on and on to the top. . . . If we will seriously call upon the Lord and ask him regularly to bless us . . . we will sense the divine hand upon our shoulder, nudging us *onward* and *upward* all the days of our lives" (*Coming to Know Christ*, 49; emphasis added).

Taking up our cross daily means moving forward— following Christ—with that "perfect brightness of hope" (2 Ne. 31:20) that leads to eternal life.

Matt. 12:36

But I say unto you, That every idle word that men shall speak, they shall give account thereof in the day of judgment.

Words are an integral part of our lives. They are the means by which we communicate our feelings, our thoughts, our wants, our needs, and our beliefs. Indeed, they disclose the very essence of who and what we are. It behooves us, therefore, to choose them wisely and well as the scriptures caution: "Be not rash with thy mouth, . . . [for] a fool's voice *is known* by multitude of words" (Eccl. 5:2–3).

Paul exhorts us to avoid "foolish talking" and "jesting, which are not convenient" (Eph. 5:4). How often do we say things that are inconvenient, whether they are words uttered in jest, in idle gossip, or in anger, and how often are these inconvenient words offensive, either to God or man or both? And haven't we all been the recipient of hurtful words casually passed off by the offender with the phrase, "Oh, I was just kidding"?

Alma reminds us that eventually we will all "be arraigned before the bar of Christ the Son, and God the Father, and the Holy Spirit . . . to be judged according to [our] works [and words], whether they be good or whether they be evil" (Alma 11:44). Then, "Let us speak the best we can" ("Nay, Speak No Ill," *Hymns*, no. 233).

Mark 6:56

And whithersoever he entered, into villages, or cities, or country, they laid the sick in the streets, and besought him that they might touch if it were but the border of his garment: and as many as touched him were made whole.

The healing touch of the Master's hand is a prevalent theme in the scriptures. And faith always precedes the miracle of healing, whether physical or spiritual. We marvel at the blind, the lame, and the afflicted whose unwavering faith, coupled with the Savior's touch, made them whole.

No less breathtaking are the accounts of healing where *spirits* were made whole and strong through the Savior's ministrations. Our minds are drawn to a young and sinful man, Alma, whose very life depended on his desire for the healing of which his spirit was so badly in need—healing that could only come through calling on the name of Jesus Christ (see Alma 36:13–20).

Through faith in the Lord Jesus Christ, we too can be healed and cleansed from infirmities that impede our spiritual progress. We too can lay our burdens in the street, so to speak, and like the young Alma, our minds and hearts can catch hold of the reality of the healing balm of Christ's Atonement as we cry out within our hearts, "O Jesus, thou Son of God, have mercy on me" (v. 18), and we can be made whole—filled with joy and light.

Luke 3:10–11

And the people asked him, saying, What shall we do then? He answereth and saith unto them, He that hath two coats, let him impart to him that hath none; and he that hath meat, let him do likewise.

John the Baptist, who was foreordained to prepare the way of the Lord, preached forthright sermons that were perfectly aligned with the One who was to come after him, even the Savior of the world.

Here in this scripture is advice that had significant application in Jesus's time and society, where usury (or lending money with high interest rates) was not unusual among those who professed to be the most pious yet whose righteousness was most often preceded by the word *self*.

And this advice is applicable in *all* times and places for all would-be Saints, regardless of their particular dispensation. It is a simple but powerful admonition to share what we have with those less fortunate, without passing judgment either on their status or their worthiness. There is no disclaiming clause that says, "If you think they deserve it," nor is there any directive suggesting that we need only give something we were just planning to throw away anyway. This advice means sharing the best of what we have, with the best of intentions.

"In the time we have it is surely our duty to do all the good we can to all the people we can in all the ways we can" (William Barclay).

Matt. 4:4

Man shall not live by bread alone, but by every word that proceedeth out of the mouth of God.

This scripture reminds us of the dangers of relying on the arm of flesh: the accomplishments of man and, more particularly, what we might deem as our own remarkable performances. We are reminded of a poem by Percy Bysshe Shelley that describes what was once a colossal stone sculpture but which now lies half buried in the sand in two crumbled pieces consisting of the "trunkless legs of stone" and the "shattered visage." "Stamped on these lifeless things" is this inscription: "My name is Ozymandias, King of Kings: Look on my works, ye Mighty, and despair!" There is little doubt that the original intent of these words was to remind others of their comparatively puny, unremarkable accomplishments, and of the futility of their efforts. However, in the greater context, we are reminded that the so-called mighty works of man most often crumble and are unworthy of emulation.

On the other hand, as we live by the words and works of the Savior—the *true* and *only* King of Kings—there is no danger of our receding into a nameless and shapeless anonymity. His desire—His only goal—is to shape us into glorious entities who will stand not only the test of time but also of all eternity.

JST Mark 2:26

Wherefore the Sabbath was given unto man for a day of rest; and also that man should glorify God, and not that man should not eat; For the Son of man made the Sabbath day, therefore the Son of man is Lord also of the Sabbath.

The concept of the Sabbath as the Lord's day and as a day of rest was established in the culminating work of the Creation: "And God blessed the seventh day, and sanctified it: because that in it he had rested from all his work which God created and made" (Gen. 2:3). The Savior again established Himself as Lord of the Sabbath through a prophet in ancient times, when He wrote the eighth commandment with His finger on tablets of stone for Moses on Mount Sinai.

Chided during His earthly ministry by self-righteous hypocrites for healing on the Sabbath (see Luke 13:14) and for plucking and eating some ears of corn (see Matt. 12:1–6), the Savior reminds them—and us—of the importance of balancing both the letter and the spirit of the law. Surely His merciful miracles of healing were meant to glorify God and expand men's spirits in gratitude and reverence for His tender mercies. Surely eating simple meals prepared with singleness of heart was not offensive. And surely our worthy endeavors on the Sabbath are likewise acceptable to God.

The Savior says the Sabbath was *given* to man, implying that it is indeed a gift to be regarded as a blessing, not a burden.

Luke 9:56

For the Son of man is not come to destroy men's lives, but to save them.

By the world's standards, we are often judged and found wanting. Maybe we are not tall enough, thin enough, smart enough, popular enough, handsome or beautiful enough, or rich enough. Whatever our perceived deficiencies, the world at large is quick and happy to point them out. And all too often, we buy into these criticisms, thus demeaning our own value.

By the Savior's standards, however, we are of infinite worth. While He kindly but firmly points out areas in which we may fall short, and while He "cannot look upon sin with the least degree of allowance" (D&C 1:31), His mission was and ever will be to lift us. He will look *beyond* (but not *over*) our flaws and see us for what we are—children of God, worth every drop of blood He shed for us in Gethsemane's garden and on Calvary's cruel cross. "For God sent not his Son into the world to condemn the world; but that the world through him might be saved" (John 3:17).

The Savior is our champion; He participates in and anticipates and congratulates our spiritual successes. "Jesus lifts us up in a world which so often puts people down" (*The Neal A. Maxwell Quote Book*, 178).

Matt. 13:3, 9

And he spake many things unto them in parables, saying, Behold, a sower went forth to sow. . . . Who hath ears to hear, let him hear.

One of the Savior's favorite teaching techniques is the use of parables, stories with layers of symbolism and varied applications, depending on each listener's spiritual maturity and desire to understand. In His parable of the sower, He categorizes varying degrees of spiritual blossoming or withering according to the soil (or condition of our spirits) in which the seed (the gospel of Jesus Christ) is sown.

At various times, our spiritual soil may fit into any of the four categories the Savior described. There may be times when our soil becomes hardened and we allow the seed to be snatched away by the adversary before it has any chance for development. Our soil may be shallow when we have not expended the time and energy to properly nourish it, and then the seed can find no depth in which to put down proper roots. Then again, soil with the potential for a good seedbed may be cluttered with worldly cares and pursuits that leave no room for pure seeds. However, when our soil is deep and rich, it can withstand any distractions, doubts, and dissension, and it is able to yield an abundant harvest.

The beauty of this parable lies in the potential of our soil, or spirits: regardless of their present states, we can change them into fertile ground that will yield a bumper crop of eternal blessings.

Matt. 21:12–13

And Jesus went into the temple of God, and cast out all them that sold and bought in the temple . . . And said unto them, It is written, My house shall be called the house of prayer; but ye have made it a den of thieves.

During His earthly ministry, the Savior twice made it crystal clear that the temple at Jerusalem was His Father's house and His house, a holy habitation not to be used or abused by unworthy people or practices. Our present-day temples bear the reverent inscription "Holiness to the Lord," reminding us once more of the Savior's ownership and our stewardship.

We enter His house *only* as invited guests. And in order to receive His sacred invitation, we must make careful spiritual preparations that require strict adherence to principles of righteous living. Before entering His temples, we are required to put our houses in order because *His* house is a house of the utmost order. It is "a house of *prayer*, a house of *fasting*, a house of *faith*, a house of *learning*, a house of *glory*, a house of *order*—a house of God" (D&C 109:8; emphasis added).

Just as Moses was directed to "put off [his] shoes from off [his] feet, for the place whereon [he stood was] holy ground" (Ex. 3:5), so we too are expected to put off our worldly cares and pursuits—anything the Lord might consider inappropriate to bring into His holy house—"that thou mayest know how . . . to behave thyself in the house of God" (1 Tim. 3:15).

Mark 9:42

And whosoever shall offend one of these little ones that believe in me,
it is better for him that a millstone were hanged about his neck,
and he were cast into the sea.

The scriptures bear sweet witness to the Savior's regard and love for little children. He held them, blessed them, healed them, prayed unto the Father for them, and exhorted all of us to emulate their pure and innocent example: "Verily I say unto you, Except ye be converted, and become as little children, ye shall not enter into the kingdom of heaven" (Matt. 18:3).

The words that should particularly capture our attention in this scripture are "little ones that believe in me." As parents, it is our duty to bring up our children in truth and light so they never lose that spark of divinity—their cloud of glory that we refer to as the Light of Christ. This divine spark warms and expands their spirits as we prepare them to receive the greater witness of the Holy Ghost, affirming to them their relationship to Jesus Christ. Surely the Savior regards it as an offense to neglect this sacred stewardship or to impede or block the progress of His little ones in any way.

"Children are the epitome of innocence . . . purity . . . love . . . hope and gladness in this difficult and troubled world" (*TGBH*, 52).

Luke 6:12–13

And it came to pass in those days, that he went out into a mountain to pray, and continued all night in prayer to God. And when it was day, he called unto him his disciples: and of them he chose twelve, whom also he named apostles.

This is only one of many scriptures where we read of the Savior going up into a mountain to pray and enjoy sacred conversations with and ministrations from His Father.

We could think of the most high and holy events as mountaintop experiences. Nephi tells us, "And I, Nephi, did go into the mount oft, and I did pray oft unto the Lord; wherefore the Lord showed unto me great things" (1 Ne. 18:3). Also, Moses ascended Mount Sinai and received the Ten Commandments, written on stone tablets by the finger of God and, in a high mountain, talked with God face-to-face (see Moses 1:2). In high and holy places, God makes known His will regarding the affairs of His children.

Surely choosing His Apostles was a matter of utmost importance to the Savior, and as such, He sought His Father's guidance on a mountain. In our day, Church leaders enjoy this same process of personal revelation. As they earnestly seek to know the Lord's will in the highest and most holy room in the temple, prophets, seers, and revelators are chosen and receive instruction. Then we are privileged to confirm and sustain those whom the Savior designates as His special witnesses.

John 12:42–43

Nevertheless among the chief rulers also many believed on him; but because of the Pharisees they did not confess him, lest they should be put out of the synagogue: For they loved the praise of men more than the praise of God.

As we read this scripture, we might feel inclined to shake our heads at these chief rulers and exclaim, "Shame on you!" We might also be reminded of Lehi's vision of the tree of life, in which those who hesitantly partook of the fruit of the tree were instantly ashamed, and they slunk away when the tenants of the great and spacious building scoffed at them (see 1 Ne. 8:25–28).

Yet this same phenomenon is alive and well in our day, when many find it unfashionable to be religious and when many find it fashionable to flout the teachings of the Savior as outmoded and provincial. There are multitudes who would be ashamed to acknowledge a relationship with or to the Savior but who think nothing of using His name in blasphemous outbursts of anger or unbridled casual exclamations.

As members of The Church of Jesus Christ of Latter-day Saints, we are asked to freely share the gospel of Jesus Christ. Will we find it fashionable to talk of Him, rejoice in Him, and preach of Him so all may know where they can "look for a remission of their sins" (see 2 Ne. 25:26), even at the risk of rejection? Will we love and seek the praise of God more than the praise of men?

Matt. 22:17, 21

Tell us therefore, What thinkest thou? Is it lawful to give tribute unto Cæsar, or not? . . . Then saith he unto them, Render therefore unto Cæsar the things which are Cæsar's; and unto God the things that are God's.

The Savior's wise reply masterfully shut down this trick question posed by wicked men who tried to back Jesus into a corner, where He would offend either the theologians or the politicians of the time. Elder Bruce R. McConkie said, "In this present world where wicked men will not repent and come unto the fulness of the Lord's perfect order of government, there must be two separate powers—ecclesiastical and civil—the one supreme in spiritual matters, the other in temporal. Neither power can dictate to the other. And men are subject to them both" (*DNTC*, Vol. I, 600–601).

In a modern revelation, we again hear the Savior's wise voice: "Wherefore, be subject to the powers that be, until he reigns whose right it is to reign, and subdues all enemies under his feet" (D&C 58:22). Elder James E. Talmage wisely tells us that what we render to God should be our souls, which are stamped with His image and superscription: "Render unto the world the stamped pieces that are made legally current by the insignia of worldly powers, and give unto God and his service, yourselves—the divine mintage of His eternal realm" (*Jesus the Christ*, 507).

Mark 6:7–8, 12

And he called unto him the twelve, and began to send them forth by two and two; and gave them power over unclean spirits; And commanded them that they should take nothing for their journey, save a staff only; no scrip, no bread, no money in their purse. . . . And they went out, and preached that men should repent.

The good news of the gospel is designed to be preached to every nation, kindred, tongue, and people until it fills the whole earth. The Lord has said, "Remember the worth of souls is great in the sight of God" (D&C 18:10). His desire is that *all* of God's children will be given the opportunity to hear and accept the full blessings of the restored gospel, to repent, and to receive the blessings available only through the Atonement of Jesus Christ.

The Prophet Joseph Smith reminds us that the Lord knows the marvelous possibilities and potential of each of His sons and daughters and that He regards each soul to be of infinite worth: "Let every one labor to prepare himself for the vineyard, sparing a little time to . . . bring back the wanderer. . . . Souls are as precious in the sight of God as they ever were" (*TPJS*, 76–77).

As the Savior reminded His chosen Twelve, missionary work moves us out of our comfort zones, off the safe sidelines, and into the arena of active involvement and participation in God's work and glory.

Luke 18:14

I tell you, this man went down to his house justified rather than the other: for every one that exalteth himself shall be abased; and he that humbleth himself shall be exalted.

Once again, the Savior teaches a lesson that is vital for "all who hath ears to hear," and that most certainly includes Saints of the latter day. We are familiar with the prayers (in the temple, no less) of the Pharisee and the publican.

One was a long and loud, self-congratulatory, spiritually prideful list of his good works, along with a great, gulping sigh of relief that he was not like the despicable tax collector who stood afar off (but probably close enough to hear the Pharisee's open condemnation). We can only hope the Pharisee could afford the services of a good chiropractor who could treat injuries inflicted by an arm twisted so awkwardly while heartily patting himself on the back!

Meanwhile, we might have had to strain to hear the publican's heartfelt and humble confession of his shortcomings as he prayed quietly for God's mercy. Yet it is this second man who earns the Savior's approval: "For not he that commendeth himself is approved, but whom the Lord commendeth" (2 Cor. 10:18). The Savior reminds us that as we congratulate ourselves on jobs well done, we deprive ourselves of Heavenly Father's rewards. "Let him therefore abase himself that he may be exalted" (D&C 124:114).

John 8:29

And he that sent me is with me: the Father hath not left me alone; for I do always those things that please him.

Many Christian sects either do not understand the Godhead or they deny the reality of a Godhead that consists of three separate and distinct Beings. They mistake the oneness or unity of purpose with there being one faceless and formless deity. We are blessed to "believe in God, the Eternal Father, and in His Son, Jesus Christ, and in the Holy Ghost (A of F 1:1), who are one in purpose but not in form.

"In what way are the Father, the Son, and the Holy Ghost one God? Though three persons are involved, they are one supreme presidency, one in creating all things, one in governing the universe, with almighty power" (*A New Witness for the Articles of Faith*, 75).

"The incidents attending the emergence of Jesus from the baptismal grave demonstrate the distinct individuality of the three Personages in the Godhead. On that solemn occasion, Jesus the Son was present in the flesh; the presence of the Holy Ghost was manifest through the accompanying sign of the dove, and the voice of the Eternal Father was heard from heaven. Had we no other evidence of the separate personality of each member of the Holy Trinity, this instance should be conclusive" (*Jesus the Christ*, 119–120).

John 4:39; 41–42

And many of the Samaritans of that city believed on him for the saying of the woman, which testified, He told me all that ever I did. . . . And many more believed because of his own word; And said unto the woman, Now we believe, not because of thy saying: for we have heard him ourselves, and know that this is indeed the Christ, the Saviour of the world.

Testimonies regarding the reality of the Savior borne by those who have had personal spiritual witnesses are welcome additions to our own testimonies—drops of oil in our spiritual lamps. However, when it comes right down to it, our lamps become full only as we come to know for ourselves that Jesus is the Christ, the Son of God, our loving and personal Savior.

The Samaritan woman at the well, whose life was in moral disarray, heard the Savior's words, and the impact on her spirit was powerful and immediate as she ran to share her discovery with her neighbors: "Is not this the Christ?" (John 4:29). Some of those who heard the woman's declaration believed her, but *all* wanted to see and know for themselves. As they heard the Savior's words, they also received their personal spiritual witnesses.

We can enjoy this same special privilege as we diligently search the scriptures. We will hear the Savior's voice and will know that He is our Shepherd, God's Only Begotten Son, and our question will become a declaration: "This is the Christ!"

John 9:39

And Jesus said, For judgment I am come into this world, that they which see not might see; and that they which see might be made blind.

In His public healing of a blind man, the Savior teaches us a significant lesson regarding His mission and ministry. He was sent by His Father into the world to judge all men according to whether they accept or reject His works and words: "I came not to call the righteous, but sinners to repentance" (Luke 5:32). In this instance, the blind man was healed both physically and spiritually, the latter being the most miraculous as we see by his simple declaration of the Savior's divinity: "I believe" (John 9:38).

Also present on that occasion and dispensing their own counterfeit brand of judgment were the Pharisees, whose spiritual blindness was more acutely debilitating than any physical handicap. And therein lies the significance of the Savior's words. The spiritually blind who open their hearts and minds to the Savior are then able to see the things of the Spirit, while those who think their spiritual eyesight is 20/20 but fail the crucial sight test of belief in the Savior and His gospel are left to grope in spiritual darkness.

It is wise for us all to periodically check our spiritual eyesight and make the necessary adjustments so we too may say, "One thing I know, that, whereas I was blind, now I see" (John 9:25).

Matt. 13:33

Another parable spake he unto them; The kingdom of heaven is like unto leaven, which a woman took, and hid in three measures of meal, till the whole was leavened.

Breadmaking is an amazing process in which a small, shapeless, sticky lump of dough is transformed into a large, fluffy, delicious, and nutritious entity that delights our olfactory senses and pleases and satisfies our palates. The means whereby such a miraculous transformation takes place is, of course, the leavening agent known as yeast, which the baker carefully kneads into the dough.

The Savior's simile comparing His kingdom to yeast has both a personal and a universal application. Elder Bruce R. McConkie explains the personal application in this way: "The leaven or yeast of eternal truth is 'kneaded' into the souls of men; then its spreading, penetrating, life-giving effect enlarges the soul and 'raises' sinners into saints" (*DNTC*, Vol. I, 299). We, like the carefully prepared loaf of bread, become, through our swelling faith and testimony, spiritual entities who are pleasing and satisfying to our Heavenly Father.

The Prophet Joseph Smith explains the universal application of this simile: "The Church of the Latter-day Saints has taken its rise from a little leaven that was put into three witnesses. Behold, how much this is like the parable! It is fast leavening the lump, and will soon leaven the whole" (*TPJS*, 100). And we see this miraculous leavening effect as the gospel continues to spread throughout the world.

Mark 10:24, 26–27

But Jesus . . . saith unto them, Children, how hard is it for them that trust in riches to enter into the kingdom of God! . . . They were astonished . . . saying among themselves, Who then can be saved? And Jesus looking upon them saith, With men it is impossible, but not with God: for with God all things are possible.

The Savior's words remind us that great wealth is not necessarily equated with spiritual poverty or deprivation. It is placing our *trust* in these riches instead of in God that proves to be our stumbling block. His words are a timely reminder that we can let the acquisition of wealth strip us of our spiritual values and replace our quest for eternal life, *or* we can use our wealth wisely in helping to build up His kingdom.

Left to our own devices, we may put our trust in the excessive accumulation of riches, leaving no room for vital, spiritual commodities; however, as we place our trust in God, His divine influence and guidance make it possible for us to divest ourselves of the excess baggage of worldly riches that would prevent our entrance into His kingdom.

When our luggage at an airport is too large for us to take on board, we have the option of paring down our excesses or of missing the flight. And so it is with our spiritual choices: sometimes we need to take inventory and keep only that which will appropriately fit us for the kingdom of God.

Luke 19:5–6

And when Jesus came to the place, he looked up, and saw him, and said unto him, Zacchæus, make haste, and come down; for to day I must abide at thy house. And he made haste, and came down, and received him joyfully.

In Jesus's time, publicans were despised and given the social cold shoulder by everyone except the Savior. Now picture a short, little man, Zacchæus, "the chief among the publicans" (see v. 2). We can almost feel the shudders of revulsion among the crowd as we picture him climbing a tree to get a glimpse of Jesus as He is passing through Jericho. And to his and everyone else's utter amazement, the Savior invites Himself to the home of Zacchæus, who is regarded as nothing but a low-down sinner. Zacchæus made haste to joyfully receive this special guest into his home.

This man, though small in stature, was large in spirit, sharing half of everything he earned with the poor and making sure he was not guilty of cheating anyone. More importantly, however, Zacchæus was willing to climb a tree (a rather arduous and indelicate task in full view of a large and pressing crowd) rather than risk missing the opportunity to see the Savior.

And the Savior looked up, which is symbolic of His regard for all of His children. He never looks down on us, regardless of our stature or status. Let us, then, like Zacchæus, "make haste" to welcome Christ into our lives.

Luke 12:15

And he said unto them, Take heed, and beware of covetousness: for a man's life consisteth not in the abundance of the things which he possesseth.

The dictionary defines *covetousness* as an inordinate desire for wealth or for someone else's wealth; in other words, it is a tendency to become disproportionately immoderate when it comes to our wants.

Referring to this malady, the poet William Wordsworth penned these words:

"The world is too much with us; late and soon,

Getting and spending, we lay waste our powers;

Little we see in Nature that is ours;

We have given our hearts away, a sordid boon!" (*A Treasury of Poems*, comp. Sarah Anne Stuart, [Galahad Books: New York, 1996], 470).

The following lines share the regrets felt by someone who spurned the Church and spent his life in the vain pursuit of fleeting pleasures, ignoring his spiritual needs: "When this big world came and called me I deserted all to follow, never noting, in my blindness, that I'd slipped my hand from His. No, I spent a lifetime seeking things I spurned when I had found them. But I'd give them all, fame and fortune, and the pleasures that surround them, for a little of the faith that made my mother what she was" (Anonymous).

"Do not spoil what you have by desiring what you have not" (Epicurus).

John 3:20–21

For every one that doeth evil hateth the light, neither cometh to the light, lest his deeds should be reproved. But he that doeth truth cometh to the light, that his deeds may be made manifest, that they are wrought in God.

We take pride in keeping our homes neat and clean. There are times, however, when we might put off cleaning those little nooks and crannies that are not immediately noticeable. We might even half jokingly say that if company comes, we'll just use the dimmer feature on our light switch to hide those imperfections. After all, no one is going to use white gloves to check for any embarrassing dust. And we often vow to take proper steps to set our houses in order—soon!

Do we make similar efforts to keep our spiritual houses in order? We all experience times when a few things might fall through the cracks, so to speak, and if we turn the lights down low, we can tell ourselves we're doing all right. Even the most observant friend or neighbor would be hard-pressed to see that anything is amiss. We might even fool ourselves into thinking we're doing just fine—and *soon* becomes *later*.

However, our deeds must be able to bear the Savior's divine scrutiny, which doesn't miss a thing. As we take care of our less-than-spotless spiritual nooks and crannies, we will feel more comfortable and confident as we bask in the Savior's light, which has no dimmer switch.

Matt. 13:31–32

Another parable put he forth unto them, saying, The kingdom of heaven is like to a grain of mustard seed, which a man took, and sowed in his field: Which indeed is the least of all seeds: but when it is grown, it is the greatest among herbs, and becometh a tree, so that the birds of the air come and lodge in the branches thereof.

A mustard seed is indeed small, but it is not the smallest seed; however, the mature plant is larger than that of any other small seed. Thus, the Savior was speaking of the relative size of fruits of this tiny seed. What a splendid comparison the Savior chose! To His contemporaries, this parable must have seemed discouraging because they did not envision the kingdom of heaven as having small and humble beginnings. Yet the lesson is both simple and powerful in meaning: "The seed is a living entity. When rightly planted it absorbs and assimilates the nutritive matters of soil and atmosphere, grows, and in time is capable of affording lodgment and food to the birds. So the seed of truth is vital, living, and capable of such development as to furnish spiritual food and shelter to all who come seeking" (*Jesus the Christ*, 271).

This simple parable was a perfect simile for the initiation and growth of Christ's kingdom during and following His earthly ministry, and it is the perfect simile for the Restoration and the growth of His kingdom in these, the latter days.

Matt. 10:34

Think not that I am come to send peace on earth: I came not to send peace, but a sword.

At first glance, this scripture may seem to conflict with the Savior's promise of "Peace I leave with you" (John 14:27). However, when we consider His disclaimer, "not as the world giveth, give I unto you" (Ibid.), there is really no contradiction. As we embrace and live the principles of the gospel of Jesus Christ, we are blessed with inner peace. It is "the peace of God, which passeth *all* understanding" (Philip. 4:7; emphasis added) and is the antidote for the rampant dissension spread abroad and even closer to home.

Sometimes converts to the Church feel the sting of bitter persecution from those nearest and dearest to them. Their anticipated spiritual inheritance in the kingdom of God is sometimes accompanied by an instant earthly disinheritance by families, friends, and entire communities. We may reflect on the conflict that accompanied the Restoration, precipitating the loss of lives and livelihoods and culminating in the cruel martyrdom of a Prophet and his brother.

Our Savior knew that not everyone would receive His good tidings with great joy, but consider His promise to those whose faith remains unshaken: "In the world ye shall have tribulation: but be of good cheer; I have overcome the world" (John 16:33).

Mark 5:22–24

And, behold, there cometh one of the rulers of the synagogue, Jairus by name; and when he saw him, he fell at his feet, And besought him greatly, saying, My little daughter lieth at the point of death: I pray thee, come and lay thy hands on her . . . And Jesus went with him; and much people followed him, and thronged him.

We may marvel at Jairus's simple and straightforward manifestation of faith: that no matter what the case may be—whether his little daughter is still alive or has already died—the Master can make it right.

Moving as quickly as He can while heeding yet other quiet petitions for healing, the Savior makes His way toward the young girl's home, only to learn that she has died. Several marvelous things then happen: Jesus comforts the grieving but faithful father with the sweet words, "Be not afraid, only believe" (v. 36); He dismisses the wailing professional mourners, allowing only the parents and three of His Apostles to accompany Him into the girl's chamber to witness the miracle of life restored; and He further demonstrates His compassion by requesting that the damsel be given something to eat.

Here is faith manifested and rewarded. While it may have seemed that timing was everything, there was no impatient demand for the Savior's immediate attention, and there was no giving up hope when it might have seemed that all was lost. Here is fulfilment of the proverb "Whoso putteth his trust in the Lord shall be safe" (Prov. 29:25).

Mark 6:41, 44

And when he had taken the five loaves and the two fishes, he looked up to heaven, and blessed, and brake the loaves, and gave them to his disciples to set before them; and the two fishes divided them he . . . And they that did eat of the loaves were about five thousand men.

After long hours of teaching in the desert's heat, the Savior and the Apostles were tired, and evening was fast approaching. The people were also tired and had yet to make their way back to their villages and homes. And everyone was hungry! The Apostles favored sending the multitude away quickly before darkness fell, but the Savior had other ideas. Why not invite them to stay and have supper? Can we guess how high the Apostles' eyebrows raised at this point? An inventory of available food indicated meager quantities of bread and fish, nothing that would even come near to feeding this large crowd.

The Savior, however, was unruffled as He first blessed the food, then broke it into pieces and directed that it be served. "And they did *all* eat, and were *filled*" (v. 42; emphasis added). The meal was simple but nourishing, and there were leftovers, which the Savior directed should be gathered up and not wasted.

This "providing of temporal food to sustain mortal life was but prelude to teaching that men must eat spiritual bread to gain eternal life" (*DNTC*, Vol. I, 344). What a blessed lesson in compassion, and what a marvelous spiritual reminder that in all ways, Jesus is the Bread of Life who guarantees we will never go away hungry.

Luke 12:22–23

And he said unto his disciples, Therefore I say unto you, Take no thought for your life, what ye shall eat; neither for the body, what ye shall put on. The life is more than meat, and the body is more than raiment.

The Lord reminds us of our highest priorities, those things that have lasting significance in both time and eternity. A delicious meal satisfies our immediate hunger, but in a few hours, we find that we are hungry again. A new suit or dress or other item of clothing brings us a sense of satisfaction about our personal appearance, but these items invariably wear out or go out of style.

Note that the Savior is not advising us to starve or go without clothing; rather, He is warning us of the dangers of thinking *only* of our physical needs and neglecting our spiritual needs. Put in everyday terms, He is saying, "The spiritual necessities are what really count in the long—and eternal—run."

President Gordon B. Hinckley understood this well when he said, "Seek for the real things, not the artificial. Seek for the everlasting truths, not the passing whim. Seek for the eternal things of God, not for that which is here today and gone tomorrow. Look to God and live" (*TGBH*, 494).

"The best things are nearest: breath in your nostrils, light in your eyes, flowers at your feet, duties at your hand, the path of God just before you" (Robert Louis Stevenson).

Luke 4:18–19, 21

The Spirit of the Lord is upon me, because he hath anointed me to preach the gospel to the poor; he hath sent me to heal the brokenhearted, to preach deliverance to the captives, and recovering of sight to the blind, to set at liberty them that are bruised. . . . This day is this scripture fulfilled in your ears.

This incident took place in a synagogue in Nazareth, where the Savior read to those assembled. As it happened, He took His text from the book of Isaiah and read the very passages that foretold His calling and mission: to free those who were in spiritual captivity on both sides of the veil and to restore spiritual eyesight to those blinded either by ignorance or by the craftiness of men.

At first, those assembled "wondered at the gracious words" (v. 22), but their wonder soon turned to anger as Jesus pointed out the particular hardness of their hearts. Now His words did not seem quite so gracious, and their anger escalated to violence as they unsuccessfully sought to throw the Savior headlong off a hill. Talk about trying to kill the Messenger!

The Nazarenes' reactions may astound us, yet they are not without duplication in our own time and, perhaps, in our own lives. Often, we bask in doctrine with which we are comfortable, but we chafe at doctrine that takes us out of our comfort zone or hits too close to home (our spiritual Achilles' heels). Is it possible that we rejoice in being children of God but wish Him to conform to our image instead of being willing to conform to His?

John 1:45–46

Philip findeth Nathanael, and saith unto him, We have found him, of whom Moses in the law, and the prophets, did write, Jesus of Nazareth, the son of Joseph. And Nathanael said unto him, Can there any good thing come out of Nazareth? Philip saith unto him, Come and see.

This short but interesting interchange between two men who would become Apostles of the Lord Jesus Christ contains a remarkable lesson. Obviously, Nathanael's experiences with the citizens of Nazareth have left him with a lasting negative impression, so he is not about to be easily impressed; however, we may admire his willingness to "come and see" at Philip's urging. Once Nathanael meets the Savior, there is an almost immediate turnaround in his attitude. In fact, he bears testimony that Jesus is the "Son of God," "the King of Israel" (v. 49).

Do we sometimes pass hasty judgments or look with a jaundiced eye on those who are called to positions in our wards and stakes because we have known them in different contexts? Do these phrases sound familiar? "You've got to be kidding! I knew him or her when . . ." or "Someone told me that he or she . . ." or "How could anyone think he or she is qualified or worthy to accept that calling?"

Are we willing to suspend judgment, to come and look beyond what we perceive as the obvious to see as Christ would see? He looked into another's heart and saw no guile. Can we do anything less?

John 8:31–32

Then said Jesus to those Jews which believed on him, If ye continue in my word, then are ye my disciples indeed; And ye shall know the truth, and the truth shall make you free.

If we listen to the philosophies of men, we hear a "doctrine" preached that decries the restrictive and prescriptive nature of religion. We hear that the Ten Commandments are out, and license to do our will is in. We hear, "Follow the crowd, free yourself from unnecessary limitations, and above all, do not worry about self-restraint." They urge a brand of discipleship that lacks leadership.

How different these are from the gentle directives of our Savior. He endorses a brand of discipleship that promises *true* freedom and safety, but it is a discipleship that demands constant fidelity to His word and works: "For you shall live by every word that proceedeth forth from the mouth of God. For the word of the Lord is truth, and whatsoever is truth is light, and whatsoever is light is Spirit, even the Spirit of Jesus Christ" (D&C 84:44–45). As we earnestly continue in His word, the Holy Ghost will witness to us the truth of all things (see Moro. 10:5).

Adherence to principles of truth brings us freedom from the bondage of the author of sin, who ever so subtly drags men "speedily . . . down to hell" (Alma 30:60). Christ's brand of discipleship is the freedom to enjoy God's richest blessings in this life and in the eternities.

Matt. 13:44

Again, the kingdom of heaven is like unto treasure hid in a field; the which when a man hath found, he hideth, and for joy thereof goeth and selleth all that he hath, and buyeth that field.

We hear stories of treasures found buried at the bottom of the ocean in sunken ships, treasures that have been hidden away for many years and perhaps even centuries. These discoveries most often involve years of exploration, considerable expense, and diligent persistence on the part of those who engage in such explorations.

In this parable, we see a man who does not necessarily go looking for the treasure but happens upon it quite by accident. The happy part of the story is that the man recognizes at once that what he has found is valuable. And what has he found? It is the gospel of Jesus Christ, which carries no temporal price tag but requires that we be willing to lay our all on God's altar. Like the father of King Lamoni, we must be willing to give away all our sins to know God and enjoy the wondrous treasures of immortality and eternal life (see Alma 22:18). We should spare no spiritual exploration, expense, or diligence in obtaining it.

"It is not a sacrifice to live the gospel of Jesus Christ. . . . It is an investment . . . a greater investment than any of which we know because its dividends are eternal and everlasting" (*TGBH*, 567–568).

Matt. 21:28–31

A certain man had two sons; and he came to the first, and said, Son, go work to day in my vineyard. He answered and said, I will not: but afterward he repented, and went. And he came to the second, and said likewise. And he answered and said, I go, sir: and went not. Whether of them twain did the will of his father?

The sons in this parable represent two classes of Heavenly Father's children. First, we see those who reject the Father's commandments but later repent and set to work to make things right. Second, we see those who pay lip service to God's laws but fail to make good on their commitments.

We may see ourselves cast at times in both roles. Sometimes we might, like the first son, say, "No, thanks, God; I don't care to do that." Upon further consideration, though, we repent and do all we can to live up to His expectations.

Then there may be times when we pretend to step right up to the plate but don't even try to hit the ball. The Savior tells us, "He that receiveth my law and doeth it, the same is my disciple; and he that saith he receiveth it and doeth it not, the same is not my disciple, and shall be cast out from among you" (D&C 41:5).

The beauty of this parable lies in the fact that both types of people have the opportunity to repent. All is never lost if we—even a bit belatedly—get back into the game.

Mark 10:6–8

From the beginning of the creation God made them male and female. For this cause shall a man leave his father and mother, and cleave to his wife; And they twain shall be one flesh: so then they are no more twain, but one flesh.

The Savior is most certainly talking about celestial marriage, which is integral to exaltation. The Prophet Joseph Smith states, "In the celestial glory there are three heavens or degrees; And in order to obtain the highest, a man must enter into this order of the priesthood [meaning the new and everlasting covenant of marriage]; And if he does not, he cannot obtain it" (D&C 131:1–3).

Regarding the charge for a man to leave his parents and cleave to his wife, President Spencer W. Kimball says, "Do you note that? She, the woman, occupies the first place. She is preeminent, even above the parents who are so dear to all of us. Even the children must take their proper but significant place" ("The Blessings and Responsibilities of Womanhood," *Ensign*, Mar. 1976, 72).

A beloved poem by Elizabeth Barrett Browning echoes the beauty of the principle of eternal love:

How do I love thee? Let me count the ways.
I love thee to the depth and breadth and height
My soul can reach, when feeling out of sight
For the ends of Being and ideal Grace.
. . . I love thee with the breath,
Smiles, tears, of all my life!—and, if God choose,
I shall but love thee better after death. (*A Treasury of Poems*, 362).

Luke 17:33

Whosoever shall seek to save his life shall lose it; and whosoever shall lose his life shall preserve it.

"These words . . . are a statement of a law of life—that as we lose ourselves in a great cause we find ourselves—and there is no greater cause than that of the Master" (*TGBH*, 587).

King Benjamin epitomized the Savior's words in his well-known sermon on service, and he was his own best visual aid. Here was a king who could have sat back and taken his ease but chose instead to lose his life in service to his fellowmen, which he characterized by saying, "I have only been in the service of God" (Mosiah 2:16).

The Savior prefaced His injunction with a succinct reminder to us all: "Remember Lot's wife" (Luke 17:32). Her claim to fame was looking back at Sodom and Gomorrah, a tragic mistake that cost her the right to move forward in the cause of the Master. She lost her life, both temporally and spiritually, and the mortgage on her salvation was forever foreclosed by the debts of her inappropriate priorities.

We are not likely to suffer the salty fate of Lot's wife for our failure to be on the Lord's errand rather than our own, but we may certainly lose our right to claim our eternal inheritance. On the other hand, priorities well placed ensure peace, safety for our soul, and the promise of God's blessings evermore (see "Choose the Right," *Hymns*, no. 239).

Matt. 10:28

And fear not them which kill the body, but are not able to kill the soul: but rather fear him which is able to destroy both soul and body in hell.

The Lord's people have always been subjected to persecution in varying degrees. And none of us is immune to influences that divide our loyalties and endanger our souls' salvation. The Prophet Joseph Smith found himself in a situation where he feared man more than God when he lost the 116 pages of the translated manuscript. The Lord reminded him, "Yet you should have been faithful; and he would have extended his arm and supported you against all the fiery darts of the adversary; and he would have been with you in every time of trouble" (D&C 3:8).

When we feel the fiery darts of persecution, whether they take the form of ridicule or something more serious, it is well to remember the Lord's comforting words found in Isaiah 51:7: "Fear ye not the reproach of men, neither be ye afraid of their revilings."

The words of one of our hymns also remind us of this comforting promise: "Fear not, though the enemy deride: / Courage, for the Lord is on our side. / We will heed not what the wicked may say, / But the Lord alone we will obey" ("Let Us All Press On," *Hymns*, no. 243).

Matt. 13:45–46

Again, the kingdom of heaven is like unto a merchant man, seeking goodly pearls: Who, when he had found one pearl of great price, went and sold all that he had, and bought it.

Unlike the parable of the man who found a treasure in a field quite by accident, this parable shows that a man found the pearl after an intense and diligent search. This is a gem highly desired and highly priced—pearls were valued above other gems—and the merchant is thrilled with its luster and quality and does not hesitate to sell *everything*, including *all* his other jewels and *all* his other possessions, to purchase this one fantastic gem.

Elder James E. Talmage clearly explains the application of this parable in our own lives: "Observe that in this parable as in that of the hidden treasure, the price of possession is one's all. No man can become a citizen of the kingdom by partial surrender of his earlier allegiances; he must renounce everything foreign to the kingdom or he can never be numbered therein. If he willingly sacrifices all that he has, he shall find that he has enough. The cost of the hidden treasure, and of the pearl, is not a fixed amount, alike for all; it is all one has. Even the poorest may come into enduring possession; his all is a sufficient purchase price" (*Jesus the Christ*, 273).

JST Matt. 22:14

For many are called, but few are chosen; wherefore all do not have on the wedding garment.

Jesus has just related the parable of the wedding feast (the Lord's millennial reign), and missionaries are hastening throughout the world to invite everyone to attend: "First, the rich and the learned, the wise and the noble; . . . then shall the poor, the lame, and the blind, and the deaf, come in unto the marriage of the Lamb, and partake of the supper of the Lord" (D&C 58:10–11).

At the dedication of the Kirtland Temple, the Prophet Joseph Smith prayed "that our garments may be pure, that we may be clothed upon with robes of righteousness" (D&C 109:76). It is significant that one particular guest at the king's wedding feast did not have on a proper wedding garment, which resulted in his being cast into outer darkness: "He had accepted the invitation (the gospel); joined with the true worshipers (come into the true Church); but had not put on the robes of righteousness (that is, had not worked out his salvation after baptism)" (*DNTC*, Vol. I, 598).

The Lord explains why some do not qualify for a seat at His table: "Because their hearts are set so much upon the things of this world, and aspire to the honors of men" (D&C 121:35) while failing to honor baptismal and priesthood covenants.

John 5:22

For the Father judgeth no man, but hath committed all judgment unto the Son:
That all men should honour the Son, even as they honour the Father.

Our earthly justice systems often leave much to be desired in the way of fairness, equality, impartiality, and consistency: a sentence imposed by one court can be overturned by another, and persons tried for identical crimes can receive completely disparate sentences. It all depends on the judge, and no two judges seem to see things the same way, nor are some of them above being bought and paid for.

How blessed we are to know that our ultimate judge will be the Savior and that we can trust His judgment to be a perfect balance of justice and mercy, because mercy cannot rob justice (see Alma 42:22–25). All judgments He awards will be fair. The reason we know this is that our perfect Father in Heaven has deemed His Beloved Son to be worthy *and* trustworthy as our ultimate judge. He cannot be bought because *He* has already bought and paid for *us* in Gethsemane's garden and on Calvary's cross.

"The Man of Galilee will finally judge each of us on the basis of a rigorous celestial theology, instead of the popular 'no-fault theology' of this telestial world" (*The Neal A. Maxwell Quote Book*, 184).

Matt. 10:16, 22

Behold, I send you forth as sheep in the midst of wolves: be ye therefore wise serpents, and harmless as doves. . . . And ye shall be hated of all men for my name's sake: but he that endureth to the end shall be saved.

As missionaries young and old go forth to preach the gospel of Jesus Christ, they are the Savior's little lambs who leave the safety of the fold and become subject to the wiles and dangers of the world. Recipients of the gospel message do not always receive it with gladness, but the gospel of Jesus Christ is always *good news*. As wise servants, ambassadors of Christ emulate His example of patience, humility, and reliance on the Holy Ghost as they spread these glad tidings.

"They shall speak as they are moved upon by the Holy Ghost. And whatsoever they shall speak when moved upon by the Holy Ghost shall be scripture, shall be the will of the Lord, shall be the mind of the Lord, shall be the word of the Lord, shall be the voice of the Lord, and the power of God unto salvation" (D&C 68:3–4). It is a marvelous promise for wise and gentle servants.

Nephi echoes the Savior's promise of salvation for wise servants who endure to the end: "Wherefore, if ye shall press forward, feasting upon the word of Christ, and endure to the end, behold, thus saith the Father: Ye shall have eternal life" (2 Ne. 31:20).

Matt. 16:4

A wicked and adulterous generation seeketh after a sign; and there shall no sign be given unto it, but the sign of the prophet Jonas. And he left them, and departed.

The Savior referred to the sin of adultery when condemning sign seekers, and the Prophet Joseph Smith added his confirming declaration: "That principle is eternal, undeviating, and firm as the pillars of heaven; for whenever you see a man seeking after a sign, you may set it down that he is an adulterous man" (*TPJS*, 157).

"Why is this so? How does a disposition to seek after signs relate to seeking after carnal pleasures? . . . Those who worship at the altar of appetite, whose thresholds for gratification are ever rising, thus demand something extraordinary to establish the truthfulness of a claim, a claim, ironically, that is verified by the quiet and unobtrusive whisperings of the Spirit. Spiritual blindness . . . and the spirit of adultery are common companions" (Joseph Fielding McConkie and Robert L. Millet, *DCBM*, Vol. 2 [Salt Lake City: Deseret Book, 1988], 88).

"Craving a sign is actually an inversion of the teacher-pupil relationship. The pupil demands of a Divine teacher that he perpetually produce proof—when it is the pupil who must produce!" (*The Neal A. Maxwell Quote Book*, 316).

John 5:8–9

Jesus saith unto him, Rise, take up thy bed, and walk. And immediately the man was made whole, and took up his bed, and walked: and on the same day was the sabbath.

The Savior healed a man who had been bedridden for thirty-eight years, earning Him a generous helping of hatred and persecution from the Jews, who either witnessed or heard of the miracle. In their eyes and from their narrow-minded and pinched point of view, two heinous crimes had been committed: the man was carrying his bed on the Sabbath, and he was healed on the Sabbath—how much more wicked could it get?

Honoring the Sabbath and keeping it holy is one of the Ten Commandments and was meant as a *gift* of appropriate rest and reverent worship. Over the centuries, however, the Jewish laws regarding Sabbath observance became so prescriptive as to be downright ridiculous and even frightening. In fact, if a Sabbath-day infraction was deemed serious enough, capital punishment could even be invoked.

In this atmosphere, where the letter of the law had long since superseded any spirit of the law, the Savior's actions were deemed worthy of death: "And therefore did the Jews persecute Jesus, and sought to slay him, because he had done these things on the sabbath day" (v. 16). Mind you, they were looking for any excuse.

And herein lies a lesson for us all—that any virtue taken to an extreme can become a vice.

JST Matt. 23:23–24

Woe unto you, scribes and Pharisees, hypocrites! for ye pay tithe . . . and have omitted the weightier matters of the law, judgment, mercy, and faith . . . Ye blind guides, . . . who make yourselves appear unto men that ye would not commit the least sin, and yet ye yourselves, transgress the whole law.

The law of tithing was a favorite of the scribes and Pharisees because they could keep it so visibly (to be seen and praised by others) and because, for them, it required no inner sacrifice. All they had to do was toss in their money, and they were good to go. "The sin of those false religious leaders lay in their ostentatious display of paying tithing on every grain of sand and blade of grass, as it were, while they transgressed the 'whole law'" (*DNTC*, Vol. I, 619).

Well might we take (or should we say "tear") a page from their book and insert instead the lesson taught by the Savior "that it is easier to pay an honest tithing than to manifest in one's soul the godly attributes of justice, mercy, and faith; the one, comparatively speaking, is lesser in importance; the others are 'the weightier matters of the law'" (Ibid.).

As with all of God's laws, paying tithing has a spiritual component. Our temporal sacrifices must be accompanied by an inner contribution and submission of our will to God, who can then bring forth the blessings of heaven (see "Praise to the Man," *Hymns*, no 27).

Luke 10:41–42

And Jesus answered and said unto her, Martha, Martha, thou art careful and troubled about many things. But one thing is needful: and Mary hath chosen that good part, which shall not be taken away from her.

We are well acquainted with the Savior's frequent visits to the home of His beloved friends Mary, Martha, and Lazarus, where He could always find a warm welcome. Of the two sisters, Martha is regarded as the one who makes sure their guest enjoys every physical comfort possible. In all likelihood, Mary is right there by Martha's side, preparing for the Savior's visit, but when He arrives, Mary chooses to sit at His feet.

Many of us can relate to Martha's request for the Savior to tell Mary to get back to her household duties. The Savior's tender response speaks volumes. He neither condemns Martha's desire to provide Him with every comfort nor hints that He would approve of Mary's neglecting her household duties. Instead, He offers a gentle reminder of priorities well paced and well placed.

He commends our efforts to create clean and orderly homes and lives; however, He also desires that we not lose sight of eternally significant matters. At times, we must lay aside our cleaning and cooking tools and bask in the refreshing, cleansing, redeeming power of gospel principles and the spiritual feast provided therein, wisely balancing the "Mary" and "Martha" in each of us.

John 5:39

Search the scriptures; for in them ye think ye have eternal life: and they are they which testify of me.

In this scripture, the Savior gives us the perfect reason to study the scriptures, for they are where we learn of Him and become acquainted with His voice: "And whoso receiveth not my voice is not acquainted with my voice, and is not of me" (D&C 84:52). The scriptures are the Lord's letters of love to us.

As we read, delight in, and ponder the holy words our Heavenly Father and His Son Jesus Christ dictated, we learn powerful lessons about ethical standards, proper spiritual living, the rewards of righteousness and the wages of sin, the nature of the Godhead, the formula for repentance, and the miracle of forgiveness, to name just a few. Most importantly, we learn about the great gift of the Savior's Atonement and the reality of His Resurrection.

President Joseph Fielding Smith teaches us that we should *treasure* the Lord's word. This means not only reading and studying but humbly and obediently seeking to do the Lord's will as well, thus inviting His wisdom and inspiration as we read (see *Doctrines of Salvation* [Salt Lake City: Bookcraft, 1954], Vol. 1, 305). The Prophet Joseph Smith made this insightful observation: "He who reads it oftenest will like it best" (*TPJS*, 56).

For the kingdom of heaven is as a man travelling into a far country, who called his own servants, and delivered unto them his goods. And unto one he gave five talents, to another two, and to another one; to every man according to his several ability; and straightway took his journey.

This parable has perennial pertinence. Talents were distributed in the amounts of five, two, and one: "The talents bestowed upon each were the gift of his Lord, who knew well whether that servant was capable of using to better advantage one, two, or five" (*Jesus the Christ*, 541). When giving their report, two of the servants reported a respectable increase on their master's investment, for which they were complimented and duly compensated. The third, however, pleading fear of failure, buried his talent in the ground, and there it stayed, collecting dust until the day of reckoning.

In a spiritual sense, we are all given talents (gifts) according to God's wisdom, and either we augment them wisely, or they atrophy. Comparison, envy, and rationalization ought not to play a role in the final tally. But like the unprofitable servant, we sometimes go on the offensive in an effort to excuse our shortcomings.

"Talents are not given to be buried, and then to be dug up and offered back unimproved, reeking with the smell of earth and dulled by the corrosion of disuse" (Ibid., 541–542). In the reckoning of profits and losses, the Lord expects us to expand our view—not only of ourselves but of Him.

Again, the kingdom of heaven is like unto a net, that was cast into the sea, and gathered of every kind: Which, when it was full, they drew to shore, and sat down, and gathered the good into vessels, but cast the bad away.

The missionary effort of The Church of Jesus Christ of Latter-day Saints casts a wide gospel net that excludes none of God's children. Naturally, missionaries teach a huge variety of people from differing social, economic, religious, and educational backgrounds. They also teach those who have varying degrees of sincerity and spiritual stability.

Some might assume that membership in the Church is all that is required for entrance into the celestial kingdom, but when it comes to judgment day, we will be judged by our righteous stewardship of that membership. Just as with the fish in this parable, there will be a day for sorting and dividing: "Insomuch as they have become immortal, they must appear before the judgment-seat of the Holy One of Israel; and then cometh the judgment" (2 Ne. 9:15). The Prophet Joseph Smith put it this way: "So shall it be at the end of the world—the angels shall come forth and sever the wicked from among the just, and . . . there shall be wailing and gnashing of teeth" (*TPJS*, 102).

The choice is ours, and the time is now to clean up our acts, for if we are righteous now, we will be righteous still on Judgment Day.

Luke 9:62

And Jesus said unto him, No man, having put his hand to the plough, and looking back, is fit for the kingdom of God.

Physical fitness is desirable, and sometimes we flourish or flounder in achieving that goal. Most of us tend to hang on to favorite items of clothing that used to fit, hoping to ease into them again. But looking back to the "good old thin days" sometimes stifles our progress and makes us discontent with our present efforts and image. Sadly, our backward glance often stalls our forward momentum.

And so it is with our spiritual fitness. Perhaps we look back at past mistakes and become bogged down in Satan-spawned regrets that blind our eyes. But focusing on the glorious, positive principle of repentance and the even more glorious blessings of Christ's Atonement, which fit us for the kingdom of God, makes us "just right," as Goldilocks says.

We might also remember previous callings where we felt important. Comparing them to what we now perceive as our lesser calls to serve, we feel underused and unappreciated. Conversely, we may look longingly back at callings that felt more comfortable compared to the spiritual expanding and stretching the Lord requires in our present service. "Forward and upward" is our safest spiritual fitness motto, and our callings to serve our Heavenly King of Glory are "just right."

Luke 9:35

And there came a voice out of the cloud, saying,
This is my beloved Son: hear him.

There are many instances in the scriptures that describe God's voice as He speaks to His children, and it is usually characterized as being still, small, and pleasant—almost a whisper: "And it came to pass that there came a voice unto them, yea, a pleasant voice, as if it were a whisper" (Hel. 5:46). We know from our own interactions with family and friends that a quiet voice is the most dramatic and effective way to get anyone's attention and to prepare them for a message of great importance.

Peter, James, and John heard the voice of God on the Mount of Transfiguration; a youthful Joseph Smith heard the voice of God in a quiet Sacred Grove; and the surviving Nephites in a land decimated by nature's destructive forces heard the voice of God as they gathered at the temple in Bountiful. In each case, Heavenly Father introduces His Beloved Son and bids us to "Hear Him," the Savior of mankind, whose message is of utmost importance to every child of God. We might even say that Christ's message is a matter of spiritual life or death. Jacob refers to it as "the pleasing word of God, yea, the word which healeth the wounded soul" (Jacob 2:8)—souls wounded by sin or sorrow or disappointment or loss.

Mark 10:45

For even the Son of man came not to be ministered unto, but to minister, and to give his life a ransom for many.

In compliance with Jewish laws and traditions, Jesus gathered with His beloved Apostles for the celebration of the final official Feast of the Passover—*final* because the Son of God was about to fulfill the law of Moses by offering Himself as a sinless sacrifice for mankind. "And he said unto them, With desire I have desired to eat this passover with you before I suffer: For I say unto you, I will not any more eat thereof, until it be fulfilled in the kingdom of God" (Luke 22: 15–16).

This was an evening marked by a holy priesthood ordinance as the Lord knelt and lovingly washed the feet of His brethren. It was an evening of sharing the sacramental cup and breaking sacramental bread with His friends. He sang hymns, imparted farewell messages, and earnestly communed with the Father on behalf of His children. It was also an evening of betrayal, and it prefaced a night of incomprehensible suffering of both body and soul and a day culminating in an ignominious death and hasty burial in a borrowed tomb. This was an evening when the sinless Son of God would signify His willingness to suffer that we might be healed and to die that we might live.

Matt. 17:1–3

Jesus taketh Peter, James, and John his brother, and bringeth them up into an high mountain apart, And was transfigured before them: and his face did shine as the sun, and his raiment was white as the light. And, behold, there appeared unto them Moses and Elias.

Far away from prying eyes, pointing fingers, and demeaning disclaimers, Peter, James, and John were privileged to witness a heavenly manifestation. This was the Transfiguration of Christ, and the mountaintop location of this sacred occurrence was spiritually significant—it was a high and holy communion.

"One purpose of the Lord's retirement was that of prayer, and a transcendent investiture of glory came upon him as he prayed. . . . Thus was Jesus transfigured before the three privileged witnesses" (*Jesus the Christ*, 343). As the astonished and humbled Apostles looked on, they also beheld the radiant, glorified personages of Moses and Elijah conversing with the Lord.

Of greatest significance is the voice of Elohim proclaiming, "This is my beloved Son, in whom I am well pleased; hear ye him" (Matt. 17:5). He is addressing "the three apostles rather than . . . Jesus, who had already received the Father's acknowledgment . . . on the occasion of His baptism" (*Jesus the Christ*, 346). It was clearly the Father's mandate to the Apostles that they "were to be guided neither by Moses nor Elijah, but by *Him*, their Lord, Jesus the Christ," who superseded all former prophets (Ibid.).

Matt. 23:37

O Jerusalem, Jerusalem . . . how often would I have gathered thy children together, even as a hen gathereth her chickens under her wings, and ye would not!

The Savior's metaphor of a mother hen with her baby chicks is tender and vivid. The wing imagery is particularly significant because we tend to think that any bird with wings will use them in flight, but a hen's wings are intended for safeguarding, not flying. The Savior is reminding us that He is ready at a moment's notice to spread His wings in our spiritual defense.

Christ is ever mindful of us and of our need to repent, and we are offered His gracious invitation to feel the tender embrace of His welcoming and protective arms: "Behold, mine arm of mercy is extended towards you, and whosoever will come, him will I receive; and blessed are those who come unto me" (3 Ne. 9:14). Will we repent and hasten to be gathered under His warm and loving wings?

"Truly, Jesus came to save sinners; and if he can take a Paul, an Alma, and a Matthew from their lowly spiritual states and raise them to apostolic and prophetic stature, surely he can pour out good things on the spiritual publicans of the world, to the end that all who will repent shall find salvation in his Father's kingdom" (*The Mortal Messiah*, 2:58).

Mark 11:11

And Jesus entered into Jerusalem, and into the temple: and when he had looked round about upon all things, and now the eventide was come, he went out unto Bethany with the twelve.

This is both a poignant and triumphant time for the Savior as He nears the completion of His mortal ministry. He has ridden into Jerusalem on a donkey as His disciples strewed His pathway with their garments and palm-tree branches and raised their voices in a Hosanna shout. These were accolades reserved only for royalty, and no one in the history of the world had ever deserved such honors more than the Son of God.

How He loved Jerusalem. We sense this as He looks "round about upon all things" and weeps over the impending doom of this beloved city (see Luke 19:41–44).

How He loved the temple, and how He resented it when, upon entering His holy habitation this one last time, He again had to forcefully clear out the irreverent and disrespectful money changers and merchants, who had made His house of prayer into a den of thieves (see Mark 11:17).

And how He loved His disciples as He blessed them as only a loving Savior could bless His beloved and faithful associates. We sense a God's heart filled with compassion for the faithful and with sorrow for those too blind to accept Him.

John 10:17–18

Therefore doth my Father love me, because I lay down my life, that I might take it again. No man taketh it from me, but I lay it down of myself. I have power to lay it down, and I have power to take it again. This commandment have I received of my Father.

When Heavenly Father presented His plan in the premortal council, Jesus Christ volunteered to be our Savior. His words are beautiful as He declares His love for our Father and for us: "But, behold, my Beloved Son, which was my Beloved and Chosen from the beginning, said unto me—Father, thy will be done, and the glory be thine forever" (Moses 4:2). Our Heavenly Father graciously accepted His offer, uncoerced and supremely unselfish, and we shouted with joy and gratitude for what was to follow.

The Savior's sacred mission necessitated that He be mortal (born of Mary) in order to die and immortal (sired by God) so He could take up His body from the grave, inseparably reuniting it with His spirit. "As the Only Begotten of the Father, he was the only person ever born into the world who could make a personal choice as to whether he should live or die, and having *voluntarily* elected to die, the only one who could *voluntarily* choose to live again as a resurrected being" (*DNTC*, Vol. I, 487; emphasis added), thus ensuring us the blessing of immortality and the potential for eternal life.

John 11:3

Therefore his sisters sent unto him, saying, Lord, behold, he whom thou lovest is sick.

"Now Jesus loved Martha, and her sister, and Lazarus" (John 11:5). Theirs is a special friendship. "It was *that* Mary which anointed the Lord with ointment, and wiped his feet with her hair" (John 11:2). There is no doubt in these sisters' minds about how the Savior feels about them. They do not express a hesitant hope that Jesus remembers and loves them, nor do they have to verbalize their desire that He come heal their beloved brother.

We stand in awe of these women with hearts and spirits so secure in the knowledge of the Savior's love and so filled with the attendant faith that He has the power to dispel what is obviously a very serious illness. And it seems logical to assume that Lazarus also knows he is in trouble and desires the touch of the Lord's healing hand.

Do we enjoy that same secure and sweet knowledge of the Savior's unconditional love for us? And does He know that we in turn love Him and trust Him to come to us in our hour of need, whether it be physical or spiritual illness that beckons His divine attention?

John 11:6

When he heard therefore that he was sick, he abode two days still in the same place where he was.

Upon receiving word of Lazarus's illness, the Savior did not go immediately to Bethany but lingered another two days in Perea before setting off on the journey of about twenty-five miles, which would require an *additional* two days of travel.

Why does He take this seemingly casual approach after receiving so poignant a communication from His beloved friends? "Then said Jesus unto them plainly, Lazarus is dead. And I am glad for your sakes that I was not there, to the intent ye may believe; nevertheless let us go unto him" (John 11: 14–15). This was to be an entirely different experience than when He raised the daughter of Jairus and the son of the widow in Nain from the dead. In neither of those instances had the bodies been brought to the point of entombment.

However, in this case, not only was Lazarus's body prepared for burial, but the funeral was also already over and the body entombed. Four days had passed since Lazarus's death, and decomposition was well underway. This was to be a bold and public demonstration to skeptics and believers alike—that He was the Son of God with power over life and death.

The faith of *all* those He loves and who love Him will be richly rewarded.

John 11:27

She saith unto him, Yea, Lord: I believe that thou art the Christ, the Son of God, which should come into the world.

Here is a woman whose testimony echoes that of a stalwart Apostle: "Thou art the Christ, the Son of the living God" (Matt. 16:16). This is the same Martha whom, on an earlier occasion, the Savior gently reminded about "that good part" when it came to spiritual matters.

All too often, Martha and Mary are stereotyped regarding their priorities; however, when their brother Lazarus dies, we see a role reversal: it is Martha who hastens to meet the Savior when He is still some distance from their home, while Mary stays in the house, attending to the needs of their guests. With sorrowful words that also give expression to her faith, Martha declares, "If thou hadst been here, my brother had not died" (John 11:21), and she then bears her testimony regarding the doctrine of resurrection, culminating in the crescendo of her powerful witness of the Savior's identity.

Shortly thereafter, Martha invites Mary to join the Lord, and "as soon as she heard *that, she arose quickly*, and came unto him" (John 11:29; emphasis added) with similar tearful expressions of her own stalwart testimony. Clearly, both of these marvelous women understood and cherished "that good part"—a gentle reminder for all of us to do likewise.

John 11:43

And when he thus had spoken, he cried with a loud voice, Lazarus, come forth.

Upon seeing the grief of Lazarus's two sisters, the Savior Himself is moved to tears: "What a scene is this—the Son of God in tears! And yet God and man are of the same race, endowed in greater or lesser degree with the same characteristics and attributes. . . . Moreover, the man Jesus . . . while he dwelt in the flesh, was subject to every normal mortal feeling and desire. . . . He rejoiced with his friends, wept with the mourners, loved those who kept his commandments" (*DNTC*, Vol. I, 533). "Then said the Jews, Behold how he loved him!" (John 11:36). And the Savior's love was about to be manifested in the most wondrous of ways.

It was both natural and fitting that prior to His command to the deceased Lazarus to come forth, the Savior prayed to His Father, thanking Him for this opportunity to use the power and authority that had already been given Him: "He gave thanks, and in the hearing of all who stood by acknowledged the Father and expressed the oneness of His own and the Father's purposes. . . . God was glorified and the divinity of the Son of Man was vindicated in the result" (*Jesus the Christ*, 460, 462).

John 12:46

I am come a light into the world, that whosoever believeth on me should not abide in darkness.

There is nothing more frustrating than a flickering or burned-out lightbulb. We live by light, and we crave its illumination for just about everything we want to accomplish. Wouldn't it be marvelous if someone could invent a lightbulb that would live up to all its promises of longevity and performance?

Fortunately, when it comes to spiritual matters, there is a light that is guaranteed never to wear out or vary in quality. And where do we find this miraculous light? It is, of course, in the Savior. His light is the light of the sun, moon, and stars combined; the light by which everything was created; the "light which is in all things, . . . which is the law by which all things are governed, even the power of God who sitteth upon his throne, who is in the bosom of eternity, who is in the midst of all things" (D&C 88:13).

In pondering the wondrous blessings of the Savior's light, we find comfort in these words: "The Lord is my light, my all and in all. / There is in his sight no darkness at all. / He is my Redeemer, my Savior and King. / With Saints and with angels his praises I'll sing" ("The Lord is My Light," *Hymns*, no. 89).

John 13:17

If ye know these things, happy are ye if ye do them.

We live in a society where happiness is too often equated with the pleasures of self-indulgence, self-gratification, and self-absorption and with the need to be instantly rewarded and entertained, regardless of personal effort or worthiness. It is a happiness that is fleeting and elusive and all too often counterfeit in its end results.

Contrast this counterfeit happiness with what the scriptures teach us about the true nature of happiness. King Benjamin equates happiness with obedience to the commandments of God: "I would desire that ye should consider on the blessed and *happy* state of those that keep the commandments of God" (Mosiah 2:41; emphasis added). The words of the Psalmist reinforce this truth: "Be glad [happy] in the Lord, and rejoice, ye righteous: and shout for joy, all ye that are upright in heart" (Ps. 32:11).

Sow a thought, and you reap an act;
Sow an act, and you reap a habit;
Sow a habit, and you reap a character;
Sow a character, and you reap [an eternal] destiny.
(Ralph Waldo Emerson)

The law of the harvest teaches us that we reap what we sow. The Savior promises that if we sow the seeds of obedience, we will reap a rich harvest of peace and happiness.

John 13:34–35

A new commandment I give unto you, That ye love one another; as I have loved you, that ye also love one another. By this shall all men know that ye are my disciples, if ye have love one to another.

As the Savior met with His beloved Apostles on the occasion of the Last Supper, He spoke of love as a *new* commandment. This may have seemed somewhat puzzling to them, since He spoke of love in His commandment given anciently to the children of Israel. In fact, the very basis of the law of Moses was love of God, self, and neighbors. Here, however, the Savior was speaking of a higher interpretation of the law of love.

The words *as I have loved you* provide the key to appropriately keeping this new commandment. When we examine how the Savior loves, we find that He loves unconditionally. He loves sinners: "Neither do I condemn thee" (John 8:11). He loves those of all social classes, rich and poor alike: He dined with publicans and conversed with members of the Sanhedrin. He loves women and children: "Forbid them not" (Luke 18:16). He loves without the promise of reciprocation, and He loves each of us purely and forever, embodying the essence of charity, for "charity is the pure love of Christ, and it endureth forever" (Moro. 7:47).

It is only our emulation of the Savior's pure love toward God and toward one another that will distinguish us as His disciples.

John 14:2

In my Father's house are many mansions: if it were not so, I would have told you. I go to prepare a place for you.

This is both a comforting and exciting promise. Even though we live in a variety of circumstances and we may not all have large and spacious abodes, we regard our earthly homes—wherever and whatever they may be—as blessings, and we are grateful for their shelter and warmth and safety.

The Savior speaks of the *mansions* in His Father's house. And His use of the word *many* assures us that such spiritually luxurious accommodations are available to all who are willing to "always remember Him, and keep His commandments" (Moro. 4:3). Otherwise, as He points out, He would not make such a bold and universal promise.

"Let not your hearts be troubled; for in my Father's house are *many* mansions, and I have prepared a place for you; *and where my Father and I am, there ye shall be also*" (D&C 98:18; emphasis added). Imagine God and His Beloved Son not only as our landlords but also as our nearest and dearest neighbors. Talk about having shelter, warmth, and safety! This is celestial housing worthy of our very finest qualifying efforts.

John 14:18

I will not leave you comfortless: I will come to you.

The word *comfort* has many meanings in our lives. We cherish our comfort zones, places or situations that give us a feeling of well-being and safety. But when the physical comforts of the world cannot console us, we yearn for spiritual comfort. It is well for us to remember that it is the Lord who provides the softening influence when we are perplexed and troubled.

The Lord spoke tender words of comfort to His confused and bewildered Apostles as they shared the Last Supper with Him on the eve of His Crucifixion: "Let not your heart be troubled, neither let it be afraid" (John 14:27).

These words of infinite compassion and comfort are meant for each one of His children. Elder Jeffrey R. Holland tells us that in spite of the Lord's innumerable words of comfort to His children, we as Latter-day Saints often resist or fail to understand His promise of peace. Surely it must apply to someone else. He goes on to say that when we fail to let the Savior's love and comfort penetrate our troubled hearts, the Savior is grieved by our lack of confidence in His loving care (see *Trusting Jesus* [Salt Lake City: Deseret Book, 2003], 68).

John 14:26

But the Comforter, which is the Holy Ghost, whom the Father will send in my name, he shall teach you all things, and bring all things to your remembrance, whatsoever I have said unto you.

When the Savior taught the Sermon on the Mount, He talked about a strait and narrow way, a straightforward path characterized by well-marked signs that lead us toward eternal life or exaltation.

Our guide on that path is the Holy Ghost, a gift freely and graciously given to all who enter the waters of baptism, but it is a gift that must be nourished and cherished. We embrace this gift by offering the Lord our contrite spirits and broken hearts, which are evidences of our true humility.

In return, the Savior promises that the Holy Ghost will bless us with comfort and peace and that we will have a remembrance of all things spiritual—things we were taught in our premortal existence as well as things we learn here. The Holy Ghost bears personal witness to us that Jesus is the Christ: "But when the Comforter is come . . . he shall testify of me" (John 15:26).

In a very personal sense, the Holy Ghost lightens our burdens and speaks peace to our souls. Nothing is too trivial for His comforting intervention and enlightenment. As Paul tells us, the Holy Ghost is "the love of God . . . shed abroad in our hearts" (Rom. 5:5).

John 14:27

Peace I leave with you, my peace I give unto you: not as the world giveth, give I unto you. Let not your heart be troubled, neither let it be afraid.

The Savior brought a type of peace into the world that confused many who heard His message. During Christ's mortal ministry, the Jews were looking for a militaristic Messiah who would break their yoke of Roman bondage and raise them triumphantly to a better position. This victory had far less to do with spiritual supremacy than with a quest for self-righteous vainglory. In present times, as wars and eruptions of violence rage at home and abroad, we long for the ending of the struggles between opposing forces. Surely the Savior's Advent will ensure this.

Amidst cataclysmic unrest, we must remember that the peace prophesied and promised and authored and published by the Savior has a personal, here-and-now application. True and abiding peace can envelop the ends of the earth, beginning in our hearts. His promise of peace is our one sure source of comfort and protection. His is the inner, eternal peace that comes from embracing the principles and ordinances of His gospel and from applying the atoning blood of His great sacrifice.

The Savior's miracles of peace in our lives are not performed to prove His divine might but to manifest His divine compassion for us.

John 15:5

I am the vine, ye are the branches: He that abideth in me, and I in him, the same bringeth forth much fruit: for without me ye can do nothing.

Branches that have been torn from trees or other plants are one evidence of the aftermath of a wind storm. There is no way to reattach those branches so they will continue to be part the original tree or vine whose roots are safely embedded in deep soil. The detached branches often become either part of a compost heap or firewood.

The Lord uses an allegory involving a divine vine and the fate of its branches that are either attached to or torn from that vine to define the relationship between Himself and His Apostles. Christ is the true vine, and His ordained prophets and Apostles are the branches, who, when safely and securely attached to the vine, carry the message of Christ's salvation to the world. "Salvation comes because of Christ. . . . But the message of salvation is carried to men by Christ's prophets. They are living branches who carry the life-giving truths to other men . . . who can then pick the fruit of eternal life from the branches. Both vine and branches are required to produce fruit . . . to make salvation available to mankind" (*DNTC*, Vol. I, 745).

John 15:10

If ye keep my commandments, ye shall abide in my love.

The Savior's promise is simple, and it never changes. It applies to all of God's children, regardless of where or when we have lived. The most exciting part of this promise is the spiritual prosperity we can enjoy as a result of our obedience: "And, if you keep my commandments and endure to the end you shall have eternal life, which gift is the greatest of all the gifts of God" (D&C 14:7). Our investment is obedience, and the return is eternal life.

When we think about the fluctuations in our present economy and the risks we face when we invest our hard-earned money, the Lord's investment plan is incomparable. The only variable is our individual performance, which we alone control. If we come up short, it is because our investment has not been enough. On the other hand, each time we choose to increase our investment in obedience, the Lord stands ready to bless us with spiritual prosperity.

King Benjamin lists some of the investments that fit us for eternal life: acknowledging God's goodness, wisdom, patience, and long-suffering; trusting in the Lord's Atonement; diligently keeping the commandments; and enduring to the end (see Mosiah 4:6).

John 15:11

These things have I spoken unto you, that my joy might remain in you, and that your joy might be full.

In these words, the Savior speaks generously of sharing His joy. Sometimes, when the burdens of life seem a bit overwhelming, when sorrows and disappointments seem to press in from all sides, we tend to forget that, as the Prophet Joseph Smith taught, "happiness is the object and design of our existence" (*TPJS*, 255).

Shepherds on a hillside were given "good tidings of great joy" (Luke 2:10), which tidings have brought great joy into the hearts of mankind through all the intervening years since Christ's birth. Isaiah speaks directly to those of us living in the last days when he says, "For ye shall go out with joy, and be led forth with peace" (Isa. 55:12). And we read the moving words of the Savior when He says, "Blessed are ye because of your faith. And now behold, my joy is full" (3 Ne. 17:20).

How can we resist the Savior's invitation to be a joyful people when our very Exemplar feels such joy? The key to finding joy in our lives and in eternity is to "pursue the path that leads to it; and this path is . . . keeping all the commandments of God" (*TPJS*, 255–256).

Howbeit when he, the Spirit of truth, is come, he will guide you into all truth: for he shall not speak of himself; but whatsoever he shall hear, that shall he speak: and he will shew you things to come. He shall glorify me: for he shall receive of mine, and shall shew it unto you.

We are admonished to seek earnestly "the best gifts, always remembering for what they are given" (D&C 46:8). "President Wilford Woodruff stated that . . . the gift of the Holy Ghost is the greatest of all the gifts of God in this life. The Spirit in our life is God's sweet certification to us that we're on course, in covenant, and in line eventually to receive eternal life. The Holy Spirit is God's down payment to us, his 'earnest money' on us, his indication that he seriously intends to save us with an everlasting salvation" (*Coming to Know Christ*, 55).

In turn, we must surrender our "whole souls as an offering unto [the Savior]" (Omni 1:26), meaning that we surrender *all* of our sins, not just a portion of them, if we are to enjoy the blessings and companionship of the Holy Ghost. Nephi tells us this great gift enables us to "speak with the tongue of angels, and shout praises unto the Holy One of Israel" (2 Ne. 31:13). Paul declares that the kingdom of God is "righteousness, and peace, and joy in the Holy Ghost" (Rom. 14:17). These are indeed magnificent promises and blessings inherent with enjoying the companionship of the Holy Ghost.

John 16:20

Verily, verily, I say unto you, That ye shall weep and lament, but the world shall rejoice: and ye shall be sorrowful, but your sorrow shall be turned into joy.

As His Crucifixion fast approached, the Savior reminded His Apostles of the universal and eternal joy that would result from His ensuing hours of suffering and sorrow. It is also a timely reminder for each of us—our joy comes because of the Lord's atoning sacrifice.

It is vital for us to remember that there are fountains of spiritual water that can replenish our drooping and thirsting spirits. And the bottom line is this: the Lord wants us to be happy and find joy in our lives. True joy lies in loving the Lord and keeping His commandments. Faithful Saints who trust in the Savior and lay hold on His Atonement know this joy is possible. "Surely he hath borne our griefs, and carried our sorrows" that we might lay hold on a fulness of joy (Isa. 53:4).

Like shepherds from long ago on a faraway hillside; like Adam and Eve, whose eyes were opened in the glorious garden; like Lehi, who partook of a desirable fruit; like Alma, who remembered His Redeemer; we too can listen for and hear and feel the "good tidings of great joy" (Luke 2:10) given to the world collectively and to each child of God individually.

John 17:3

And this is life eternal, that they might know thee the only true God, and Jesus Christ, whom thou hast sent.

It is well for us to *know* God and Jesus Christ, not just know *about* Them. The scriptures are our greatest source of information on this sacred topic. The Savior bears witness of this: "Search the scriptures; for in them ye think ye have eternal life: and they are they which testify of me" (John 5:39). Elder D. Todd Christofferson tells us that the main purpose of the scriptures is to fill us with faith in our Heavenly Father and His Beloved Son, to guide us in knowing Them and loving Them (see "The Blessing of Scripture," *Ensign*, May 2010, 34).

The Apostle Paul admonishes us, "Rejoice in the Lord alway: and again I say, rejoice" (Philip. 4:4). The more we come to know the Savior, the more reasons we find to rejoice in Him, our Lord and God. We rejoice in His central role in the great plan of happiness. We rejoice in His birth and earthly ministry. We rejoice that He is our Savior, who wrought the great and infinite Atonement in our behalf. We rejoice that He is our merciful mediator with the Father. We rejoice that He loves us. And we rejoice in the Restoration of His everlasting gospel.

Mark 14:26

And when they had sung an hymn, they went out into the mount of Olives.

The Savior's final Feast of the Passover culminated with the singing of a hymn before the Master moved toward the garden in which His great act of atoning love would begin (see Mark 14:26). So much in the way of suffering and sacrifice lay ahead for Him, so it is lovely to know that it was prefaced by the strains of a beautiful hymn, just as His birth was heralded by angelic anthems. On both occasions, surely the heavens resounded in reverent replicating echoes.

Singing hymns soothes our spirits, invites the Holy Ghost, and relays our heartfelt praise to our Heavenly Father and His Beloved Son. Our musical talents may not measure up to the standard and quality of other voices in the congregation, but if our hearts are in tune, it will not matter if our voices are a little off-key. All that matters is that we are having a musical conversation with the Lord, whose heart receives our more or less melodic offerings in perfect pitch: "For my soul delighteth in the song of the heart; yea, the song of the righteous is a prayer unto me, and it shall be answered with a blessing upon their heads" (D&C 25:12).

Mark 14:32–33

And they came to a place which was named Gethsemane: and he saith to his disciples, Sit ye here, while I shall pray. And he taketh with him Peter and James and John.

At the conclusion of the Last Supper, Jesus and His eleven Apostles made their way to the Garden of Gethsemane, a quiet and secluded place, where Jesus often went with His disciples.

Despite the sacred events that had occurred during the private time they had just shared with the Savior, despite the Savior's great intercessory prayer and despite His final intimate and powerful sermon, His Apostles still felt some confusion in their hearts regarding His title of *Messiah*. There was no doubt that He was the Son of God, but was He the deliverer the Jews had so fervently desired? They had not yet received the gift of the Holy Ghost, so it is understandable that a member of the Godhead's constant companionship had not yet solidified their testimonies.

Knowing the confusion in their minds, Jesus bade eight of His beloved companions to sit and wait while He took with Him the three who had been privileged to be with Him on the Mount of Transfiguration. "And when he was at the place, he said unto them," chiding them gently for their doubtful hearts and minds, "Pray that ye enter not into temptation. And he was withdrawn from them about a stone's cast, and kneeled down, and prayed" (Luke 22:40–41).

JST Luke 22:42, 44

Father, if thou be willing, remove this cup from me: nevertheless not my will, but thine, be done. . . . And being in an agony he prayed more earnestly: and he sweat as it were great drops of blood falling down to the ground.

In our premortal existence, Jesus, our Elder Brother, stepped forward, knowing the Fall would separate us from God both physically and spiritually and that our only rescue would come through a savior. The Lord said, "Here am I, send me" (Abr. 3:27). Those five words held mankind's hope for an eternal destiny.

"Christ's agony in the garden is unfathomable by the finite mind. . . . He struggled and groaned under a burden such as no other being who has lived on earth might even conceive as possible. It was not physical pain, nor mental anguish alone, that caused Him to suffer such torture as to produce an extrusion of blood from every pore; but a spiritual agony of soul such as only God was capable of experiencing. . . . In that hour of anguish Christ met and overcame all the horrors that Satan . . . could inflict. . . . In some manner, actual and terribly real though to man incomprehensible, the Savior took upon Himself the burden of the sins of mankind from Adam to the end of the world" (*Jesus the Christ*, 568–569).

There was no other good enough
To pay the price of sin.
He only could unlock the gate
Of heav'n and let us in.
("There is a Green Hill Far Away," *Hymns*, no. 194).

Luke 22:43

And there appeared an angel unto him from heaven, strengthening him.

"There was a tragic irony surrounding this night of nights. He who had always pleased the Father (John 8:29) and had thus never been alone (that is, separated spiritually from his Father) was subjected to the forces and effects of sin that he had never known, forces that must have been poignantly and agonizingly intense. . . . [Then,] an angel, sent from the courts of glory, came to strengthen the God of Creation in this hour of greatest need" (*Coming to Know Christ*, 36–37).

Elder Bruce R. McConkie lends special insight to this occurrence: "The angelic ministrant is not named . . . [but] if we might indulge in speculation, we would suggest that the angel who came into this second Eden was the same person who dwelt in the first Eden. At least Adam, who is Michael, the archangel—the head of the whole heavenly hierarchy of angelic ministrants—seems the logical one to give aid and comfort to his Lord on such a solemn occasion. Adam fell, and Christ redeemed men from the fall; theirs was a joint enterprise, both parts of which were essential for the salvation of Father's children" (*The Mortal Messiah*, 4:125).

John 18:4

Whom seek ye?

On several occasions during the Lord's mortal ministry, He asked this question in various forms. The word *seek* implies an earnest search, and the good news is that He is not hard to find. One of the surest ways to find Him is through searching the scriptures.

The names of all our standard works of scripture reflect the focus of their content—our Savior Jesus Christ. Three of them testify of His coming and His mortal mission, His work and His glory, and the fourth comprises a compilation of His latter-day doctrines and covenants. He is the main focus in all of these works; His name is prominent and pre-eminent throughout their pages. *He is not hard to find.*

To disciples everywhere, the Savior issues this invitation: "Come, follow me" (Luke 18:22). His footprints are clear and easy to find throughout the scriptures. He never covers His tracks in order to confuse or deceive or disappoint us. He promises that our search will always be successful: we will always find Him. We treasure the words of the Psalmist: "When thou saidst, Seek ye my face; my heart said unto thee, Thy face, LORD, will I seek" (Ps. 27:8).

Matt. 26:75

And Peter remembered the word of Jesus, which said unto him, Before the cock crow, thou shalt deny me thrice. And he went out, and wept bitterly.

This senior Apostle had walked and talked with his Master, had borne witness of Jesus's divinity, had raised his sword in defense of the Savior in the Garden of Gethsemane, and, when all the other disciples fled, followed Jesus afar off to the high priest's palace. No doubt he was thoroughly exhausted by the alarming turn of events and frightened by the confusing uproar of Jesus's arrest, which culminated in his denial of Christ in a moment of weakness.

"Recognizing his error, repenting of his weakness, he turned about and became a mighty voice in bearing witness of the risen Lord. He . . . dedicated the remainder of his life to testifying of the mission, the death, and the Resurrection of Jesus Christ, the living Son of the living God. . . . And he it was who, with James and John, came back to earth in this dispensation to restore the holy priesthood, under which divine authority the Church of Jesus Christ was organized in these latter days" (*TGBH*, 533).

His marvelous example offers hope to all of us, who have our momentary lapses of courage and faith. Our tears may be bitter too, but we, like Peter, can go on in the cause of our Savior.

John 18:37–38

To this end was I born, and for this cause came I into the world, that I should bear witness unto the truth. Every one that is of the truth heareth my voice. Pilate saith unto him, What is truth?

Is there an answer to this all-important question? At an earlier time during His ministry, the Savior said, "If ye continue in my word . . . ye *shall* know the truth, and the truth shall make you free" (John 8:31–32; emphasis added). "A knowledge of truth will help men to be free, whether it come by direct revelation . . . of the prophets, from the written word of God as recorded in the scriptures . . . or as revealed to a prayerful youth upon his knees in the sanctuary of a grove" (Hugh B. Brown, *The Abundant Life* [Salt Lake City: Bookcraft, 1965], 280–281).

The word *continue* in the Savior's promise suggests that knowing the truth is an eternal quest, which our ninth article of faith clearly corroborates: "We believe all that God *has revealed*, all that He *does now reveal*, and we believe that He *will yet reveal* many great and important things pertaining to the Kingdom of God" (emphasis added).

"Truth cuts across all three time zones—our premortal state, our second state (mortality), and the eternal future that is fashioned for us" (*The Neal A. Maxwell Quote Book*, 353).

Matt. 26:50

Then came they, and laid hands on Jesus, and took him.

As Jesus emerged from His garden of suffering, victorious in His determination to keep His promise to His Father and to us, there followed a night filled with indignities and abuses heaped one upon another in a cumulation of shameful inhumanities.

His parody of a trial made a mockery of Jewish law. He was interrogated with the utmost arrogance. "And the men that held Jesus mocked him, and smote *him*. And when they had blindfolded him, they struck him on the face, and asked him, saying, Prophesy, who is it that smote thee?" (Luke 22:63–64). He was taken before the Roman governor, who lacked the strength of character to withstand the crazed crowd's lust for the blood of this innocent Man and who even stooped to political games by delivering Christ to stand before Herod, a ruler so depraved and bereft of common humanity and decency that the Savior, in all His divine dignity, refused to speak to him.

Convicted of blasphemy, Jesus was then delivered into the hands of soldiers, who scourged Him, a punishment so cruel that men often died when this beating was administered prior to their crucifixion. Then a crown of thorns was placed on the Savior's head, and He began the agonizing trip to Calvary.

Mark 15:22, 25

And they bring him unto the place Golgotha, which is, being interpreted, The place of the skull. . . . And it was the third hour, and they crucified him.

"Death by crucifixion was at once the most lingering and most painful of all forms of execution. The victim lived in ever increasing torture, generally for many hours, sometimes for days" (*Jesus the Christ*, 608). For Christ, the agony of the cross began at about nine o'clock in the morning and ended at around three o'clock in the afternoon, during which time he suffered not only the pain of the nails, unrelenting thirst, and horrible strain on His internal organs but also the recurring agonies of Gethsemane.

As if to add insult to injury, Satan rallied all of his hellish forces in one last tormenting and tempting taunt: "If thou be the king of the Jews, save thyself" (Luke 23:37). But in heaven, all of God's children must have held their breath and then exhaled in one glorious and grateful sigh of relief as love triumphed. The Savior saw His sacrifice through to the end, willingly completing His infinite Atonement. So He who had stepped forth in heaven in our behalf once again forced Satan to slink away in defeat.

The gift of the Savior's infinite Atonement is universal yet intimately personal. It was not completed for a large, faceless crowd but for each well-known and dearly loved child of God.

John 19:25–26

Now there stood by the cross of Jesus his mother. . . . When Jesus therefore saw his mother, and the disciple standing by, whom he loved, he saith unto his mother, Woman, behold thy son!

Mary's deep grief as she watched her Son's agony while He was on the cross must have been intense. This may also have been a time for remembering the joy of holding her tiny, newborn son—the Son of God—as well as for remembering the many scenes of healing and preaching that brought comfort and hope to so many lives and quiet joy and pride to her own heart.

"At this moment of supreme suffering, Jesus reached out with words to the one who had given Him life, who had loved Him as only a mother could, and whom He adored above all others . . . 'Woman, behold thy son'" (S. Kent Brown, *Mary and Elisabeth* [American Fork, UT: Covenant Communications, Inc., 2002], 76).

Jesus may also have been telling her that He wanted her to watch Him finish this final chapter of His earthly life. When Heavenly Father momentarily withdrew His presence at the apex of the Savior's suffering, "Mary, who had given birth to Him . . . and loved Him with a mother's love, would not let Him die alone. At this intense moment, she became a witness of His death as she had been a witness of His birth" (Ibid.).

Matt. 27:46

And about the ninth hour Jesus cried with a loud voice,
saying, Eli, Eli, lama sabachthani? that is to say, My God,
my God, why hast thou forsaken me?

The Father withdrew His Spirit, intensifying Christ's suffering on the cross, as evidenced by Christ's lonely cry. He was utterly and completely alone. Elder Tad R. Callister suggests that the "withdrawal of God's Spirit . . . may have been a natural response to the avalanche of evil heaped upon the Innocent One. When the Savior reached the climax of his ordeal—when the infinite sins of infinite worlds pressed upon Him—God's Spirit retreated from the consequences of such universal evil" (*The Infinite Atonement*, 138–139).

Elder James E. Talmage makes this observation: "It seems, that in addition to the fearful suffering incident to crucifixion, the agony of Gethsemane had recurred, intensified beyond human power to endure. In that bitterest hour the dying Christ was alone, alone in most terrible reality. That the supreme sacrifice of the Son might be consummated in all its fullness, the Father seems to have withdrawn the support of His immediate Presence, leaving the Savior of men the glory of complete victory over the forces of sin and death" (*Jesus the Christ*, 613).

Then His triumph over sin was complete, and that awful loneliness ended as the Savior commended His Spirit into the outstretched arms of His Father (see Luke 23:46).

Matt. 27:54

Now when the centurion, and they that were with him, watching Jesus, saw the earthquake, and those things that were done, they feared greatly, saying, Truly this was the Son of God.

The Roman soldiers who carried out the mechanics of crucifixion were men hardened by acts of brutality. So Christ's execution was just business as usual. And this crucifixion had started out this way. The Romans had mocked Jesus, spit on Him, hit Him, and gambled for His only earthly belonging, a robe: "They part my garments among them, and cast lots upon my vesture" (Ps. 22:18). Then they sat down to watch Him die.

But somehow, this event was different. Even these ruthless and callous men knew that something was different. Although crucifixion was a common form of capital punishment in those times, there had never been one to match this one in its diabolical injustice and its attendant natural disasters. Christ's Crucifixion was accompanied by storms and earthquakes and darkness as the very elements themselves poured out their grief.

And the majestic dignity of the One being crucified was like no other these soldiers had ever seen. Jesus had asked for God's forgiveness for these hardened brutes, then had voluntarily given up His life. They had no choice but to recognize His divine status and parentage. It was testimony borne of compulsion, but it *was* testimony.

JST 1 Pet. 4:6

Because of this, is the gospel preached to them who are dead, that they might be judged according to men in the flesh, but live in the spirit according to the will of God.

At the very moment of Jesus's death, "his mortal ministry ended and his ministry among the spirits in prison began. . . . Then it was that he who had now suffered for our sins, the Just for the unjust, having been put to death in the flesh but continuing to live in the spirit, 'went and preached unto the spirits in prison' (1 Pet. 3:18–20)" (*The Mortal Messiah*, 4:241).

All the millions who had died without a knowledge of Christ were now to become the recipients of the full and glorious message of the gospel of Jesus Christ as the Savior organized a vast network of missionaries in the spirit world.

It was also a time of rejoicing for the long-departed righteous, who had awaited the reuniting of their spirits and bodies. The scriptures bear witness that this blessing began to be fulfilled immediately following the Savior's resurrection: "Jesus, when he had cried again with a loud voice, yielded up the ghost. . . . And the graves were opened; and many bodies of the saints which slept arose, And came out of the graves after his resurrection" (Matt. 27:50, 52–53).

Luke 24:5–6

Why seek ye the living among the dead? He is not here, but is risen.

When it was determined that Jesus was indeed dead, Joseph of Arimathea and Nicodemus took His body down from the cross. Joseph had begged Pilate for Jesus's body and had kindly offered to lay it in his family's unused tomb. He and Nicodemus, both honorable and devout men, who, because of fear of the Jews, kept their discipleship secret, hastily washed the body of the lifeless Lord, wrapped Him in clean linens, and anointed Him with spices. It was imperative for this process to be accomplished before the observance of the Jewish Sabbath began.

At the first indication of dawn's light on the most significant Sunday morning in all the history of mankind, Mary Magdalene and other women went to the tomb. They went for the purpose of anointing the Lord's body with additional spices and ointments, making sure that the men's hasty ministrations were given the tender, refined final touches that only these women could properly and compassionately accomplish.

Upon finding that the stone had been rolled away, they went into the tomb only to find it empty. Their consternation deepened when two men in shining garments announced that the Lord was risen. At that point, grief clouded their comprehension as they ran to tell the Apostles that He was not there.

John 20:15

Woman, why weepest thou? whom seekest thou?

Mary Magdalene followed Peter and John back to the tomb as they ran to see for themselves if the women's report was indeed true. Lingering behind in the garden, Mary expressed her grief, which turned into unrestrained weeping. A person she mistook for the gardener asked Mary those two poignant questions. It was only when the man addressed her by name that joyful comprehension finally dawned, and Mary recognized the voice of her beloved Shepherd, Jesus Christ.

He simply spoke her name, but "the recognition was instantaneous. Her rivers of tears became a sea of joy" (*The Mortal Messiah*, 4:363).

"How much there is incident to the death, burial, and resurrection of our Lord which ennobles and exalts faithful women. They wept at the cross, sought to care for his wounded and lifeless body, and came to his tomb to weep and worship for their friend and Master. And so it is not strange that we find a woman, Mary of Magdala, chosen and singled out from all the disciples, even including the apostles, to be the first mortal to see and bow in the presence of a resurrected being. Mary, who had been healed of much and who loved much, saw the risen Christ!" (*DNTC*, Vol. I, 843).

Luke 24:39

Behold my hands and my feet, that it is I myself: handle me, and see; for a spirit hath not flesh and bones, as ye see me have.

After the sorrowful scene of death that had seemed to Christ's followers so final and futile, the appearance of the resurrected Christ was a joyous affirmation that there is eternal hope for all of God's children.

The Apostle Paul bears testimony of this: "But now is Christ risen from the dead, *and* become the firstfruits of them that slept. . . . For as in Adam all die, even so in Christ shall all be made alive" (1 Cor. 15:20, 22). Moroni adds his testimony to the blessings of the Resurrection as well: "The death of Christ bringeth to pass the resurrection, which bringeth to pass a redemption from an endless sleep, from which sleep all men shall be awakened by the power of God when the trump shall sound" (Morm. 9:13).

"Christ came; he was crucified, died, and rose again the third day; he worked out the infinite and eternal atonement, all with but one end in view: to bring to pass the immortality and eternal life of man, to enable men to repent and be baptized and gain eternal life" (*The Mortal Messiah*, 4:281). He lives, and because He lives, we too shall live!

Matt. 7:3

And why beholdest thou the mote that is in thy brother's eye, but considerest not the beam that is in thine own eye?

As we age, we may be alarmed when our eyesight is simply not what it used to be. However, the Savior is far more concerned about our spiritual eyesight and draws our attention to the unhappy fact that when it comes to discerning the faults and failings of others, our vision seems to be 20/20. But when it comes to our own shortcomings, we are often left groping (quite happily) in the dark.

There is something of a natural tendency in us to want to put on our rose-colored glasses and ignore our own faults while sharply scrutinizing where someone else may be (in our humble opinion) falling short. We all like to occasionally give ourselves a little pat on the back and tell ourselves we're okay, especially when compared to someone else who doesn't seem quite as okay as we are.

By so doing, we earn the Savior's label as hypocrites who would do well to cast the beam (a heavy piece of timber) out of our own eye in order to see more clearly the mote (a tiny sliver) in another's eye (see Matt. 7:5), thereby earning the *Savior's* pat on our back.

Matt. 28:19

Go ye therefore, and teach all nations, baptizing them in the name of the Father, and of the Son, and of the Holy Ghost.

The media bombards us daily with stories of frightening and unholy events—all of which tend to overshadow the positive, unchanging, and glorious news that God is in His heaven and He is mindful of all His children and is desirous that they have the blessing of the gospel in their lives. The power of the worldwide missionary effort will make this blessing possible.

"This sick world cries out for healing. Christ, the Son of God, was the Master Healer, and he has shown us the way. It is his message of peace and reconciliation that we teach. His is the gospel of charity and peace and love. Ours is a mission . . . of reconciliation . . . to a needy world" (*TGBH*, 373).

Our mandate is the same as that which the Savior gave to His ancient Apostles and to those in the early days of the Restoration: "The Gospel must roll forth, and it will until it fills the whole earth. . . . You have a work to do that [none other] can do; you must proclaim the Gospel in its simplicity and purity" (Joseph Smith, *History of the Church*, Vol. 2, 196, 198).

Acts 1:8

But ye shall receive power, after that the Holy Ghost is come upon you: and ye shall be witnesses unto me both in Jerusalem, and in all Judæa, and in Samaria, and unto the uttermost part of the earth.

Prior to His Crucifixion, the Savior promised His Apostles that He would send the Comforter, "*which is* the Holy Ghost, whom the Father will send in my name, [and] he shall teach you all things, and bring all things to your remembrance, whatsoever I have said unto you" (John 14:26).

Now the resurrected Christ's ascension is imminent, and after a glorious forty-day ministry among them, He is reminding His Apostles that they "shall be baptized with the Holy Ghost not many days hence" (Acts 1:5). By the power of the Holy Ghost, these stalwart ambassadors of Christ will be witnesses of the gospel in all the world, thus spreading it far beyond the hitherto prescribed Judæan boundaries. And by the power of the Holy Ghost, all who hear the gospel of Jesus Christ may know of its truthfulness (see Moro. 10:5).

The gift of the Holy Ghost was a blessing to these faithful followers of Jesus Christ and is a blessing to *all* disciples of Christ: "[He] is Christ's minister; he speaks and acts in the place and stead of the Son; his mission is to testify of Jesus, to reveal the mind and will of the Lord, to say what Christ would say if personally present"(*DNTC*, Vol. II, 22).

Acts 1:9–11

And when he had spoken these things . . . he was taken up; and a cloud received him out of their sight. And while they looked . . . behold, two men stood by them in white apparel; Which also said, Ye men of Galilee, why stand ye gazing up into heaven? this same Jesus, which is taken up from you into heaven, shall so come in like manner as ye have seen him go into heaven.

In His final glorious farewell from the Mount of Olives—a favorite and sacred location for meetings with His Apostles—the Savior and His holy angels teach a beautiful lesson regarding His Second Coming. There is first an assurance to these faithful and adoring eleven that the Savior's words to them on a previous occasion will all be fulfilled, "for the Son of man shall come in the glory of his Father with his angels" (Matt. 16:27).

Second, the angels reassure the Apostles that Christ will be *the same Jesus* they have known and loved: "that Jesus whom the apostles knew intimately, whose immortal body they had felt and handled . . . who had eaten fish and an honeycomb before them . . . [shall] come again, on the Mount of Olivet, literally, personally, in the flesh, as a glorified Man" (*DNTC*, Vol. II, 28).

And finally, the angels' words, "Why stand ye looking up?" are a great reminder that we must be up and doing; like disciples in all dispensations, we must be about our Father's business.

Luke 24:52–53

And they worshipped him, and returned to Jerusalem with great joy. And were continually in the temple, praising and blessing God.

Reluctant as the Apostles may have been to have the Savior depart from their midst, knowing that His personal earthly ministry with them had reached its conclusion, their hearts were nevertheless filled with joy and gratitude: *joy* because theirs had been the privilege of being called to serve with the Son of God, and it would now be their privilege to carry on His work in His sacred name; and *gratitude* because they knew they had not been left alone but would be guided and empowered by the gift of the Holy Ghost. Imagine their conversation as these beloved brethren made their way down from the Mount of Olives! They were, without doubt, excited to be "anxiously engaged" (D&C 58:27).

Upon returning to Jerusalem, their destination of choice was the temple—and what better place to *praise* and *bless* God and prepare themselves for diligent service. It is in His holy temples that we all receive His most pleasing words and learn the eternal principles of salvation and exaltation. Isaiah says it beautifully: "Come ye, and let us go up to the mountain of the LORD, to the house of the God of Jacob; and *he will teach us of his ways, and we will walk in his paths*" (Isaiah 2:3; emphasis added).

Acts 2:1–4

When the day of Pentecost was fully come, . . . suddenly there came a sound from heaven as of a rushing mighty wind, and it filled all the house . . . And there appeared unto them cloven tongues like as of fire, and it sat upon each of them. And they were all filled with the Holy Ghost, and began to speak with other tongues, as the Spirit gave them utterance.

On special spiritual occasions, signs manifest the presence of the Holy Ghost. When John baptized Jesus, a dove signified that the Holy Ghost had witnessed and endorsed that ordinance (see John 1: 32–34). Likewise, after the Nephite Twelve were baptized, "the Holy Ghost did fall upon them. . . . And behold, they were encircled about as if it were by fire; and it came down from heaven, and the multitude did witness it" (3 Ne. 19:13–14).

During the dedication of the Kirtland Temple, "a bright light like a pillar of fire rest[ed] upon the Temple," and "a noise . . . like the sound of a rushing mighty wind . . . filled the Temple," and "many began to speak in tongues and prophesy" (see *HC*, Vol. 2, 428; see also D&C 109:36–37).

On the day of Pentecost, the Apostles received the gift of tongues due to the bestowal of the gift of the Holy Ghost, and everyone present in that linguistically varied crowd understood their words. Thus began the fulfillment of the Savior's parting words that the gospel would be preached to every nation, kindred, and tongue.

Act 2:37–38

*Now when they heard this, they were pricked in their heart, and said . . .
Men and brethren, what shall we do? Then Peter said unto them, Repent and
be baptized . . . in the name of Jesus Christ for the remission of sins, and ye
shall receive the gift of the Holy Ghost.*

"What shall we do?" is a question we may well ask ourselves from time to time as we take inventory of our spiritual condition. And the answer is always as straightforward as was Peter's: "Repent." We have continual need to repent of various sins in varying degrees, whether they be sins of commission or omission.

We are reminded of Alma's powerful sermon, in which he asks some soul-searching questions, not to the world at large but to members of the Church. Have we been spiritually born of God, received His image in our countenances, experienced a mighty change of heart, exercised faith in the atoning mission of Jesus Christ, or checked to see whether our hands are clean and our hearts pure? And last but certainly not least, has our testimony stood the test of time (see Alma 5:14–26)?

When we enter into the waters of baptism, it is with the promise that we will serve God and our fellowmen and keep His commandments to the end that "he may pour out his Spirit more abundantly upon [us]" (Mosiah 18:8–10). What a wonderful privilege it is to partake of the sacrament each week; it is our opportunity to renew our baptismal covenant and strengthen our resolve to repent to enjoy the companionship of the Holy Ghost.

Acts 3:19

Repent ye therefore, and be converted, that your sins may be blotted out, when the times of refreshing shall come from the presence of the Lord.

It is always alarming when we spill something on clean clothes, and we naturally wonder whether we will be able to remove or blot out the stain. We choose a cleansing agent and apply our best efforts to the task. When it comes to *spiritual* stains, there is one Cleansing Agent whose guarantee of perfect results for everyone—every time—can be trusted.

The Lord's cleansing process is arduous and requires effort on our part. It is not one-sided, nor are we promised a quick fix: "To every forgiveness there is a condition. . . . There must be a washing of robes to get them white and there must be a new consecration and devotion to the living of all the laws of God" (*The Miracle of Forgiveness*, 353).

Then, after all we can do, the Savior in His kind and tender mercy—manifested by His great atoning sacrifice—heals, washes, and purges us, preparing us for the blessings of eternal salvation. What a glorious promise, and what a spectacular result! There is no residue of sin, no lingering stain, no fear of further recriminations: "Behold, he who has repented of his sins, the same is forgiven, and I, the Lord, remember them no more" (D&C 58:42).

Acts 3:6–7

Then Peter said, Silver and gold have I none; but such as I have give I thee: In the name of Jesus Christ of Nazareth rise up and walk. And he took him by the right hand, and lifted him up: and immediately his feet and ankle bones received strength.

A crippled man had just asked Peter and John for money. Peter's humble reply contains the beauty of great understatement, and perhaps it discourages the poor man into thinking that he might not get something that would be of any value to him. But Peter's seemingly apologetic and even self-deprecating dismissal of the man's request builds to a stunning crescendo as, by the power of the priesthood bestowed on him by the Son of God, Peter lifts the man to his feet, instantly healing his limbs that had been useless since birth.

It is the same kind of miraculous healing we find in the pages chronicling the Savior's earthly ministry. And just as with so many such demonstrations of compassion, spiritual healing accompanies the miracle of physical healing. The recipient is indeed "lifted up" as both body and spirit receive an infusion of strength hitherto unknown: "And he leaping up stood, and walked, and entered with them into the temple, walking, and leaping, and *praising God*" (v. 8; emphasis added).

The treasure of the Savior's healing power enables us to rise above our spiritual infirmities, to walk in His ways, and to be lifted to breathtaking spiritual heights.

Acts 4:12

Neither is there salvation in any other: for there is none other name under heaven given among men, whereby we must be saved.

Peter's testimony is echoed in these powerful words as he reminds us that there is a name that is universally and eternally significant, a name that is the epitome of all that is good and worthy of emulation. He who bears this name is Jesus Christ, the Son of God. It is a name with which all of us can safely and proudly claim a connection, "for God so loved the world, that he gave his only begotten Son, that whosoever believeth in him should not perish, but have everlasting life" (John 3:16). This doctrine was revealed to Enoch, to whom the Father testified that Jesus Christ was "the only name which shall be given under heaven, whereby salvation shall come unto the children of men" (Moses 6:52).

Taking upon us the Lord's name involves a sacred responsibility on our part, one that we are reminded of each week as we partake of the sacrament: "[We] are willing to take upon [us] the name of [Heavenly Father's] Son, and always remember him and keep his commandments which he has given [us]." We are then given the glorious promise "that [we] may always have his Spirit to be with [us]" (see D&C 20:77) and thereby be worthy partakers of His salvation.

Acts 4:18–20

And they called them, and commanded them not to . . . teach in the name of Jesus. But Peter and John answered . . . Whether it be right in the sight of God to hearken unto you more than unto God, judge ye. For we cannot but speak the things which we have seen and heard.

Here is a most splendid example of courage under pressure, and we note the marvelous spiritual stature of these fearless and bold ambassadors of the Savior Jesus Christ. By the power of the Holy Ghost, they have already publicly shamed Annas, Caiaphas, and their cohorts with their bold declaration: "Be it known unto you all, and to all the people of Israel, that *by the name of Jesus Christ of Nazareth, whom ye crucified*, whom God raised from the dead, *even* by him doth this man stand here before you whole" (v. 10; emphasis added).

Now Peter and his fellow Apostle John again fearlessly face down these cowardly, fearful, would-be bullies on their own turf: "So when they had further threatened them, they let them go, finding nothing how they might punish them, because of the people: for all *men* glorified God for that which was done" (v. 21). Talk about losing face!

How we love and admire these spiritually strong men of God, who could not be swayed by cowardly threats or derision, whose only fidelity is to their Master.

In the face of belittling ridicule or outright confrontation, will we too stand strong in our allegiance to God and His Son?

Acts 7:55–56

But he, being full of the Holy Ghost, looked up steadfastly into heaven, and saw the glory of God, and Jesus standing on the right hand of God.

Among the disciples of Christ, Stephen stands out as one whose love for the Savior is legendary. The Apostles and all true followers of Christ loved him, and Jewish religious leaders hated and even feared him in consequence of false testimonies of heresy and blasphemy suborned against him.

Stephen answered these charges with a broad recitation of the history of Israel down through the generations and a bold accusation of his accusers' crimes against God, which culminated in the murder of His Only Begotten Son. Then, in the eyes of these wicked men, Stephen committed the unpardonable sin, claiming to see in vision Jesus standing on the right hand of God: "In one brief glimpse of heaven and its chief inhabitants, Stephen learned more about God and his glory than could be acquired through eons of research by uninspired philosophers" (*DNTC*, Vol. II, 78).

Stephen's magnificent speech and glorious vision won him neither converts nor accolades; rather it was answered with a violent frenzy of uncontrolled wrath and a hideous death by stoning. Dignified and emulating Christ's example right to the end, this saintly disciple asked that this grievous sin be not laid to the charge of his murderers (see Acts 7:60).

Acts 9:5

And he said, Who art thou, Lord? And the Lord said, I am Jesus whom thou persecutest: it is hard for thee to kick against the pricks.

Why would the Lord bother with Saul? Here was a man who was fanatically dedicated to the persecution of the Saints, who "[breathed] out threatenings and slaughter against the disciples of the Lord" (v. 1), the very same man who consented wholeheartedly to the death of Stephen.

In the book of Abraham, we read of the noble and great souls who stood in the presence of God in our premortal existence. Surely Saul (Paul) stood out in this vast throng of valiant souls, and the Lord, in His infinite mercy, knew his potential and saw fit to chasten Paul, to allow him to make a gigantic course correction.

How very fitting and symbolic it is that after seeing the "light," Paul was blinded for several days to allow him the opportunity for the spiritual introspection and instruction that would open his eyes to the truth. This prepared him for the priesthood blessing that restored his sight and for his immediate baptism, after which would follow the gift and blessing of the Holy Ghost (see v. 17). Of a surety, this was a drastic shift in perspective, and it is available to all of God's children through the miracle of Christ's Atonement.

Acts 9:6

And he trembling and astonished said, Lord, what wilt thou have me to do?

There is no hesitation on Paul's part as he asks the Lord this all-important question. There is no argument, no request from this learned and brilliant man for a theological or philosophical discussion; there is no lingering trace of the arrogant and self-important purveyor of persecution. Paul simply and humbly acknowledges his messenger and waits for the message.

Paul's question also embodies an unspoken acknowledgment of his weakness. He knows he is no longer in charge, nor does he wish to be. He is ready for the spiritual make-over that will fit him for the Lord's errand and enable him to become what the Lord wants him to be.

This is the very embodiment of the Lord's words to Moroni: "And if men come unto me I will show unto them their weakness . . . that they may be humble; and my grace is sufficient for all men that humble themselves before me . . . then will I make weak things become strong unto them" (Ether 12:27).

Our willingness to ask this question and then listen humbly for the answer demonstrates our faith in an "all-loving Being who wants more than anything for us to be all that we are intended to be" (*Coming to Know Christ*, 51).

Acts 10:15

And the voice spake unto him again the second time, What God hath cleansed, that call not thou common.

In preparation for the gospel being taken to the Gentiles, Peter receives a vision in which he is commanded to eat types of meat and fowl that have hitherto been designated as common—or forbidden—under the Mosaic law. Now, with one simple but effective visual aid, the Lord is teaching a lesson that will have eternal consequences for all of His children.

Cornelius, a devout centurion who carries the genetic label of "Gentile," is told by an angel to find Peter. "'He will teach you the gospel; he will baptize you in water and bring you into the fold of Christ where you can become a new creature by the power of the Holy Ghost, thus putting off the natural man and becoming a saint through the atonement of Christ the Lord.' What a message thunders forth to the pious and good among all churches from this heaven-directed experience of Cornelius!" (*DNTC*, Vol. II, 97–98).

Nephi states this principle plainly and beautifully: "And he inviteth them all to come unto him and partake of his goodness; and he denieth none that come unto him, black and white, bond and free, male and female; and he remembereth the heathen; and all are alike unto God, *both Jew and Gentile*" (2 Ne. 26:33; emphasis added).

Acts 10:35

But in every nation he that feareth him, and worketh righteousness, is accepted with him.

Heavenly Father knows each of us by name. He loves us and rejoices in our diversities, whether they be of race, color, height, weight, appearance, marital status, social standing, educational opportunities, or physical, mental, and emotional needs.

While serving as a member of the Quorum of the Twelve, President Howard W. Hunter stated that we are all literally brothers and sisters, spirit children of our Heavenly Father. In our premortal state, we were one large eternal family, and we enjoyed a familial relationship there. Our Heavenly Parents give us a common paternity as well as a literal brotherhood and sisterhood (see "All Are Alike unto God," *Ensign*, June 1979, 72).

Alma tells us, "Now my brethren, we see that God is mindful of every people, whatsoever land they may be in; yea, he numbereth his people, and his bowels of mercy are over all the earth" (Alma 26:37). We are each valuable and important in the eyes of our Heavenly Father and His Son, even when we stumble, fall, or lose our way. Though we may not look or feel or act exactly like anyone else, Heavenly Father and Jesus Christ love us and accept us and see our potential as valuable family members.

Acts 11:17–18

Forasmuch then as God gave them the like gift as he did unto us, who believed on the Lord Jesus Christ; what was I, that I could withstand God? When they heard these things, they . . . glorified God, saying, Then hath God also to the Gentiles granted repentance unto life.

After centuries of being taught the spiritual safety of separatism when it came to mingling with other nations, the Apostles and Saints in Jerusalem were suddenly faced with a new dilemma, namely, digesting the doctrine that the gospel of Jesus Christ was to be shared with everyone so that all of God's children would have the opportunity to return to God's presence and become like Him.

As always, Peter's conversion as He received the will of the Lord on this matter was swift and sure. He was ready once again to "walk on water" as he reassured his brethren that the Atonement of their beloved Savior is infinite and universal, not selective and exclusive. It promises resurrection for all mankind, provides an opportunity for repentance, and propels us toward perfection.

The lovely words of a hymn remind us that regardless of who, where, or what we are, the blessings of the Savior's Atonement are meant specifically and personally for each one of us: "That he should extend his great love unto such as I, / Sufficient to own, to redeem, and to justify. / Oh, it is wonderful that he should care for *me* / Enough to die for *me*!" ("I Stand All Amazed," *Hymns*, no. 193; emphasis added).

Acts 15:11

But we believe that through the grace of the Lord Jesus Christ we shall be saved.

At times we are prone to make our lists and breathe sighs of spiritual relief that we are successfully meeting all of the requirements for a passing grade in the course of salvation. We might even go so far as to say that we need only a certain percentage of the Savior's Atonement because of our strict adherence to His rules.

Jacob calls this attitude "looking beyond [or missing] the mark" (Jacob 4:14), that *mark* being the Savior. The focus of all we do or accomplish should be Jesus Christ and His Atonement. Of course, it is important for us to be anxiously engaged when it comes to obedience to the principles and ordinances of the gospel, but the Lord wants us to *become* something good, not just *do* good things.

What we *become* in the eternal sense is *only* through His grace—"*above and beyond* all we can do . . . *in spite of* all we can do—which will never be enough" (*Coming to Know Christ*, 120). What we *do* is simply our humble gesture of accepting His grace. "It has been wisely said that grace is God's acceptance of us, *while faith is our acceptance of God's acceptance of us*" (Ibid., 136).

Acts 17:2

And Paul, as his manner was, went in unto them, and three sabbath days reasoned with them out of the scriptures.

It is no surprise that Paul relied on the scriptures. We read that Adam kept a book of remembrance, "for it was given unto as many as called upon God to write by the spirit of inspiration" (Moses 6:5). "The thing which they first wrote, and which of all their writings was of the most worth unto them, was a Book of Remembrance, a book in which they recorded what the Lord had revealed about himself, about his coming, and about the plan of salvation, which plan would have force and validity because of his atonement. This was the beginning of the Holy Scriptures" (Bruce R. McConkie, *The Promised Messiah* [Salt Lake City: Deseret Book, 1978], 86).

Like the Saints in all dispensations, we are directed to search the scriptures for ourselves: "Wherefore, if ye shall press forward, *feasting* upon the word of Christ, and endure to the end, behold, thus saith the Father: Ye shall have eternal life" (2 Ne. 31:20; emphasis added). The scriptures provide us with a bounteous banquet of God's works and words.

"The scriptures are doors with immense truths behind them, divine insights of major proportions; there is an eternal curriculum—things God would have all men and women upon the face of the earth learn for their happiness" (*The Neal A. Maxwell Quote Book*, 298).

Acts 17:11

These were more noble . . . in that they received the word with all readiness of mind, and searched the scriptures daily, whether those things were so.

After the signs and wonders of the Savior's birth cast their radiance over many souls in the promised land, it was only a matter of a few short years before people became easy prey for Satan's tactics of doubt and skepticism, causing them to rationalize their sacred experiences as less than miraculous and astonishing.

What sacred thing might *we* treat lightly? It may not be a sign in the heavens, but maybe it is another wonder, such as the scriptures, the First Vision, or the prophets' words. If we receive the word of the Lord with all readiness of mind, as Paul counseled, there is no room for doubt or equivocation, nor is there a desire to water down God's laws to suit our own rationalizations. Once our minds are ready to receive and treat with ongoing reverence and astonishment the marvelous works and wonders of the Lord, the Holy Ghost can carry them "unto [our] hearts" (2 Ne. 33:1), where they will never be forgotten, cast aside, or relegated to the folder of unbelief. Our delight will be in the law of the Lord as we meditate on the wonders of His gospel by day and night (see Ps. 1:2).

Acts 17:22–23

Then Paul . . . said, Ye men of Athens, I perceive that in all things ye are too superstitious. For as I passed by, and beheld your devotions, I found an altar with this inscription, TO THE UNKNOWN GOD. Whom therefore ye ignorantly worship, him declare I unto you.

On a first reading, Paul's words may seem a bit abrupt. (And sometimes they were. He was not a man who minced words.) However, his words also contain an element of respect. Instead of berating these people for what they didn't know, he congratulated them for believing in *something* and magnanimously offered to add to their scanty store of beliefs. Paul then proceeded to reveal truths about a personal and loving God and Godhead that astounded some, disgusted others, and raised a righteous curiosity in a select few.

As missionaries teach, they build upon what people already know or think they know. More often than not, God is mostly an unknown and obscure entity and is thus unfortunately held at arm's length. We are not apt to embrace or trust a total stranger; we save our open arms and hearts for someone we know and love.

God desires that all of His children know and love Him just as He knows and loves each one of us: "I give unto you these sayings that you may understand and know *how* to worship, and know *what* you worship, that you may come unto the Father in my name, and in due time receive of his fulness" (D&C 93:19; emphasis added).

Acts 20:33

I have coveted no man's silver, or gold, or apparel.

The tenth and final commandment of the Lord to the children of Israel reads: "Thou shalt not covet [desire or take pleasure in] thy neighbour's house, thou shalt not covet thy neighbour's wife, nor his manservant, nor his maidservant, nor his ox, nor his ass, nor any thing that *is* thy neighbour's" (Ex. 20:17). We would agree that this all-inclusive list covers the entire gamut of what was "hands off." And when the Lord gave the parable of the good Samaritan, He made the meaning of the word *neighbour* very clear—it's not just the people next door!

Every "Thou shalt not" also implies an equal and opposite positive action: "As to coveting, the Lord has made it clear that not only should we not lust for something belonging to another, but we should gladly share our own possessions. Our welfare work, our fast offerings, our tithing programs, our missionary work—all these have in them this element of sharing the benefits with those less fortunate" (*The Miracle of Forgiveness*, 99).

Our hearts and minds should be filled with gratitude as opposed to inappropriate longing. Well might we say with the Psalmist, "Incline my heart unto thy testimonies, and not to covetousness" (Ps. 119:36).

Acts 20:29–30

For I know this, that after my departing shall grievous wolves enter in among you, not sparing the flock. Also of your own selves shall men arise, speaking perverse things, to draw away disciples after them.

Paul's words are sobering and even frightening as he speaks of the coming Apostasy, which began even before the demise of all the Apostles. It was a gradual and subtle process accompanied by creeping secularism and subtle distortion of true doctrine within the Church itself. The greatest dangers always arose from within—the proverbial fox in the henhouse. The dimming of the gospel light continued until the utter darkness of apostasy enveloped the whole earth.

Hundreds of years earlier, Lehi watched in vision as the inhabitants of the great and spacious building (a large majority of whom were most likely disaffected members of the Church) pointed their fingers and mocked those who held to the iron rod. Are there such dangers within the Church today? Most assuredly!

"Occasionally a member of the Church who is weak in the faith struggles with his other questions and circumstances and loses the battle. Those few members who desert the cause are abandoning an oasis to search for water in the desert. Some of them will not just wander off but will become obsessed critics occupying offices in the 'great and spacious building' . . . that large but third-class hotel" (*The Neal A. Maxwell Quote Book*, 16).

Acts 26:28

Then Agrippa said unto Paul, Almost thou persuadest me to be a Christian.

When Agrippa makes this interesting "almost" declaration, he is most certainly referring to Paul's teachings regarding the gospel of Jesus Christ. We might speculate about what held him back. Why didn't his *almost* become *of a surety* (see Acts 12:11)?

Probably the most logical answer to this question lies in the fact that this was Herod Agrippa II, the last of the infamous Herodian dynasty. We remember with disgust and horror Herod the Great, who ordered the slaughter of the innocents, and Herod Antipas, who had John the Baptist beheaded and before whom Jesus maintained a dignified silence while this despicable despot "mocked *him,* and arrayed him in a gorgeous robe, and sent him again to Pilate" (Luke 23:9, 11). And Agrippa II perpetuates this Herodian legacy of cruelty, decadence, and political expedience. It would not do for Agrippa II to align himself with these religious fanatics.

As devout Christians, we would do well to check whether *we* have any "almosts" in our allegiance to the Savior. Do we *almost* believe in the law of tithing? In the Word of Wisdom? In keeping the Sabbath day holy? In loving and serving our fellowmen? In faithful temple attendance? Or in following the prophet? Our greatest strength lies in the strength of our complete conversion.

Rom. 1:16

For I am not ashamed of the gospel of Christ: for it is the power of God unto salvation to every one that believeth.

The story of Paul's miraculous conversion is legendary. In embracing the Light of Christ, Saul also fully embraced a new way of life and a new name. We may marvel at the strength of his conversion and unshakable testimony as he became one of the Lord's most stalwart Apostles.

Was he an unlikely candidate for conversion? Yes. Was he a fit candidate for salvation? Yes. And so are all of God's children. Lehi affirms this quite eloquently: "Wherefore [Christ] is the firstfruits unto God, inasmuch as he shall make intercession for all the children of men; and they that believe in him shall be saved" (2 Ne. 2: 9). The Savior adds His personal witness that this is true: "For behold, by me redemption cometh" (3 Ne. 9:17).

Paul recognized the saving power of Christ's Atonement and governed the remainder of his life accordingly. What a great example for all members of The Church of Jesus Christ of Latter-day Saints. Do our actions and speech set us apart as children of God, or do they brand us as simply being part of the worldly crowd? The antithesis of being ashamed is being proud and unabashed in declaring in word and deed that the gospel of Jesus Christ is the power of God unto salvation.

Romans 2:29

But he is a Jew, which is one inwardly; and circumcision is that of the heart, in the spirit, and not in the letter; whose praise is not of men, but of God.

Paul is here reminding us that it is not the outward rituals of our religion that set us apart as followers of Christ but what is in our hearts. Under the law of Moses, circumcision signified eligibility for the blessings and responsibilities of the Abrahamic covenant, with no divided loyalties. Upon Christ's completion of His great atoning sacrifice, the law of Moses was fulfilled, and outward rituals and sacrifices were replaced with the circumcision of the heart.

During His visit to the Nephites, the Savior explained what this meant: "And ye shall offer for a sacrifice unto me a broken heart and a contrite spirit. And whoso cometh unto me with a broken heart and a contrite spirit, him will I baptize with fire and with the Holy Ghost" (3 Ne. 9:20). The Holy Ghost can only offer companionship when our thoughts are synchronized with our words and deeds, when our hearts are right before the Lord, "for as he thinketh in his heart, so is he" (Prov. 23:7).

And we should consider the lovely promise the Savior makes to those whose hearts are pure: "They shall see God" (Matt. 5:8). What greater motivation do we need to put our hearts in order?

Rom. 3:23–24

For all have sinned, and come short of the glory of God; Being justified freely by his grace through the redemption that is in Christ Jesus.

The whole purpose of the gospel of Jesus Christ is to change lives; if we had no need for change, there would be no need for a Redeemer. We experience that change only through repentance. How very great, then, is our need for a Redeemer, as attested to by Nephi: "Wherefore, all mankind were in a lost and in a fallen state, and ever would be *save they should rely on this Redeemer*" (1 Ne. 10:6; emphasis added).

We sometimes mistakenly believe that after all our commendable efforts, Jesus will make up the difference, but "that is incorrect and misleading, inasmuch as it causes us to overstate our own role in salvation and grossly understate the role of him who has bought us with his blood. . . . We are saved by the grace of Jesus Christ—his unmerited divine favor, his unearned divine assistance, his enabling power—*above and beyond* all we can do . . . *in spite of* all we can do—which will never be enough. . . . Christ is our . . . Redeemer. . . . He is God, and if it were not so, he could not save us. . . . Without him, we have nothing. With him, we have everything" (*Coming to Know Christ*, 119, 120, 121).

Romans 6:4

Therefore we are buried with him by baptism into death: that like as Christ was raised up from the dead by the glory of the Father, even so we also should walk in newness of life.

King Benjamin tells us that "the natural man is an enemy to God, and has been from the fall of Adam, and will be, forever and ever, unless he yields to the enticings of the Holy Spirit, and putteth off the natural man and becometh a saint through the atonement of Christ the Lord" (Mosiah 3:19).

Elder Bruce R. McConkie tells us how this is achieved. "Baptized members of God's earthly kingdom . . . are born again; they become new creatures of the Holy Ghost; they die as pertaining to sin and live in the realm of righteousness; they . . . become saints through the atonement; they crucify the man of sin, bury their sins in the watery grave of baptism, and come forth resurrected, as it were, to righteousness" (*DNTC*, Vol. II, 249).

The Prophet Joseph Smith tells us that the gift of the Holy Ghost is an inseparable part of this process: "You might as well baptize a bag of sand as a man, if not done in view of the remission of sins and getting the Holy Ghost. Baptism by water is . . . good for nothing without the other half—that is, the baptism of the Holy Ghost" (*TPJS*, 314).

Romans 6:23

For the wages of sin is death; but the gift of God is eternal life through Jesus Christ our Lord.

Given the choice, which of us would be content with receiving minimum wages compared to a substantially higher salary? Imagine someone saying to their employer, "Oh, no, thanks. Keep the silver dollar; I'll just take the penny and run." By the same token, which of us, when given the choice, would stay in a substandard hotel room when offered the penthouse?

Are we as selective when it comes to spiritual wages and accommodations? Alma tells us that "every man receives wages of him whom he listeth to obey. . . . And now if ye are not the sheep of the good shepherd, of what fold are ye?" (Alma 3:27; 5:39). Are we content with pennies and small rooms when spiritual fortunes and mansions are available?

Paul's choice of words is significant—he speaks of *wages* and *gifts*. Wages are earned; gifts are granted. Depending on our choice of shepherd, we receive either wages or gifts, the one being spiritual death, *earned* by evil works and paid by Satan ("Here's your paycheck, and too bad if you expected more."); and the other being eternal life, a gift granted through the mercy and Atonement of our Savior Jesus Christ ("Your good works and obedience have qualified you to receive my *gift* of salvation and one of my Father's many mansions.").

Romans 8:6, 13

For to be carnally minded is death; but to be spiritually minded is life and peace. . . . For if ye live after the flesh, ye shall die: but if ye through the Spirit do mortify the deeds of the body, ye shall live.

God's equations are simple and straightforward: carnal behavior equals spiritual death; spiritual behavior equals eternal life and peace. We are the only variable, and the choice is ours. That does not mean we can have it both ways: "Wherefore, men are free . . . to choose liberty and eternal life, through the great Mediator of all men, *or* to choose captivity and death, according to the captivity and power of the devil" (2 Ne. 2:27; emphasis added).

Being "natural" men and women, (see Mosiah 3:19), we might say our carnal behavior comes naturally, so Moroni exhorts us to "come unto Christ, and be perfected in him, and deny [ourselves] of all ungodliness" (Moro. 10:32).

C. S. Lewis also reminds us that we really can't have it both ways: "Christ says, 'Give me All. . . . No half-measures are any good. . . . I don't want to drill the tooth, or crown it, or stop it, but to have it out. Hand over the whole natural self, all the desires which you think innocent as well as the ones you think wicked—the whole outfit. I will give you a new self instead. In fact, I will give you Myself: my own will shall become yours'" (*Mere Christianity* [New York: Simon and Schuster, 1996], 169).

Romans 8:16–17

The Spirit itself beareth witness with our spirit, that we are the children of God. And if children, then heirs; heirs of God, and joint-heirs with Christ; if so be that we suffer with him, that we may be also glorified together.

One of the very best things we know about ourselves is that we are literally the spirit sons and daughters of God. "So God created man in his own image, in the image of God created he him; male and female created he them" (Gen. 1:27). Who does not thrill at the words of Moses when he boldly declares, "For behold, I am a son of God, in the similitude of his Only Begotten" (Moses 1:13), especially after he has conversed with God face-to-face?

Thus, in a spiritual sense, we are God's heirs, with Jesus Christ being the Chief Heir. And this makes us His joint-heirs. Just as Jesus did not receive of the "fulness at first, but continued from grace to grace, until he received a fulness" (see D&C 93:13), so must we, through obedience to the gospel of Jesus Christ, progress toward fulness.

So what do we stand to inherit? What is in our Father's will? God Himself answers this question, and we must pause a moment to catch our breath at the glorious revelation of our legacy: "For behold, this is my work and my glory—to bring to pass the immortality and eternal life of man" (Moses 1:39).

Romans 8:35

Who shall separate us from the love of Christ? shall tribulation, or distress, or persecution, or famine, or nakedness, or peril, or sword?

If anyone ever knew firsthand about God's love, bestowed through His Only Begotten Son, it was Paul. He had worked zealously and relentlessly to destroy the Church of Christ, and, like Alma the younger and the sons of Mosiah, nothing short of the Savior's personal intervention would stop him: "And thus did the Spirit of the Lord work upon them, for they were the very vilest of sinners. And the Lord saw fit in his infinite mercy to spare them" (Mosiah 28:4).

God knew and loved them. He doesn't want them or us to perish in our sins, "for God so loved the world, that he gave his only begotten Son, that whosoever believeth in him should not perish, but have everlasting life" (John 3:16). In Enoch's glorious vision, the God of heaven wept tears for His wayward children, "the workmanship of [His] own hands" (Moses 7:32). He knows us and loves us intimately; even "the very hairs of [our] head are all numbered" (Matt. 10:30). We thrill as Nephi bears tender testimony of God's love: "I have beheld his glory, *and I am encircled about eternally in the arms of his love*" (2 Ne. 1:15; emphasis added).

Romans 8:38–39

For I am persuaded, that neither death, nor life, nor angels, nor principalities, nor powers, nor things present, not things to come, Nor height, nor depth, nor any other creature, shall be able to separate us from the love of God, which is in Christ Jesus our Lord.

There is no greater evidence of God's love for His children than the gift of His Son to the world. This gift is not selectively bestowed on only a few of God's favorites; in fact, we are *all* His favorites and can participate in the blessings of the Atonement. Christ came into the world "that through him all might be saved whom the Father had put into his power and made by him" (D&C 76:42).

"Salvation comes because of the Atonement. Without it the whole plan of salvation would be frustrated. . . . With it the eternal purposes of the Father will roll forth, the purpose of creation be preserved, the plan of salvation made efficacious, and men will be assured of a hope of the highest exaltation hereafter" (*Mormon Doctrine*, 61).

How grateful we are for a loving Father who gave us His Son, knowing that Christ would suffer exquisite agony on our behalf. How grateful we are for Him who willingly laid down His life that we might not perish spiritually. "Greater love hath no man than this, that a man lay down his life for his friends" (John 15:13).

Romans 10:13–14

For whosoever shall call upon the name of the Lord shall be saved. How then shall they call on him in whom they have not believed? and how shall they believe in him of whom they have not heard? and how shall they hear without a preacher?

As members of The Church of Jesus Christ of Latter-day Saints, we have been graciously invited to participate in the great missionary effort, the wages for which are richly rewarding: "And if it so be that you should labor all your days in crying repentance unto this people, and bring, save it be one soul unto me, how great shall be your joy with him in the kingdom of my Father!" (D&C 18:15). Whether that one soul we bring unto Christ is a spouse, a child, a sibling, a friend, or a complete stranger, the Savior promises the same reward of both earthly and eternal joy.

As President Hinckley points out, the eternal significance of missionary service is awe-inspiring: "I have seen miracles in my time. The greatest miracle of all, I believe, is the transformation that comes into the life of a man or woman who accepts the restored gospel of Jesus Christ. . . . It is indeed a marvelous work and a wonder, which has been brought to pass by the power of the Almighty in behalf of His sons and daughters. We . . . can serve in a work of salvation in behalf of the whole human family" (*TGBH*, 242).

Romans 12:2

And be not conformed to this world: but be ye transformed by the renewing of your mind, that ye may prove what is that good, and acceptable, and perfect, will of God.

We love stories where the hero or heroine is changed either from a lowly state to one of respect or from being physically unattractive to being beautiful or handsome. Without exception, the protagonist must follow some rules and put forth great personal effort to become the princess or prince we are cheering for.

However, it is not just in fairy tales that these kinds of things happen. The gospel of Jesus Christ has the power to transform ordinary men and women into something spiritually remarkable—even beautiful and handsome—if we are willing to conform ourselves to its principles, ignoring the siren calls of the world. Paul describes this process as coming out of the darkness and walking in the light of the Lord (see Eph. 5:8).

Once we prove our willingness to conform, the Atonement of Jesus Christ has the power to transform and lift us to a godly status: "To him that overcometh will I grant to sit with me in my throne, even as I also overcame, and am set down with my Father in his throne" (Rev. 3:21). We can become the princesses and princes our Savior is cheering for.

Rom. 12:9

Abhor that which is evil; cleave to that which is good.

Our instinctive reaction to something repulsive or frightening is to turn away and run as fast as possible in the other direction; however, the least hesitation on our part can slow that run to a jog, then to a walk, and then to a standstill that gradually becomes a pivoting turn toward the very thing we had once found so abhorrent. Alexander Pope penned these succinct lines that capture the essence of this incremental decline:

> Vice is a monster of so frightful mien,
> As to be hated, needs but to be seen;
> Yet seen too oft, familiar with her face,
> We first endure, then pity, then embrace.
> (*The Poems of Alexander Pope*, Vol. 2, 48)

Abhorring evil means making up our minds firmly about what we truly believe and embrace. Do we believe in being *sort of* honest, true, chaste, and benevolent? Do we *sometimes* seek after that which is praiseworthy and lovely and of good report? Or are we fully committed in our desire to give sin the cold shoulder?

The evidence of our gratitude and love for the Lord's atoning sacrifice, His redeeming love, and amazing grace lies in the degree to which we are willing to give sin a wide berth.

Romans 13:8

Owe no man any thing, but to love one another: for he that loveth another hath fulfilled the law.

The Apostle Paul's lessons on love are legendary, reminding us that the Savior taught and practiced love as the highest gospel law: "By this shall all *men* know that ye are my disciples, if ye have love one to another" (John 13:35). Every act the Savior performed, whether healing the sick, feeding thousands of hungry people, or clearing unholy merchandise from the temple, was motivated by love. And every lesson He taught, whether it was a treatise on forgiveness or a tutorial on gratitude, had as its objective the power and eternal importance of love.

Jesus was and is the perfect example of everlasting love for all mankind. And He asks us this soul-searching question and provides its profound answer: "Therefore, what manner of men ought ye to be? Verily I say unto you, even as I am" (3 Ne. 27:27).

"Love is the security for which children weep, the yearning of youth, the adhesive that binds marriage, and the lubricant that prevents devastating friction in the home; it is the peace of old age, the sunlight of hope shining through death. How rich are those who enjoy it in their associations with family, friends, church, and neighbors" (*TGBH*, 317).

Rom. 13:13

Let us walk honestly, as in the day . . . not in strife and envying.

It seems to be a natural reaction for us to feel diminished by someone else's success. The familiar parable of the prodigal son comes to mind. The older, steady, loyal brother "was angry" (Luke 15:28). To his way of thinking, he was suddenly esteemed as less lovable than his wastrel brother, who had experienced a mighty change of heart. The older brother bought into Satan's politics of envy, whose campaign slogan goes something like this: "If God loves *him*, He surely cannot love you as much."

Envy might very well be referred to as "heart trouble" that needs corrective surgery. In contrast, we read of the Nephites, who, after the resurrected Savior's visit, experienced "no envyings," because of the "love of God which did dwell in the *hearts* of the people" (4 Ne. 1:16, 15; emphasis added).

The antidote for envy, then, is the pure love of Christ. This love is the corrective surgery that softens hearts that have been hardened by the Satan-spawned false notions that someone else's success diminishes us, that we are constantly being measured according to others' accomplishments, and that we are found wanting. The Savior's heart is large and loving enough to extend unconditional love to all of His children. Nothing will be withheld from those who seek Him, follow Him, and love Him.

Romans 14:17

For the kingdom of God is not meat and drink; but righteousness, and peace, and joy in the Holy Ghost.

Most of us have what are sometimes referred to as *gospel hobbies*—those aspects of the gospel we enjoy most and at which we feel we excel. Maybe we are devoted to observing what we feel are the fine points of the Word of Wisdom, or perhaps we feel strongly about Sabbath observance or any number of other important gospel observances.

However, we must be ever vigilant that the letter of the law does not crowd out the spirit of the law. We are saddened when we hear of heated gospel debates and disputes as one member contends against another on what they believe are the fine (and in their opinion, the *finest*) points of doctrine. The truth is, we are all striving in the best way we know how to find our way along the pathway that leads to eternal life.

There is only one direction in which we should be looking, and that is *not* down our noses at others who we feel are woefully wanting in the correct ways of doing and thinking. Rather, our focus should be on our Savior, who is *the* way, *the* truth, and *the* One who breathes *gentle* life into our understanding of the principles of His gospel and sheds light on that understanding through the powerful witness of the Holy Ghost.

1 Cor. 1:27

But God hath chosen the foolish things of the world to confound the wise; and God hath chosen the weak things of the world to confound the things which are mighty.

We all have weaknesses that can be turned into strengths; however, it is only as we turn to the Savior for guidance that He helps us become aware of what those weaknesses are. Humility allows us to have faith in the Lord so He can teach us, thereby increasing our spiritual strength.

We see a daily fulfillment of this for missionaries called to preach the gospel in all parts of the world. The majority of them are young and inexperienced in the ways of the world and in gospel knowledge: they often struggle to learn a foreign language; their formal college educations may not even have begun; and their experience in human relationships is very basic. But through their faith, obedience, and humility, these weak missionaries become strong in all the ways that truly count. The Lord is able to teach them, and in turn, they are able to teach the things of the Spirit: "That the fulness of my gospel might be proclaimed by the weak and simple unto the ends of the world, and before kings and rulers" (D&C 1:23).

Our strength comes through humbly learning and doing the will of the Lord, relying always on His grace.

1 Cor. 2:9

But as it is written, Eye hath not seen, nor ear heard, neither have entered into the heart of man, the things which God hath prepared for them that love him.

Paul may very well have been quoting the writings of Isaiah when he said, "It is written," for Isaiah makes this wondrous promise of unimaginable blessings the Lord has in store for those "that waiteth for him" (see Isa. 64:4), or, in other words, who love Him. This is a magnificent promise: He will reveal to us the mysteries and the wonders of eternity; will grant us great wisdom, understanding, and knowledge "by the unspeakable gift of the Holy Ghost"; and will share with us all the secrets of His will—"nothing shall be withheld" (D&C 121:26–28; see also 76:5–10). Who would not wish to claim these great blessings?

We live in a day of lotteries, when huge fortunes are promised to whoever buys the winning ticket. All that person has to do is come forward and show their proof of purchase. How very different is the Lord's "lottery." We *all* hold the winning ticket, and our proof of purchase is our manifestation of love for Him, who loved us first and best.

The Savior says, "If ye love me, keep my commandments" (John 14:15). Love for the Savior logically leads to obedience, which in turn gives us the privilege of claiming His glorious promises.

1 Cor. 2:16

For who hath known the mind of the Lord,
that he may instruct him? But we have the mind of Christ.

We are familiar with the old saying "Great minds think alike." When we readily agree with the ideas of a close friend or spouse, or when our spirits respond to a fine lecture or lesson that reinforces truths we already embrace, we are gratified by these closely knit mental processes that produce a meeting of the minds.

But how often do we think of this in terms of our minds being in tune with the Savior's mind? "Knowing God towers above all earthly attainments. . . . Those who nurture a lifelong trust and confidence in Jesus Christ and sustain their efforts to keep [His] commandments and walk in the Light will come to know their Lord and become partakers of the heavenly gift. . . . In short, we come to know the Master as our lives more closely parallel his life, as we gain 'the mind of Christ'" (*Coming to Know Christ*, 158–160).

For the Apostle Paul—and for us—the greatest meeting of minds is to "think what [Christ] thinks, know what he knows, say what he would say, and do what he would do in every situation—all by revelation from the Spirit" (*DNTC*, Vol. II, 322).

1 Cor 6:19–20

Know ye not that your body is the temple of the Holy Ghost which is in you, which ye have of God, and ye are not your own? For ye are bought with a price: therefore glorify God in your body, and in your spirit, which are God's.

When new temples are announced during a general conference of the Church, there is a unanimous and delighted intake of breath among Church members. Why does the building of temples generate such excitement? Because they are God's highest and holiest places on earth. They are the edifices wherein we are taught the doctrines and principles of salvation and where we are endowed with power from on high to claim the attendant blessings.

Temples are palaces of spiritual cleanliness, just as is the kingdom of God. The Lord, then, is paying us a high compliment when He tells us that *we* are the temples of God; thus, the same rules of spiritual cleanliness apply to us. The Psalmist offers insight into the meaning of inner cleanliness: "Who shall ascend into the hill of the Lord? or who shall stand in his holy place? He that hath clean hands, and a pure heart" (Ps. 24:3–4).

The words of a hymn remind us of this principle: "While of these emblems we partake / In Jesus' name and for His sake, / Let us remember and be sure / Our hearts and hands are clean and pure" ("While of These Emblems We Partake," *Hymns*, no. 173).

Inner purity prepares our personal temple to be a comfortable dwelling place for God's Spirit.

1 Cor. 10:67

Now these things were our examples, to the intent we should not lust after evil things. . . . Neither be ye idolaters . . . as it is written, The people sat down to eat and drink, and rose up to play.

The word *lust* is most often associated with unhealthy or inappropriate longings or desires, often for that which may bring momentary gratification but, in the long run, results in spiritual damage. Lust and idolatry are closely related in their short-term payoff and long-term penalties.

We may be dismayed by the unholy examples of the children of Israel, which earned them a long and weary wandering in the wilderness of sin and a denial of the keys to the gates of the promised land. But while our lusts and idols may be less visible, they are no less spiritually harmful. An unhealthy desire for anything that takes precedence over our love of God—be it fame, fortune, social status, power, or personal gratification in any of its many forms—can be classified as lustful and idolatrous. Golden calves, or idols, can take on many forms, most of them subtle and alluring and seemingly small and harmless until they assume proportions that can even obscure the face of God.

The Lord gives us the antidote for these spiritual disorders: "Look unto me in every thought; doubt not, fear not. . . . Be faithful, keep my commandments, and ye shall inherit the kingdom of heaven" (D&C 6:36–37).

1 Cor. 10:10

Neither murmur ye, as some of them also murmured, and were destroyed of the destroyer.

When we hear the word *murmur*, we are apt to think of Laman and Lemuel, the monarchs of murmuring. The very sound of the word carries a subtle ring of low-key discontent, a malady that is ever so closely related. It is a spiritual sniffle that starts out small but, when left untreated, can turn into full-blown, uncontrollable carnal coughing. Nephi tells us that when Satan's toehold of murmuring proceeds unchecked, he then "rage[s] in the hearts of . . . men, and stir[s] them up to anger against that which is good" (2 Ne. 28:20).

This problem is not hard to see in Laman and Lemuel, but perhaps on close inspection (or introspection), we might also recognize some signs of this problem in ourselves. Do we detect what we consider to be flaws in our leaders or in their counsel? Do we suspect that others get preferential treatment, either in our families or in our wards and stakes? Do we chafe under the so-called restraints of the Word of Wisdom or the law of tithing or Sabbath observance, failing to see the blessings of obedience?

Paul again reminds us that we should "do all things without murmurings and disputings: That ye may be blameless and harmless, the sons [and daughters] of God" (Philip. 2:14).

1 Cor. 10:13

There hath no temptation taken you but such as is common to man: but God is faithful, who will not suffer you to be tempted above that ye are able; but will with the temptation also make a way to escape, that ye may be able to bear it.

The Lord tells us that temptation is an integral part of our agency: "And it must needs be that the devil should tempt the children of men, or they could not be agents unto themselves; for if they never should have bitter they could not know the sweet" (D&C 29:39). Relentless forces of Satan and his minions are constantly attacking our vulnerabilities. Having failed in one area to win us over, they will strike again and again, hoping to wear us down by the sheer force of their cunning perseverance: "That is part of the human experience—facing temptations on a daily, almost moment-by-moment basis—facing them not only on the good days but on the days we are down, the days we are tired, rejected, discouraged, or sick" (*The Infinite Atonement*, 106).

We cannot, however, become sin's landlord and then leave it to the Lord to give the eviction notice. We must personally fight against sin, and thankfully, we have the Lord's promise that He will strengthen us and help us come off conquerors: "The righteous cry, and the Lord heareth, and delivereth them out of all their troubles" (Ps. 34:17).

1 Cor. 13:13

And now abideth faith, hope, charity, these three;
but the greatest of these is charity.

The three great virtues of faith, hope, and charity are rarely spoken of separately because they incrementally build on one another, with charity being the most important. Charity is a virtue most often associated with good works. The Savior taught, "Whosoever will lose his life for my sake, the same shall save it" (Luke 9:24).

Consider the Savior's example of service: He healed the sick, caused the blind to see, bade the cripples to walk, cast out evil spirits, raised the dead, loved and comforted the sinner, washed His Apostles' tired and dusty feet, reached out to His mother with His pure love in the last hours of His suffering on the cross, and ultimately ransomed us all in Gethsemane and on Calvary.

Elder Dallin H. Oaks adds wise counsel on this topic. He cautions us against service that seeks the recognition and accolades of men, service that is motivated by selfishness rather than selflessness. He counsels us that it is only through service that is motivated by love of God and our fellowmen that we qualify as recipients of God's promise of eternal life (see "Unselfish Service," *Ensign*, May 2009, 93–96).

1 Cor. 12:1, 4, 31

Now concerning spiritual gifts, brethren, I would not have you ignorant. . . . There are diversities of gifts, but the same Spirit. . . . But covet earnestly the best gifts.

In modern revelation, the Lord tells us we should seek *earnestly* for the best gifts, "always remembering for what they are given" (D&C 46:8). He is talking about the gifts of the Spirit, and He does not leave us to guess at their purpose. The Savior goes on to say, "They are given for the benefit of those who love me and keep all my commandments, *and him that seeketh so to do*" (v. 9; emphasis added). The Lord's generosity and love are evident in these words, especially when He acknowledges that we are all at varying points on the pathway to perfection.

"Spiritual gifts come from God . . . by the power of the Holy Ghost. . . . Men must receive the gift of the Holy Ghost before that member of the Godhead will take up his abode with them and begin the supernal process of distributing his gifts to them. . . . Thus the gifts of the Spirit are for believing, faithful, righteous people; they are reserved for the saints of God. . . . Spiritual gifts are endless in number and infinite in variety" (*A New Witness for the Articles of Faith*, 270, 370, 371).

1 Cor. 14:10

There are, it may be, so many kinds of voices in the world.

We are surrounded by voices that compete for our attention, voices that would have us buy this or that, voices that entice us to engage in one type of activity or another, voices that plant the seeds of doubt about our worth as children of God. The one voice, however, upon which we can always rely to lead us in paths of truth and righteousness is that of our Savior.

"The sheep hear his voice: and he calleth his own sheep by name, and leadeth them out. . . . And the sheep follow him: for they know his voice" (John 10:3–4). His voice is neither harsh nor loud, yet it can pierce our souls and cause our hearts to burn (see 3 Ne. 11:3). When the Savior speaks, His words are carried into our hearts and our spirits with a message we can trust, a message of love that reassures us that we are valued and valuable. The message is always the same; it is the message of repentance and faith in the Lord Jesus Christ.

We can hear His voice as we tune our hearts to His spiritual frequency and receive His pleasing word through the privilege of quiet and personal revelation.

1 Cor. 15:29

Else what shall they do which are baptized for the dead, if the dead rise not at all? why are they then baptized for the dead?

In September 1823, the angel Moroni appeared to Joseph Smith three times in one night. Moroni quoted the prophecy in Malachi regarding the coming of Elijah to "plant in the hearts of the children the promises made to the fathers," saying that "the hearts of the children shall turn to their fathers" (JS—H 1:39). Obviously, this important doctrine bore repeating because it had been lost in the shuffle of the dark night of the Apostasy.

This prophecy was fulfilled in the Kirtland Temple on April 3, 1836, when Elijah restored the sealing keys of the priesthood—keys that turned the lock in the door of spirit prison for countless spirits who anxiously awaited the privilege of being born again in the baptismal fonts of our temples.

While various other religious sects have hotly contested the practice of baptism for the dead in the temples of The Church of Jesus Christ of Latter-day Saints, it was, as the Prophet Joseph Smith clearly stated: "certainly practiced by the ancient churches. . . . The Saints have the privilege of being baptized for those of their relatives who are dead . . . and who have received the Gospel in the spirit, through the instrumentality of those who have been commissioned to preach to them while in prison" (*TPJS*, 179).

1 Cor. 15:41

There is one glory of the sun, and another glory of the moon, and another glory of the stars: for one star differeth from another star in glory.

Prophets knew and taught the doctrine of the three degrees of glory anciently. Prophets in Book of Mormon times also understood and preached this doctrine: "And he cometh into the world that he may save all men if they will hearken unto his voice; for behold, he suffereth the pains of all men. . . . And he suffereth this that the resurrection might pass upon all men, that all might stand before him at the great and judgment day" (2 Ne. 9:21–22).

We will then be assigned to a degree of glory commensurate with our works and our testimony of Jesus Christ. God is bound by law, and we will be judged according to the law of justice: "And it is requisite with the justice of God that men should be judged according to their works; and if their works were good in this life, and the desires of their hearts were good, that they should . . . be restored unto that which is good. And if their works are evil they shall be restored unto them for evil. Therefore, all things shall be restored to their proper order" (Alma 41:3–4).

Where do *we* stand in relation to our testimony of Jesus Christ? Sunbeam, moonbeam, or star?

1 Cor. 15:55–57

O death, where is thy sting? O grave, where is thy victory? The sting of death is sin; and the strength of sin is the law. But thanks be to God, which giveth us the victory through our Lord Jesus Christ.

The doctrine of resurrection is sweet and comforting, and death is not a frightful specter that lurks menacingly just around the corner, waiting to carry us off to an uncertain fate. How glorious is this truth that only our Savior Jesus Christ can make possible.

"Men are born, they live for an hour of glory, and die. Most throughout their lives are teased by various hopes; and among all the hopes of men in all ages of time, none is so great as the hope of immortality. The empty tomb that first Easter morning brought the most comforting assurance that can come into man's heart. This was the affirmative answer to the ageless question raised by Job, 'If a man die, shall he live again?' (Job 14:14). . . . This is the promise of the risen Lord. This is the relevance of Jesus to a world in which all must die. . . . His death sealed the testimony of His love for all mankind. His resurrection opened the gates of salvation to the sons and daughters of God of all generations" (*TGBH*, 551–552).

Well might we thank God, our Heavenly Father, who gave His Only Begotten Son that we might not perish but have everlasting life (see John 3:16).

1 Cor. 15:58

Therefore, my beloved brethren, be ye steadfast, unmoveable, always abounding in the work of the Lord, forasmuch as ye know that your labour is not in vain in the Lord.

"The conditions of conquest are always easy. We have but to toil awhile, endure awhile, believe always, and never turn back" (Marcus Annaeus Seneca). How true this is when it comes to our service in the Lord's vineyard. We don't have the option of giving up or giving out; in fact, *abounding* means we will always be looking for ways to serve above and beyond the minimum requirements of our callings.

We might wonder whether our call to serve is really important. The Lord assures us that the quality of our service is measured by the intent of our hearts: "Verily I say, men [and women] should be anxiously engaged in a good cause . . . and bring to pass much righteousness; For the power is in them, wherein they are agents unto themselves. And inasmuch as men [and women] do good they shall in nowise lose their reward" (D&C 58:27–28).

"Suppose Peter had not left his nets 'straightway'? (See Mark 1:18.) He might have become the respected president of the local Galilean fishermen's association. But he would not have been on the Mount of Transfiguration with Jesus, Moses, and Elias and heard the voice of God (See Matthew 17:4)" (*The Neal A. Maxwell Quote Book*, 55).

1 Cor. 16:14

Let all your things be done with charity.

Paul's sermons on charity are powerful. In this simple statement, he leaves no doubt about the role of charity, or the pure love of Christ, in our lives. On another occasion, Paul wrote, "We then that are strong ought to bear the infirmities of the weak, and not to please ourselves" (Rom. 15:1). Two interpretations of his words come to mind: our thoughts and actions should be focused outward and not inward; or, perhaps Paul is also telling us that our charity should not be self-congratulatory.

Our Savior's pure love is eternal and nonpartisan. There should be no confusion, then, about His new commandment: "As I have loved you, that ye also love one another" (John 13:34).

"Charity, or love, is the greatest principle in existence. If we can lend a helping hand to the oppressed, if we can aid those who are despondent and in sorrow, if we can uplift and ameliorate the condition of mankind, it is our mission to do it, it is an essential part of our religion to do it" (Joseph F. Smith, *The Prophets Have Spoken*, Vol. 2 [Salt Lake City: Deseret Book, 1999], 390).

2 Cor. 1:3

Blessed be God, even the Father of our Lord Jesus Christ, the Father of mercies, and the God of all comfort.

"We believe in God, the Eternal Father" (A of F 1:1). The word *Father* denotes perfect love, comfort, guidance, mercy, kindness, and generosity, to name but a few of His attributes, because He is a perfect Father.

We believe in Him because He manifested His love for us in our premortal existence, when He provided a plan whereby we could come to earth and receive bodies just like His. He eagerly awaits the day of our return, which our Savior and Elder Brother, Jesus Christ, made possible through the Atonement, "for God so [loves us]" (John 3:16).

We believe in Him because He manifested Himself in this dispensation, thus dispelling all mysticism about who and what He is. He *is* a God with a body and passions, and He knows each of us by name: "All things are numbered unto me, for *they are mine and I know them*" (Moses 1:35; emphasis added).

We believe in Him because He is interested in the very details of our lives, and He weeps with us and for us. We "are the workmanship of [His] own hands" (Moses 7:32), and He is grieved when we make mistakes.

We believe in Him because He created us—we are His "begotten sons and daughters" (D&C 76:24).

2 Cor. 4:8–9

We are troubled on every side, yet not distressed; we are perplexed, but not in despair; Persecuted, but not forsaken; cast down, but not destroyed.

This scripture reminds us of the "glass half full" philosophy. It is a timely reminder about feeling contentment and expressing gratitude.

Contentment is a complementary condiment to gratitude; it is the ability to "stop and smell the roses," remembering to count our blessings as opposed to enumerating our trials. Henry Ward Beecher said, "Let the thankful heart sweep through the day and, as the magnet finds the iron, so will it find, in every hour, some heavenly blessings."

A short poem by Henry van Dyke offers a positive perspective on contentment:

"These are the gifts I ask of thee, Spirit serene: Strength for the daily task / Courage to face the road / Good cheer to help me bear the traveler's load /And for the hours of rest that come between /An inward joy for all things heard and seen."

Like Nephi of old, we can express our joy, gratitude, and contentment to Him who graciously gives us the gift of each day: "Rejoice, O my heart, and cry unto the Lord, and say: O Lord, I will praise thee forever; yea, my soul will rejoice in thee, my God, and the rock of my salvation" (2 Ne. 4:30).

2 Cor. 5:7

For we walk by faith, not by sight.

When "we were in the presence of God; we saw him and knew the course he had charted for us. Now we are out of his personal presence . . . [and we] are being tested under circumstances where we must accept him and his laws on faith" (*DNTC*, Vol. II, 420). A favorite scripture tells us that "faith is the substance of things hoped for, the evidence of things not seen" (Heb. 11:1). We have to believe some things before we can see them.

President Wilford Woodruff explains the second part of that scripture in Hebrews 11:1, which says that faith is "the substance of things hoped for"—"the resurrection, the eternal judgment, the celestial kingdom, and the great blessings that God has given in the holy anointings and endowment in the temples, are all for the future, and they will be fulfilled, for they are eternal truths. We will never while in the flesh, with this veil over us, fully comprehend that which lies before us in the world to come" (*The Prophets Have Spoken*, 1013).

A quote by Saint Augustine seems to sum faith up quite nicely: "Faith is to believe what we do not see; the reward of this faith is to see what we believe."

2 Cor. 5:17–18

Therefore if any man be in Christ, he is a new creature: old things are passed away; behold, all things are become new. And all things are of God, who hath reconciled us to himself by Jesus Christ.

Looking back on times when we were estranged from loved ones or friends, we may recall the sadness we felt until the problem was resolved. Then we may remember our feelings of joy as those differences were reconciled and we could once again enjoy those sweet associations.

The Fall of Adam brought spiritual death into the world and our estrangement from the presence of God. We died a spiritual death and became "carnal, sensual, and devilish" (Alma 42:10), which made us enemies to God (see Mosiah 3:19) and which condition was pleasing neither to ourselves nor to God, who loves us and longs for a reconciliation.

So He sent His Son to bring spiritual life back into the world through His atoning sacrifice. There is no other way to repair the rift between God and ourselves—no other way to become new creatures, worthy once again to associate with our Heavenly Father.

"And we rejoice in the knowledge—a doctrine that is indeed the burden of scripture—that Jesus Christ came into the world to save sinners, to rescue and redeem people like you and me, to make up the difference, to make *all* the difference, and thus to make *us* different" (*Coming to Know Christ*, 56; emphasis added).

2 Cor. 5:20

Now then we are ambassadors to Christ, as though Christ did beseech you by us: we pray you in Christ's stead, be ye reconciled to God.

While we are more commonly known as Mormons, our official name identifies us as disciples—or ambassadors—of Christ. Those who subscribe to other religions or to no religion at all closely watch our words and actions because we are members of The Church of Jesus Christ of Latter-day Saints. When someone of our faith is involved in less-than-exemplary activities, the media is quick to pick up on it. The world is watching!

A group of early-morning seminary students who were definitely in the religious minority at their schools were challenged to wear badges labeled "I Am a Child of God" to school for just one day. Some students feared the ridicule of their classmates; however, some accepted the challenge and later reported that, for the most part, their classmates were respectfully curious and attentive as they explained their beliefs. The students who dared to be ambassadors for Christ were blessed with an increase of faith and testimony in the cause of Christ.

How about our own track records? Do our actions and speech set us apart as children of God, or do they brand us as simply being part of the worldly crowd? Do we fear that we might fall out of favor with our friends or colleagues?

"I will speak of thy testimonies also before kings, and will not be ashamed" (Ps. 119:46).

2 Cor. 7:10

For godly sorrow worketh repentance to salvation not to be repented of; but the sorrow of the world worketh death.

Different types of sorrow are connected with sin. There is the sorrow that is mainly regret because we have been caught or exposed, and we might be denied some privileges or rewards. Then there is the "sorrowing of the damned, because the Lord [will] not always suffer [us] to take happiness in sin" (Morm. 2:13). In all such cases, worldly rationalizations quickly replace repentance.

Godly sorrow, however, is that which leads to true and honest repentance. It is the kind of sorrow Alma the younger expressed when he said he was "racked with torment" and "harrowed up" (Alma 36:17). It is the sorrow he explained to his son some years later: "Only let your sins trouble you, with that trouble which shall bring you down unto repentance" (Alma 42:29).

Allowing us to feel godly sorrow, the Lord gives us the formula for true repentance: "By this ye may know if a man repenteth of his sins—behold, he will confess them and forsake them" (D&C 58:43). And the most wondrous news of all is that the Savior has "power given unto him from the Father to redeem [us] *from* [our] sins because of repentance" (Hel. 5:11; emphasis added).

2 Cor. 9:7

Every man according as he purposeth in his heart, so let him give; not grudgingly, or of necessity: for God loveth a cheerful giver.

True generosity is the product of perfect harmony between the intents of our hearts and our outward performances. When the Lord told Samuel that he judges us by what is in our hearts rather than by our outward appearances, it might well mean that He knows when we are just going through the motions of good works without having a good heart (see 1 Sam. 16:7).

Mormon tells us the consequences of grudging generosity: "God hath said a man being evil cannot do that which is good; for if he offereth a gift . . . except he shall do it with real intent it profiteth him nothing. . . . For behold, if a man being evil giveth a gift, he doeth it grudgingly; wherefore it is counted unto him the same as if he had retained the gift" (Moro. 7:6, 8). King Benjamin also warns against meanness of heart and spirit when it comes to giving. He reminds us that generosity is not judgmental (see Mosiah 4:16–17).

As always, the Lord has the final and best advice of all: "Fear not to do good . . . for whatsoever ye sow, that shall ye also reap; therefore, if ye sow good ye shall also reap good for your reward" (D&C 6:33).

2 Cor. 9:15

Thanks be unto God for his unspeakable gift.

We have probably all watched game shows on television. Sometimes the prizes are spectacular—cars, trips, and cash—and a small part of us wishes we could be one of the lucky winners. Most of us, however, win the prizes that are the most precious, not by spinning a wheel of chance but by diligent and sometimes daunting labor, often when it is not really convenient. A quick check of our spiritual priorities reminds us that the service the Savior rendered was tempered by love and compassion, not by expedience. How convenient was it for Him to suffer in Gethsemane and on Calvary?

Some commercial contests offer a final grand prize, which only one winner can hope to claim. Not so with the Savior's grand prize. Our Heavenly Father desires to favor *all* of his children with the "unspeakable gift" of eternal life through the Atonement of His Only Begotten Son.

For our part, the Savior invites us to do good and to deny ourselves of all ungodliness, making the commitment to "love and serve him, the only living and true God" (D&C 20:19). By so doing, we can most assuredly claim eternal life, the grandest of all prizes.

2 Cor. 12:9–10

My grace is sufficient for thee: for my strength is made perfect in weakness. Most gladly therefore will I rather glory in my infirmities, that the power of Christ may rest upon me. Therefore I take pleasure in infirmities, in reproaches, in necessities, in persecutions, in distresses for Christ's sake: for when I am weak, then am I strong.

No one is immune from the storms of adversities and infirmities that blow through our lives, sometimes with alarming ferocity and often with frustrating frequency. The infirmities of which Paul writes can take many forms. They might be physical and very visible, or they might be inner struggles, known only to us and our Heavenly Father.

We cannot always choose the obstacles we face, but we can always decide whether we will allow them to discourage us or lead us to a closer relationship with and dependence on our Savior. He gives us this marvelous promise: "I give unto men weakness that they may be humble . . . for *if they humble themselves before me, and have faith in me*, then will I make weak things become strong unto them" (Ether 12:27; emphasis added).

When we feel that our endurance has been tested to the breaking point, it is well to remember that the Lord, through His grace, will grant us strength to weather the winds of adversity. It is a promise and gift reserved for each one of us because He knows us and loves us.

JST Gal. 1:10

For do I now please men, or God? or do I seek to please men? for if I yet pleased men, I should not be the servant of Christ.

True servants of Christ do not subscribe to the hedonistic and self-serving philosophies of the world, philosophies authored by Lucifer, the father of all lies, who would have us deny or ignore any significant eternal consequences.

However, we need to be aware of the *subtle* nuances of the "eat, drink, and be merry" train of thought that moves quickly, quietly, and efficiently. Once on board, it is easy to relax and enjoy the ride while listening to the clever ads: "God . . . will justify in committing a little sin . . . lie a little, take the advantage of one because of his words, dig a pit for thy neighbor . . . and if it so be that we are guilty, God will beat us with a few stripes, and at last we shall be saved in the kingdom of God" (2 Ne. 28:8).

Unfortunately, the conductor of that train is intent on driving it "carefully down to hell," where passengers are unceremoniously tossed out without so much as a backward glance.

Satan's flattery cannot hold a candle to the Lord's approbation. It is imperative that we board the right train, the ultimate destination of which is the kingdom of God.

Gal. 1:11–12

But I certify you, brethren, that the gospel which was preached of me is not after man. For I neither received it of man, neither was I taught it, but by the revelation of Jesus Christ.

Every person who is a member of The Church of Jesus Christ of Latter-day Saints is a convert whether or not we are born into an LDS family. Each of us must gain a testimony for ourselves, and we achieve this only through personal revelation, which comes to every earnest seeker of truth by the power of the Holy Ghost: "God shall give unto you knowledge by his Holy Spirit, yea, by the unspeakable gift of the Holy Ghost" (D&C 121:26).

"Thus revelation—personal revelation—is the rock foundation upon which the church and kingdom of God is built. . . . It was with Paul as it is with us—of course we are taught the gospel by others, of course we study it out of the revealed word; but in the final analysis, it comes to us by revelation, the Holy Spirit of God bearing witness to the spirit within us that the holy word is true. In the ultimate and true sense, it does not come to us by the power of man, but by the power of God. And thus we build our house of salvation upon the rock of revelation" (*A New Witness for the Articles of Faith*, 489).

Gal. 3:26–27

For ye are all the children of God by faith in Christ Jesus. For as many of you as have been baptized into Christ have put on Christ.

What is more precious and more exciting than the birth of a new baby! It is an event parents and siblings joyfully anticipate. The tiny new son or daughter is welcomed with open arms and hearts and with a priesthood blessing that stipulates they now belong to a specific family, with all the privileges of that particular heritage.

As exciting as this first birth is, without a second birth, we cannot claim the privileges of our Heavenly Father's family. The Savior stated that "except a man be born *again*, he cannot see the kingdom of God" (John 3:3; emphasis added). Our baptism signifies this *new birth* into a *new family*—the family of Christ—where we are welcomed with the joyous embrace of divine parental approval and a promise of all the Father hath if we remain true to this spiritual heritage.

"And now, because of the covenant which ye have made ye shall be called the children of Christ, his sons, and his daughters; for behold, this day he hath spiritually begotten you; for ye say that your hearts are changed through faith on his name; therefore, ye are born of him and have become his sons and his daughters" (Mosiah 5:7).

Gal 5:22–23

But the fruit of the Spirit is love, joy, peace, longsuffering, gentleness, goodness, faith, Meekness, temperance.

We all may have a favorite fruit, and we eagerly anticipate enjoying its abundance when the season is right, hoping the crop will be sweet and satisfying. And we may be saddened when the season for that fruit is past or when it was not quite as sweet and satisfying as we had hoped. So we long for the time when we will again be able to enjoy that special treat at its peak of goodness.

The fruit of the Spirit, of which Paul speaks, is always in season; its quality is consistently pleasing and delicious, and the Holy Ghost is the supplier of this abundance. There are no disappointing crops or harvests, nor do we ever feel empty or hungry once we have tasted it.

President Gordon B. Hinckley tells us, "You recognize the promptings of the Spirit by the fruits of the Spirit—that which enlighteneth, that which buildeth up, that which is positive and affirmative and uplifting and leads us to better thoughts and better words and better deeds is of the Spirit of God. . . . I think it is just that plain, just that simple" (*TGBH*, 261).

Gal. 5:25

If we live in the Spirit, let us also walk in the Spirit.

This scripture, when put in modern vernacular, probably comes close to saying "Put your money where your mouth is" or "You talk the talk, but can you walk the walk?" It is a "let us be up and doing" scripture that reminds us that it is one thing to hear and know the will and word of the Lord but quite another to be doing something about it. The Apostle Paul, whose walk was as straightforward and bold as his talk, also said, "For not the *hearers* of the law *are* just before God, but the *doers* of the law shall be justified" (Rom. 2:13; emphasis added).

It is well for us to regularly take personal inventory to see whether we are walking in the Spirit. Are we trying to emulate Jesus—to walk in His footsteps—or just simply to talk about Him? The words of a favorite hymn emphasize the importance of our godly walk:

"Come, *follow* me," the Savior said.
Then let us in his footsteps *tread*,
For thus alone can we be one
With God's own loved, begotten Son.
("Come, Follow Me," *Hymns*, no. 116; emphasis added).

Gal. 5:26

Let us not be desirous of vain glory, provoking one another, envying one another.

Vanity is defined as inflated pride in oneself or one's accomplishments, leaving no room for appreciating the achievements of others. Pride looks in any other direction rather than up to God. It is a tsunami bent on the destruction of that which is precious and sacred.

When pride looks inward, love of self is one of its best accomplishments. Paul characterized it as a loss of natural affection (see 2 Tim. 3:2–3).

When pride looks sideways, it spawns contention and competition; however, it always demands to be the winner. Its disdainful glance is filled with envy and denies the equality of brotherhood. C. S. Lewis said, "Pride gets no pleasure out of having something, only out of having more of it than the next man" (*Mere Christianity* [New York: Macmillan, 1952], 110).

When pride looks downward, its arrogant stare warns that its learning and wisdom exceed that of all others. There is nothing worth learning that it doesn't already know.

"Who shall ascend into the hill of the Lord? or who shall stand in his holy place? He . . . who hath not lifted up his soul unto vanity" (Ps. 24:3–4).

Gal. 6:2

Bear ye one another's burdens, and so fulfill the law of Christ.

We read in Proverbs 17:17 that "a friend loveth at all times," not just when it is easy or convenient. This is the measure of the Lord's friendship and sets the standard for our own. As mankind's greatest friend, the Savior freely shares that which is most precious—his love, His tender mercy, His redeeming gospel, His friendship. Can we as His friends do any less?

That great Book of Mormon prophet Jacob entreats us, "Think of your brethren like unto yourselves, and be familiar with all and free with your substance, that they may be rich like unto you" (Jacob 2:17). The word *brethren* is an intimate term that carries with it a connotation of compassion and friendship, and the broad interpretation of *substance* goes far beyond our material goods.

A radiant smile, a genuine expression of concern, a listening ear that is not mindful of the ticking of the clock, a heart that hears what is hidden beneath the words, lips fastened against hasty expressions of judgment—these are all Christlike gestures of compassion that link our hearts and spirits in friendship with our children, our siblings, our spouses, our coworkers, our neighbors, the stranger in need, and thus with the Savior Himself.

Gal. 6:7

Be not deceived; God is not mocked: for whatsoever a man soweth, that shall he also reap.

The Savior plainly tells us, "For every tree is known by [its] own fruit. For of thorns men do not gather figs, nor of a bramble bush gather they grapes" (Luke 6:44). There are those who unwisely test this immutable law of the harvest, who hope they can pass a course without attending classes or studying, who anticipate the blessings of eternal life without keeping the commandments of God.

If nothing is sown, then there is no harvest. It is like admiring our neighbor's beautiful garden and impending bounteous harvest, then saying, "You're so lucky to have a nice garden like that; I wish I had one." But luck and wishing have absolutely nothing to do with it. How about the day-to-day hard work of preparing the soil, planting the seeds, fertilizing, watering, and weeding? This attitude might also be compared to admiring (even envying) the spiritual gardens of our neighbors, who earnestly work and sacrifice to bring forth the blessings of heaven, while we procrastinate our spiritual plantings.

Consider Alma's positive and encouraging words: "But if ye will nourish the word, yea, nourish the tree as it beginneth to grow, by your faith with great diligence, and with patience, looking forward to the fruit thereof, it shall take root; and behold it shall be a tree springing up unto everlasting life" (Alma 32:41).

Eph. 2:8

For by grace are ye saved through faith; and that not of yourselves: it is the gift of God. Not of works, lest any man should boast.

We read in the Book of Mormon that "we know that it is by grace that we are saved, after all we can do" (2 Ne. 25:23). "Some have misunderstood this scripture, supposing that the Atonement provides the cleansing power, while our works alone provide the perfecting power; thus, working hand in hand, exaltation is achieved. But such an interpretation is not correct. It is true that the Atonement provides the cleansing power. It is also true that works are a necessary ingredient of the perfecting process. *But without the Atonement, without grace, without the power of Christ, all the works in the world would fall far short of perfecting even one human being. . . .* In other words, grace is not only necessary to cleanse us, but also to perfect us" (*The Infinite Atonement*, 263–264; emphasis added).

"The works of man will never be enough to qualify one for the eternal prize; acting alone, without the grace and mercy and condescension of God, these deeds are but paltry offerings and are thus not *sufficient* for salvation. . . . Christ seeks to reconcile finite men with their infinite Heavenly Father. He is Mediator, Intercessor, and Redeemer" (Robert L. Millet, *By Grace Are We Saved* [Salt Lake City: Bookcraft, 1989], 70, 102).

Eph. 2:19

Now therefore ye are no more strangers and foreigners, but fellowcitizens with the saints, and of the household of God.

Countless poems and songs have been written about the happiness and love found in our homes. A few such idyllic lines follow:

Home is where there's one to love!
Home is where there's one to love us. . . .
Home is sweet, and only sweet,
When there's one we love to meet us!

(Charles Swain, "Home Is Where There Is One to Love Us," *A Treasury of Poems*, 270).

Regardless of our earthly family affiliations or situations, which are varied and can sometimes be complicated, disappointing, or even painful, there is one perfect household to which we are all invited to belong. It is the household of God, where we can all gather safely under the protective roof of the gospel and where we are welcomed with our Savior's open arms.

Through the blessings of the Abrahamic covenant, the gospel becomes that safe household for all of God's children who desire the fellowship of Jesus Christ: "Behold, I will lead thee by my hand, and I will take thee, to put upon thee my name . . . and my power shall be over thee" (Abr. 1:18).

Eph 4:10

He who descended is the same also that ascended up far above all heavens, that he might fill all things.

Christ's *descension* and *ascension* were both integral parts of His *condescension*. One of our hymns says it beautifully: "Jesus, the Anointed, / *Descended* from above / And gave himself a ransom / To win our souls with love" ("O God, the Eternal Father," *Hymns*, no. 175; emphasis added).

In Nephi's great, panoramic vision, he beheld a beautiful virgin carrying a child whom the angel identified as the Son of God. Then Nephi watched the Savior's earthly ministry unfold, culminating in His Crucifixion "for the sins of the world" (see 1 Ne. 11:14–33). Here we see the *condescension* of Christ as He *descended* to earth: "God the Son traded his heavenly home with all its celestial adornments for a mortal abode with all its primitive trappings. . . . It was a trade of unparalleled dimension, a condescension of incredible proportions, a descent of incalculable depth" (*The Infinite Atonement*, 64) into a world with its attendant temptations, pain, suffering, and inevitable death.

Once again, the words of the hymn describe this quite splendidly: "How infinite that wisdom, / The plan of holiness, / That made [our Father's plan of] salvation perfect / And veiled the Lord in flesh, / To walk upon his footstool / *And be like man, almost*, / In his exalted station, / And die, or all was lost" ("O God, the Eternal Father," *Hymns*, no. 175; emphasis added).

Eph. 4:31–32

Let all bitterness, and wrath, and anger, and clamour, and evil speaking, be put away from you, with all malice. And be ye kind to one another, tenderhearted, forgiving one another, even as God for Christ's sake hath forgiven you.

The Savior enlarged the commandments that we love God and our neighbor to include our enemies as well, which is usually easier said than done. When we are mistreated, we usually want to retreat in hurt silence or retaliate. Jesus reminds us that we should behave in an entirely different way—His way—extending love, blessings, good deeds, and prayers to those inclined to treat us badly and focusing on what they might need instead of on what we think they deserve. Considering our own shortcomings, we need to pray that *we* don't get what we deserve!

It seems a tall order, but as with all of the Lord's commandments, compliance is achieved incrementally. It can start with something as simple as being the first to speak a kind word after a quarrel. It can be as easy as kneeling in prayer to plead for the spiritual well-being of someone who has wounded our spirits. It can even be as straightforward as a smile or a handshake, a kind and friendly word, or a card. There may be times when none of these gestures has the desired effect, but compliance with God's law of love sows seeds that may only blossom fully in eternity.

Eph. 5:33

Nevertheless let every one of you in particular so love his wife even as himself; and the wife see that she reverence her husband.

Following the Savior's visit to the Nephites, the people enjoyed two hundred years of peace and happiness, and this included happy marriages: "And they were married, and given in marriage, and were blessed according to the multitude of the promises which the Lord had made unto them. . . . And surely there could not be a happier people among all the people who had been created by the hand of God" (4 Ne. 1:11, 16). It would be wonderful if that could be said of every marriage relationship!

President Hinckley—whose marriage to Sister Hinckley was blessed with an abundance of love, longevity, and happiness—has this to say on the subject: "I have long felt that happiness in marriage is not so much a matter of romance as it is an anxious concern for the comfort and well-being of one's companion. That involves a willingness to overlook weaknesses and mistakes" (*TGBH*, 325).

The Lord's instructions are clear and sweet. Consider the words of He who is the perfect example of perfect love: "Thou shalt love thy wife [or husband] with all thy heart, and shalt cleave unto her [or him] and none else" (D&C 42:22).

Eph. 5:6–7

Let no man deceive you with vain words: for because of these things cometh the wrath of God upon the children of disobedience. Be not ye therefore partakers with them.

Our minds can be easily swayed by the use of language that appeals to our emotions rather than to our common sense. We are bombarded with cleverly designed advertisements, where the wonders of a product are touted in persuasive formats that are hard to resist.

Purveyors of iniquity throughout the scriptures use these same techniques. Sherem "was learned, that he had a perfect knowledge of the language of the people; wherefore, he could use much flattery, and much power of speech, according to the power of the devil" (Jacob 7:4), and some followers of Christ were deceived. Korihor the anti-Christ also comes to mind: "And he did rise up in great swelling words" (Alma 30:31) that had the power to persuade many followers of Christ to abandon their beliefs and testimonies and their very eternal salvation.

The Lord exhorts us to "beware lest [we] are deceived," and then he gives us the perfect formula: "And that ye may not be deceived seek ye earnestly the best gifts, always remembering for what they are given" (see D&C 46:8). The gifts of the Spirit, bestowed by the power of the Holy Ghost, are given to help us discern between deceitful doctrine and the word of God.

Eph. 6:11

Put on the whole armour of God, that ye may be able to stand against the wiles of the devil.

The combined strength of the components of the armor of righteousness is more than sufficient to enable us to shake off Satan's chains and to walk uprightly instead of struggling in the dust. Satan would have us believe there is fame and fortune awaiting us in a future spent with him; however, he advertises no protective armor that guarantees the fulfillment of his empty promises. There is only the ominous clank of his chains that would bind us to a destination of obscurity and misery. On the other hand, the armor of God gives us the strength to shake off Satan's chains, to arise, and to move upward toward God—toward a celestial destination.

Basically, the call to put on the armor of God is a call to repentance. President Spencer W. Kimball urges us as Latter-day Saints to recognize that none of us is immune from the need to repent (see *The Miracle of Forgiveness*, 31). Repentance is one of the first principles of the gospel of Jesus Christ, and it is indeed a principle with a promise of the Lord's help and forgiveness.

The armor of God is tailored to every individual's size and needs; it fits each one of us perfectly and comfortably, and fits us for the kingdom of God.

Philip. 4:7

And the peace of God, which passeth all understanding, shall keep your hearts and minds through Christ Jesus.

In all instances, the message of peace is the same: it is the message of repentance and faith in the Lord Jesus Christ. It is this peaceful message that keeps—or guards—our hearts and minds. To those who are humble and willing to listen, the voice of the Messenger is gratifying and satisfying in its message. Hearts are softened, and misguided lives are changed. "I will hear what God the LORD will speak: for he will speak peace unto his people, and to his saints" (Ps. 85:8).

Jacob refers to the message as "the pleasing word of God, yea, the word which healeth the wounded soul" (Jacob 2:8). The Savior's voice and message can calm all the storms that rage in our lives. It is a message that carries with it a promise of peace no other source can match.

In a movingly beautiful passage of scripture, the prophet Abinadi tells us, quoting the prophet Isaiah, "For O how beautiful upon the mountains are the feet of him that bringeth good tidings, that is the founder of peace, yea, even the Lord, . . . yea, him who has granted salvation unto his people" (Mosiah 15:18). Surely this message of salvation can speak nothing but peace to our souls.

Philip. 4:8

Whatsoever things are true, whatsoever things are honest, whatsoever things are just, whatsoever things are pure, whatsoever things are lovely, whatsoever things are of good report; if there be any virtue, and if there be any praise, think on these things.

In this scripture, an impressive list of virtues is brought to our attention, which then builds to a most stunning and climactic mandate: *Think on these things.* There are so many things that vie for position in our minds, not all of which are pure and wholesome.

We can never afford to let down our guard when it comes to sorting and sifting and tossing out thoughts that are not virtuous or lovely. It is said we cannot always prevent unsavory thoughts from coming into our minds, but we do not need to invite them to stay for dinner!

Our thoughts are the precursors of our speech and actions: "For as he thinketh in his heart, so is he" (Prov. 23:7). Alma's words on this subject carry a powerful warning: "Our words will condemn us, yea, all our works will condemn us . . . and our thoughts will also condemn us; and in this awful state we shall not dare to look up to our God" (Alma 12:14).

The Lord's instruction regarding this principle also carries a powerful and reassuring promise: "Let virtue garnish thy thoughts unceasingly; *then shall thy confidence wax strong in the presence of God*" (D&C 121:45; emphasis added).

Philip. 2:5–6

Let this mind be in you, which was also in Christ Jesus: Who, being in the form of God, thought it not robbery to be equal with God.

Throughout His mortal ministry, the Savior taught the doctrine that His Father is the supreme Ruler of the universe: "My Father is greater than I" (John 14:28). In doing so, He is verifying that He worships the same God we all do.

"Wherein, then, lies our Lord's equality with his God and our God? Is it not in that Jesus, crowned now himself with exaltation, has received from the Father all knowledge, all truth, all wisdom, all power? Is it not in the same sense that all of the sons of God, as joint-heirs with Christ, shall receive all that the Father hath? . . .

"President Lorenzo Snow, early in his ministry, received by direct, personal revelation the knowledge that (in the Prophet Joseph Smith's language), 'God himself was once as we are now, and is an exalted man, and sits enthroned in yonder heavens,' and that men 'have got to learn how to be Gods . . . the same as all Gods have done before' ([*TPJS*,] 345–346)" (*DNTC*, Vol. II, 531). President Snow later summarized it this way: "As man now is, God once was; / As God now is, man may be" (Ibid., 531).

This is glorious and lofty doctrine to be further comprehended, "even beyond the grave" (*TPJS*, 348).

Col. 2:6–7

As ye have therefore received Christ Jesus the Lord, so walk ye in him: Rooted and built up in him, and stablished in the faith, as ye have been taught, abounding therein with thanksgiving.

In His parable about seeds and soil, the Savior spoke of seeds that fell on a thin layer of soil atop a stony surface. They grew quickly into plants, but the scorching rays of the sun caused them to wither away because they had no deep roots. Other seeds fell among thorns and weeds that choked them. Jesus then described seeds that fell into deep, rich soil, put down strong roots, and yielded an abundant harvest (see Matt. 13:6, 8).

How deep do *our* roots go? Does our spiritual soil barely cover a hard and rocky surface that allows our testimonies no real roots? Does the heat of adversity or disappointment or despair cause our faith in Christ to wither on weak vines? Is our faith weakened by worldly weeds of scorn or peer pressure?

Or do we nourish and dig our spiritual soil so it is a deep and rich base for the roots of our testimonies of and faith in Jesus Christ? Do we acknowledge Him as the Son of God? Do we believe in His Atonement and Resurrection? Can we say without hesitation that He lives? If so, we should "offer unto God thanksgiving; and pay [our] vows unto the most High" (Ps. 50:14).

Col. 3:20–21

Children, obey your parents in all things: for this is well pleasing unto the Lord. Fathers, provoke not your children to anger, lest they be discouraged.

The fifth commandment, written by the finger of the Lord on tablets of stone atop Mount Sinai, says, "Honour thy father and thy mother: that thy days may be long upon the land which the LORD thy God giveth thee" (Ex. 20:12). Whether in time or in eternity, obedience to this commandment will earn the Lord's divine stamp of approval.

In another long-ago dispensation, Isaiah said, "And all thy children *shall be* taught of the LORD; and great *shall be* the peace of thy children" (Isa. 54:13). Homes where the gospel of Jesus Christ is lived and taught with love, mercy, and respect are the seedbeds of the peace of which Isaiah speaks.

A parent's greatest responsibility is teaching children to love the Lord and to live and espouse values that their children can safely emulate: "Fathers and mothers are needed who will rise and stand upon their feet to make of their homes sanctuaries in which children will grow in a spirit of obedience, industry, and fidelity to tested standards of conduct. If our society is coming apart at the seams, it is because the tailor and the seamstress in the home are not producing the kind of stitching that will hold under stress" (*TGBH*, 200).

1 Thes. 4:1

Furthermore then we beseech you, brethren, and exhort you by the Lord Jesus, that as ye have received of us how ye ought to walk and to please God, so ye would abound more and more.

In answer to cynical questions the Pharisees hurled at Him, the Savior's reply concerning His identity and His submission to the Father was quietly magnificent: "And he that sent me is with me: the Father hath not left me alone; *for I do always those things that please him*" (John 8:29; emphasis added).

Pleasing God can surely be equated with obedience, and the Savior is reminding us of the blessings of obedience to God's commandments—*He will not leave us alone.* "Therefore, let your hearts be comforted; for all things shall work together for good to them that *walk uprightly*" (D&C 100:15; emphasis added).

"At times when we are inclined to think it is vain to serve the Lord, we should stir our faith, believe in the rich promises of God, and obey—and patiently wait. The Lord will fulfill all his rich promises to us. Paul says, 'Eye hath not seen, nor ear heard, neither have entered into the heart of man, the things which God hath prepared for them that love [and obey] him' (1 Cor. 2:9)" (*The Miracle of Forgiveness*, 305).

1 Thes. 5:8

But let us, who are of the day, be sober, putting on the breastplate of faith and love; and for an helmet, the hope of salvation.

The history of the world is a history of battles fought and won and lost. It is a history begun in a premortal setting, where the adversary sought to dethrone God the Father, usurp His glory, and deny us our agency; however, the forces of truth and righteousness soundly defeated him.

Among the ongoing battles between good and evil, we thrill at the story of David and Goliath, where a young boy, armed with only a slingshot and his faith in God, brought down a bully whose only claims to fame were a massive physique and an even more colossal ego. David's words were a courageous preface for what was to follow: "This day will the Lord deliver thee into mine hand. . . . And all this assembly shall know that the Lord saveth not with sword and spear: for the battle *is* the Lord's, and he will give you into our hands" (1 Sam. 17:46–47). And the rest of the story is sacred history.

Temptations, societal ills, the subtle pressures and overt tyrannies of kingdoms, thrones, and principalities, all spawned by the adversary, who would have us forget our Champion—these can never overthrow the power of personal faith in the Lord Jesus Christ when we are spiritually armed.

1 Thes. 5:16

Rejoice evermore.

The word *rejoice* is liberally sprinkled throughout the pages of scripture and is always associated with lifting our heads and hearts to Jesus Christ: "Therefore, lift up your heads, and rejoice, and put your trust in God" (Mosiah 7:19). The admonition to lift up our heads is beautifully symbolic, reminding us of the direction from whence our help comes: "I will lift up mine eyes unto the hills, from whence cometh my help" (Ps. 121:1).

To receive the Savior's guidance and comfort, our heads, hearts, minds, and eyes must be lifted up. In a quiet grove of trees, a young boy saw a light and heard a voice because he lifted his head to the Source of light and truth. The prophet Nephi bowed in humble—even desperate—petition to God, then lifted his head to hear the joyous news of the imminent birth of the Savior.

Such scriptural examples speak of Jesus Christ and His power to deliver us from bondage—in all of its nefarious forms—and to rescue us from the grasp of the adversary. We truly have reason to rejoice, to lift up our heads in a grateful upward glance: "Lift up your hearts and be glad, your redemption draweth nigh" (D&C 35:26).

1 Thes. 5:17

Pray without ceasing.

The Prophet Joseph Smith gave this counsel regarding prayer: "Seek to know God in your closets, call upon him in the fields. Follow the directions in the Book of Mormon, and pray over, and for your families, your cattle, your flocks, your herds, your corn, and all things that you possess; ask the blessing of God upon all your labors, and everything that you engage in" (*TPJS*, 247).

Developing a regular habit of morning and evening prayers keeps us connected with Deity. Our families and friends need to know that our prayers in their behalf are consistent and heartfelt. We need to really mean it when we tell family members and friends, "I'll keep you in my prayers."

To His Saints of the latter days, the Savior gives this commandment: "Pray *always*, lest you enter into temptation and lose your reward" (D&C 31:12; emphasis added). Note the use of the word *always* as opposed to *occasionally* or *when it's convenient*.

Our Heavenly Father is interested in all aspects of our lives, and He eagerly awaits our daily calls. The Psalmist reminds us of the order and power of consistent prayer: "Evening, and morning, and at noon, will I pray, and cry aloud: and he shall hear my voice" (Ps. 55:17).

1 Thes. 5:18

In every thing give thanks: for this is the will of God in Christ Jesus concerning you.

On the occasion of the Last Supper, Jesus expressed His gratitude and love for His Apostles in His great intercessory prayer, once again setting the pattern and example for the attitude of gratitude we should cultivate.

Elder Henry B. Eyring challenges us to make "thank you" a priority in our prayers. He explains that verbal expressions of gratitude increase our recollections of blessings received, making our prayers more heartfelt and less rushed (see *To Draw Closer to God* [Salt Lake City: Deseret Book, 1997], 78).

We might occasionally feel hard-pressed to think of something for which we are grateful when negative circumstances surround us. A few moments of quiet reflection on our knees will bring to our remembrance what might at first be a trickle of thanks—which, when humbly expressed, will open the floodgates of gratitude.

Let us be grateful children of God at all times and in all circumstances, in times of need and turmoil as well as in times of personal peace and plenty. Let us joyfully count our blessings and "name them one by one" ("Count Your Blessings," *Hymns*, no. 241). Let us remember with gratitude that the world is glorious, truth has been restored, and God lives and loves us.

1 Thes. 5:22

Abstain from all appearance of evil.

Taking the initiative against evil is far wiser than waiting for its approach and then trying to rally our defenses against it and far wiser than going in for a closer look, hoping to be able to back away in time.

The fable of the gingerbread man and the fox is an entertaining and edifying case in point. Despite his boastful words, "Run, run as fast as you can. You can't catch me; I'm the gingerbread man," he succumbed to the fox's offer to ferry him across the river on his back. As the water got deeper, the fox urged the gingerbread man to hop up closer to his shoulders, then his neck, and closer still until he finally had nowhere to go but into the fox's mouth. His invincibility became susceptibility.

Whether we are talking about what we wear, what we eat or drink, what we watch, listen to, and read, or what our dealings are with our fellowmen, the guidelines from the Lord are clear: "And I give unto you a commandment, that ye shall forsake *all* evil [no picking and choosing] and cleave unto *all* good [again no picking and choosing], that ye shall live by *every word* which proceedeth forth out of the mouth of God" (D&C 98:11; emphasis added).

JST 2 Thes. 2:3

Let no man deceive you by any means: for there shall come a falling away first, and that man of sin be revealed, the son of perdition.

There are many means of deceit afoot among the children of men; in fact, we look on in horrified awe as one wicked trend follows another in rapid succession, each one seemingly more daring, blatant, and bold than its predecessor. Yet, amidst all this gloom and doom and despite these being the worst of times, they are also the best of times.

How can this be so? The answer is simple: it is because the Restoration of the gospel of Jesus Christ came after a long night of apostasy. This restored the glorious knowledge that the Savior came in the meridian of time and atoned for the sins of all mankind. It also restored the reassuring knowledge that we have the divine gift of agency, granted by a merciful and loving Heavenly Father, that empowers us to choose the right, to "let God and heaven"—rather than sin and sorrow—"be [our] goal" (see "Choose the Right," *Hymns*, no. 239).

A prophet pleads, "God give us the strength, the courage, the faith in all our choices to choose that which will enrich the mind, strengthen and discipline the body, nourish the spirit, and thus give us growth and joy in this life and eternal life in the world to come" (*TGBH*, 54–55).

2 Thes. 3:13

But ye, brethren, be not weary in well doing.

"Then wake up and do something more / Than dream of your mansion above" ("Have I Done Any Good?," *Hymns*, no. 223). With days filled to overflowing with tasks to complete, places to go, meetings to attend, appointments to keep, and people to please, there are probably few of us who have time to dream of our mansions above. There is barely time to snatch a few hours of sleep before it is time to start the relentless routine again!

Could it be that we might be missing the *well-doing* point of the Savior's injunction? In His parable of the sower, we read how the seeds that fell among thorns "are they, which, when they have heard, go forth, and are choked with cares and riches and pleasures of this life, and bring no fruit to perfection" (Luke 8:14). Do our cares and pleasures ever fill our days so completely that our well-doing is postponed for less busy times?

The foundations of our mansions above might well be laid by following this simple guideline: "Do all the good you can, / By all the means you can, / In all the ways you can, / In all the places you can, / To all the people you can" (Ella Wheeler Wilcox in *Treasury of Poems*, 120).

JST 1 Tim. 2:4

Who is willing to have all men to be saved, and to come unto the knowledge of the truth which is in Christ Jesus, who is the only Begotten Son of God, and ordained to be a Mediator between God and man; who is one God, and hath power over all men.

"Jesus saith . . . I am the way, the truth, and the life: no man cometh unto the Father, but by me" (John 14:6). Using the shepherd metaphor found so often in His teachings, the Savior explains what He means by "the way": He is "the door of the sheep. . . . by me if any man enter in, he shall be saved . . . and find pasture" (John 10: 7, 9). There is no other way.

Because of the Fall, we are all estranged from the presence of God, both physically and spiritually. But through the Atonement of Jesus Christ, we "may be saved [privileged once again to enjoy the pleasure of God's presence], by obedience to the laws and ordinances of the gospel" (see A of F 1:3).

As our Mediator with the Father, Christ has the power (to which He was premortally ordained) to bring about our reconciliation with our Heavenly Father: "Wherefore, he is the firstfruits unto God, inasmuch as he shall make intercession for all the children of men; and they that believe in him shall be saved" (2 Ne. 2:9).

"O the wisdom of God, his mercy and grace!" (2 Ne. 9:8).

1 Tim. 4:12

Be thou an example of the believers, in word, in conversation, in charity, in spirit, in faith, in purity.

"In our dialogues with others we must be an example of the believer. Conversation is the substance of friendly social activity. . . . But it must not be salty, or uncouth, or foul if one is in sincerity a believer in Christ" (*TGBH*, 494).

A young woman overheard a conversation among friends at school in which coarse language was prevalent. One of the young men involved was a member of her ward. She approached him and offered a gentle rebuke with these words: "Is that the same mouth I heard you use on Sunday when you were blessing the sacrament?" In other words, abstinence from bad language must be a seven-day habit.

Taking the Lord's name in vain is *particularly* offensive and unbecoming. Regarding this unholy practice, the Lord issues a stern warning: "Let all men beware how they take my name in their lips" (D&C 63:61). "[God] does not want us . . . to take His name in vain, but this is because of what happens to *us* when we do. Our profanity cannot diminish His Godhood, His love, His omnipotence, or His omniscience. But our profanity does damage us and can damage us *profoundly*" (*The Neal A. Maxwell Quote Book,* 269; emphasis added).

1 Tim. 4:14

Neglect not the gift that is in thee, which was given thee by prophecy.

When we look at each other's more obvious gifts—the gift of music, of speaking, of miracles, of tongues, of wisdom and knowledge, of faith, of healing—we may wonder whether our gifts are worthy of praise or mention.

The Savior reassures us that all gifts are praiseworthy and significant because of the source from which they come: "For there are many gifts, and to every man is given a gift by the Spirit of God" (D&C 46:11). To be a good listener, to be patient in suffering, to find joy in service, to be discerning in our choices, to be strong in our testimony, to make our homes a haven where others feel safe and welcome, to enjoy the beauties of the earth, to enjoy the gifts and accomplishments of others, to know how to touch and comfort or teach and bless—these are all good gifts.

Elder Marvin J. Ashton gave us wise counsel when he reminded us that we sell ourselves short when we measure our gifts according to external standards such as social standing, physical appearance, or intellectual status. We all have God-given gifts, which we must recognize, develop, and use wisely (see "There Are Many Gifts," *Ensign*, Nov. 1987).

1 Tim. 6:10

For the love of money is the root of all evil: which while some coveted after, they have erred from the faith, and pierced themselves through with many sorrows.

Before pointing an accusing finger at anyone with an abundance of this world's wealth, we should remember that it is the *love of money* that is pinpointed as the root of all evil. If the accumulation of wealth takes precedence over our love of God and our fellowmen, it becomes a spiritual burden—even a spiritual malady—which the Lord calls a *canker* and which the dictionary defines as an erosive or spreading sore: "Wo unto you rich men, that will not give your substance to the poor, for your riches will canker your souls" (D&C 56:16).

In perfect harmony with Proverbs 27:24, which states that "riches *are* not for ever," Alma gives this wise counsel that echoes the old adage "You can't take it with you": "Seek not after riches nor the vain things of this world; for behold, you cannot carry them with you" (Alma 39:14). To date, there has been no sighting of a hearse towing a treasure-filled trailer to the cemetery!

The Savior has the final and finest counsel: "Seek not for riches, but for wisdom, and behold, the mysteries of God shall be unfolded unto you, and then shall you be made rich. Behold, he that hath eternal life is rich" (D&C 6:7).

2 Tim. 2:23

But foolish and unlearned questions avoid, knowing that they do gender strifes.

There is nothing more unsettling than when gospel discussions deteriorate into contentions regarding speculative interpretations of doctrine. According to President Joseph F. Smith, this type of discussion is characteristic of those who are in or heading toward a state of apostasy (see *Gospel Doctrine*, 372).

The Lord cautions us: "And of tenets thou shalt not talk, but thou shalt declare repentance and faith on the Savior, and remission of sins by baptism, and by fire, yea, even the Holy Ghost" (D&C 19:31). In other words, stick to the safety of gospel doctrine. This does not preclude thoughtful study and pondering of the works of gospel scholars, the list of which is most certainly headed by Apostles and prophets.

Sometimes, however, we might be so carried away in all we have learned that we "hearken not unto the counsel of God" and "set it aside, supposing" that we have surpassed even God in our spiritual expertise (see 2 Ne. 9:28–29). Paul refers to this state as "ever learning, and never able to come to the knowledge of the truth" (2 Tim. 3:7).

Finally, Paul reminds us, "Avoid foolish questions . . . and contentions, and strivings about the law; for they are unprofitable and vain" (Titus 3:9).

JST 2 Tim. 3:16

And all scripture given by inspiration of God, is profitable for doctrine, for reproof, for correction, for instruction in righteousness.

In the Lord's preface to the Doctrine and Covenants, we read these stunning words—an invitation and a declaration to all the world: "Search these commandments, for they are true and faithful, and the prophecies and promises which are in them shall all be fulfilled" (D&C 1:37).

The scriptures bear testimony of Jesus Christ through the mouths of prophets and Apostles and through the words of the Savior Himself. We are admonished to feast upon the words of Christ and to let our souls "delight in fatness" (2 Ne. 9:51). Too often, we put ourselves on a stringent scripture-study diet, neglecting to enjoy this enlargement of spirit that can only increase our inner beauty.

As we prayerfully search the scriptures, they become a familiar voice, a pleasing melody we want to hear often. We read inspired tutorials on course corrections, repentance, and the miracle of the Lord's forgiveness. We are filled with understanding and warmth and a recollection of truths previously and premortally taught, as witnessed by the Holy Ghost. Additionally, we have the Lord's assurance that the scriptures are our ultimate protection against the adversary's darts of deception: "And whoso treasureth up my word, shall not be deceived" (JS—M 1:37).

Hebrews 2:18

For in that he himself hath suffered being tempted, he is able to succor them that are tempted.

Alma describes the scope of the Savior's Atonement when he says, "And he shall go forth, suffering pains and afflictions and *temptations of every kind*; and this that the word might be fulfilled which saith he will take upon him the pains and sicknesses of his people (Alma 7:11; emphasis added). Paul says the Savior "was in all points tempted like as *we are*" (Heb. 4:15). For Him, as for us, this was more than a one-time confrontation with Satan, but there was one crucial difference: "He suffered temptations but *gave no heed unto them*" (D&C 20:22; emphasis added). He *never* pondered His options; He *never* entertained the notion of response or indulgence. There was no resting place or even temporary lodging in His heart for these sins as would-be tenants.

The Savior's mortality enabled Him to *understand* and, ultimately, in the Garden of Gethsemane, to *feel* the pain of all *our* battles with temptation. This was crucial to His becoming our advocate with the Father, to know how to provide relief, comfort, help, and merciful love in our times of temptation, be they hourly, daily, or weekly. He beautifully reminds us that He is our "advocate, who knoweth the weakness of man and how to succor them who are tempted" (D&C 62:1).

Heb. 5:8–9

Though he were a Son, yet learned he obedience by the things which he suffered; And being made perfect, he became the author of eternal salvation unto all them that obey him.

Whether we make plans on the spur of the moment or well in advance of our anticipated activity, we can never be completely sure how everything will turn out. There are so many variables that can get in the way, no matter how carefully we follow the formula.

However, there is one plan that is absolutely flawless, which, if followed according to its divine design, has a perfectly predicted outcome. It is the plan of salvation, a plan our Heavenly Father clearly, carefully, and lovingly conceived and presented to us for our sustaining vote in our premortal existence: "At the first organization in heaven we were all present, and saw the Savior chosen and appointed and the plan of salvation made, and we sanctioned it" (*TPJS*, 181).

The plan of salvation promises us kinship with the Savior, made possible through the light and power of His Atonement and Resurrection. It is a perfect plan with the promise of a glorious outcome for all who experience a mighty change of heart. This change enables and ennobles us to become spiritually begotten sons and daughters with all the rights, privileges, and obligations that come with such a holy heritage.

Heb. 8:10

I will put my laws into their mind, and write them in their hearts: and I will be to them a God, and they shall be to me a people.

When Moses ascended the mount to learn the Lord's will, a most wonderful thing occurred. Not only was the Lord's presence manifested to Moses and the Israelites by fire and smoke, but all the people heard His voice. Surely they would now be obedient to His laws. Yet, not too long afterward, these same people erected a golden calf and engaged in unrestrained and inappropriate revelry. There was obviously some kind of disconnect between what they had seen and what they had internalized.

Like the children of Israel, we sometimes chafe under laws we believe are confining and outmoded simply because we fail to internalize them. If we receive the words of the Lord with "all readiness of mind," as Paul counseled (Acts 17:11), there is no room for doubt. We must then make sure our hearts are softened sufficiently for the words to enter, where they will never be forgotten—"written not with ink [that can be blotted and erased], but with the spirit of the living God [whose words are eternal and unchangeable]; not in tables of stone [that can crumble, break, and erode], but in fleshy tables of the heart [where they become a living, breathing, and internalized entity]" (2 Cor. 3:3).

Heb. 10:22

Let us draw near with a true heart in full assurance of faith, having our hearts sprinkled from an evil conscience, and our bodies washed with pure water.

Planning a road trip is exciting, and we look forward to arriving at our carefully selected destinations. Our preparations for these journeys are usually intense. We ensure that our vehicle is in top-notch traveling condition, consult road maps, plan how far we want to travel each day, decide on suitable accommodations along the way, and choose the appropriate personal necessities we will need. Neglecting any of these preparations can result in a disappointing or an aborted journey.

Our journey home to our Heavenly Father involves no fewer intense and careful preparations and no less excitement as we anticipate our final destination. And what might these preparations involve? Knowing where we want to go and who we wish to spend time with, putting on the whole armor of righteousness (see Eph. 6:14–17), setting suitable and realistic goals for each leg of the journey (it can't be done in a day or week or year—it takes a lifetime of faith and patience), regularly consulting the scriptures for course corrections, and taking no inappropriate baggage, for our eternal destination is truly holy ground (see Ex. 3:5).

Finally, "let us remember and be sure / Our hearts and hands are clean and pure" ("While of These Emblems We Partake," *Hymns*, no. 173).

Heb. 11:1

Now faith is the substance of things hoped for, the evidence of things not seen.

We are all familiar with the saying "Seeing is believing," but when applied to the principle of faith, it is really better expressed the other way around: "Believing is seeing." Thomas, who would only believe once he had seen, was gently chided by the Lord: "Thomas, because thou hast seen me, thou hast believed: blessed *are* they that have not seen, and *yet* have believed" (John 20:29).

There are those who claim they would believe if they could see, and our thoughts turn to the well-known sign seekers in the scriptures: Sherem, whose demand for a sign cost him his life (see Jacob 7:13–20); the unbelieving Nephites, whose fixation on signs rather than on faith in Christ led them to the brink of destroying their faithful neighbors (see 3 Ne. 1:9); and the stiff-necked Pharisees, who saw but, in their pride, denied even the most miraculous signs of the Son of God.

Faith in the Lord Jesus Christ is the undergirding principle upon which all gospel growth is built. Hoping for things not seen defines faith perfectly: "Faith is the total trust, complete confidence in, and ready reliance upon the perfect merits, tender mercy, and endless grace of Jesus Christ for salvation" (*Coming to Know Christ*, 146).

Heb. 11:6

But without faith it is impossible to please him: for he that cometh to God must believe that he is, and that he is a rewarder of them that diligently seek him.

There is only one way to come unto God, and that is through the intercession of our Savior, Jesus Christ. And it is our Savior in whom we demonstrate our faith and our desire to please God and thereby enjoy His rewards.

The Savior rewards those who diligently seek Him "in faith, nothing wavering" (James 1:6). This is demonstrated countless times throughout the scriptures. It was faith that allowed the brother of Jared to *seek* and then *see* the Lord. It was faith in Christ that allowed lepers to be healed, the blind to see, and the woman with the issue of blood to be made whole. Through a prophet's great faith in the Lord, the waters of the Red Sea were parted. Faith enabled Nephi to behold the wondrous vision of the tree of life as he sought confirmation of Lehi's vision. Because of faith, the young Joseph Smith saw and heard God the Father and His Beloved Son, Jesus Christ.

> If with all your hearts ye truly seek me,
> Ye shall ever surely find me,
> Thus saith our God.
> ("If with All Your Hearts," *CSB*, 15).

Heb. 12:5–7

My son, despise not thou the chastening of the Lord, nor faint when thou art rebuked of him: For whom the Lord loveth he chasteneth. . . . For what son is he whom the father chasteneth not?

When the Nephites began to suffer enormous defeats in their battles with the Lamanites, "there began to be a . . . lamentation in all the land" (Morm. 2: 11). Mormon was optimistic that their sorrowing signified repentance: "But behold this my joy was vain, for their sorrowing was not unto repentance, because of the goodness of God; but it was rather the sorrowing of the damned, because the Lord would not always suffer them to take happiness in sin" (Morm. 2:13). Our wise and loving Father saw fit to chasten His people, whom He refused to support in their wickedness.

Earthly parents do not always follow this heavenly example of wise stewardship. We hear of instances where parents seek to excuse, rationalize, and even condone their children's inappropriate behavior. They mistake indulgence for love, turning a blind eye for turning the other cheek, and the absence of consequences for mercy—the *eternal* consequences of which could prove disastrous.

As painful as the Lord's chastening may be, it is always motivated by love. He is never willing to sever the brake lines of obedience in order to gratify our sometimes headlong rush around the dangerous curves of defiance. "I have loved you—Wherefore, ye must needs be chastened" (D&C 95:1–2).

Heb. 12:1

Wherefore . . . lay aside every weight, and the sin which doth so easily beset us, and let us run with patience the race that is set before us.

When it comes to spiritual matters, there are no quick fixes on the road to salvation, despite what Satan would have us believe. We are all familiar with, but not fooled by, his old "eat, drink, and be merry" (2 Ne. 28:7) philosophy that leads us to believe we can shed pounds of sin in the twinkling of an eye.

Paul reminds us that we need to be constantly vigilant: "I find then a law, that, when I would do good, evil is present with me" (Rom. 7:21). We all need to keep our lives as lean and sin free as possible, and the Savior offers us the flawless method that never fails—repentance and endurance in the race to His finish line.

All of us run or walk spiritually at different speeds: some of us run unwearyingly, some of us walk briskly, some of us shuffle along slowly, and some of us need the support of canes or walkers. But the reward is the same for all who triumph over Satan. Good spiritual runners are spiritually born of God and look forward to claiming the prize of eternal life. We rejoice in the Savior's universal sin-loss promise: "For behold, I, God, have suffered these things for all, that they might not suffer if they would repent" (D&C 19:16).

Heb. 12:12

Wherefore lift up the hands which hang down, and the feeble knees.

In a heated battle against the Amalekites, the children of Israel relied on Moses, who stood at the top of a hill with the rod of God extended in his hand. As long as he held up his hand, Israel prevailed. Understandably, Moses's hands became heavy, and his knees became feeble. So Aaron and Hur sat Moses down on a stone; then they stood on either side of him and held his hands steady until the battle ended successfully (see Ex. 17:8–13).

Are there hands around us that hang down under the weight of unbearable burdens? Can we help someone find a comfortable resting place, where faith and courage can be renewed? It is not for us to judge whether someone is worthy of our helping hands; instead, it is our privilege to reach out, even when it does not seem convenient.

Aaron and Hur saw a need and addressed it, even though it very likely exhausted them as well. The Savior reminds us of our need to be on His errand, regardless of personal sacrifice: "Wherefore, be not weary in well-doing, for ye are laying the foundation of a great work" (D&C 64:33). One of our greatest works is to lend one another our helping hands.

Heb. 13:5

Let your conversation be without covetousness; and be content with such things as ye have: for he hath said, I will never leave thee, nor forsake thee.

Too often we focus on our deficiencies and don't appreciate the qualities that make us who and what we are. Samuel Johnson once said, "It is common to overlook what is near by keeping the eye fixed on something remote." We become like the child who hastily opens a pile of gifts and then wonders aloud, "Is that all there is?"

And when it comes to comparing our lot in life with someone else's, it is well to remember that "what makes us discontented with our condition is the absurdly exaggerated idea we have of the happiness of others" (anonymous). When we pause to consider the things the Lord allots to us, it leaves very little time or room for discontent. Consider His glorious promises: "Ye are little children, and ye have not as yet understood how great blessings the Father hath in his own hands and prepared for you. . . . The kingdom is yours and the blessings thereof are yours. . . . And he who receiveth all things with thankfulness shall be made glorious" (D&C 78:17–19). And when we consider the Lord's promise that He will never forsake us, our cup of contentment is filled to overflowing.

James 1:5

If any of you lack wisdom, let him ask of God, that giveth to all men liberally, and upbraideth not; and it shall be given him.

How fitting that these words were penned by Jesus's half brother—words that "led Joseph Smith to his knees in the Sacred Grove in the Spring of 1820, when the dispensation of the fulness of times was ushered in by the personal appearance of the Supreme Rulers of the Universe" *(DNTC, Vol. II, 243)*.

Joseph's faith never wavered, even when the very forces of hell combined to destroy him. Exerting all of his energy and faith, he called on God to deliver him. His was a prayer heard and answered with the most profound results: "I saw two Personages . . . standing above me in the air. One of them spake unto me, calling me by name and said, pointing to the other—*This is My Beloved Son. Hear Him*" (JS—H 1:16–17).

Joseph's prayer of faith set the pattern for ensuing and ongoing heavenly communication as he became the instrument of the Restoration. As the Lord's Prophet and seer, Joseph Smith "has done more, save Jesus only, for the salvation of men in this world, than any other man that ever lived in it" (D&C 135:3).

James 1:6

But let him ask in faith, nothing wavering.

It may be that some of our most earnest petitions to the Lord are about our desire for increased faith. "The consequences of righteous, persistent asking are staggering. Who could have had more faith than the Savior's original Twelve—yet they came to him and implored, 'Lord, increase our faith' (Luke 17:5). . . . It was a simple, honest request for the gift of . . . 'exceedingly great faith' (Moro. 10:11). And what faith came by the asking!" (*The Infinite Atonement* [Salt Lake City: Deseret Book, 2000], 275).

"The law of prayer operates by faith; it is perfected by obedience; it has greater power when there is conformity and uprightness in the lives of those who petition their God. . . . Thus, prayers are heard and prayers are answered when those who seek their God do so in righteousness. . . . As with all else that he does, he is bound by the laws of obedience and faith and personal righteousness that he himself has ordained" (*A New Witness for the Articles of Faith*, 384–385).

James 1:8

A double minded man is unstable in all his ways.

How reliable are the words of people who speak out of both sides of their mouths? Or how comfortable do we feel trusting a person who lists to every wind that blows? Would we rely on the loyalty of someone who is as "unstable as water" (Gen. 49:4)?

Who can forget the unforgettable challenge Elijah issued to the children of Israel, some of whom had defected from the Lord's side and joined with the wicked worshipers of Baal: "How long halt ye between two opinions? if the LORD be God, follow him" (1 Kgs. 18:21). In other words, "You can't have it both ways!"

And Elijah's words still hold true in our day: "Even if we decide to leave Babylon, some of us endeavor to keep a second residence there, or we commute on weekends" (*The Neal A. Maxwell Quote Book*, 25). Absolute single-mindedness is required of every true disciple of Christ. We cannot be a little bit chaste, a little bit honest, or a little bit virtuous.

Fidelity to righteousness brings rich rewards, for thus saith the Lord, "I will be on your right hand and on your left, and my Spirit shall be in your hearts, and mine angels round about you, to bear you up" (D&C 84:88).

JST James 1:12

Blessed is the man that resisteth temptation: for when he is tried, he shall receive the crown of life, which the Lord hath promised to them that love him.

In June 1830, the Prophet Joseph Smith undertook the translation of the King James Version of the Bible, making inspired changes that were sometimes as small as the replacement of a single word. These alterations enrich the intended meaning of the scriptures. Such is the case in this verse, where the Prophet replaced the word *endureth* with the word *resisteth*. This small change replaces a passive word with one of positive action.

The laws of physics tutor us in the principle of resistance—an equal and opposite force can deflect an opposing power. Consider the example of Joseph, who found favor in Pharaoh's Egyptian court. He withstood the force of moral temptation and took positive action as he fled for his very eternal life. His courageous resistance to temptation focused on eternal rewards in contrast to worldly gratification or fear of man-made reprisals.

Peter warns us that the adversary is "a roaring lion, [who] walketh about, seeking whom he may devour" (1 Pet. 5:8). The Apostle Paul reminds us, however, that "in all these things we are more than conquerors through him that loved us" (Rom. 8:37). The promise of eternal life is sure for those of us who are immovable against the force of temptation because of our love for our Savior, Jesus Christ.

James 1:22

But be ye doers of the word, and not hearers only, deceiving your own selves.

Our hearts and spirits respond gratefully to messages of truth, and we resolve to follow the Savior more faithfully and to abandon the less-than-pleasing habits that have taken up comfortable residence within us. This is often more easily said than done, which is exactly the point James makes in this succinct but richly meaningful directive. Put in more earthy terms, it is a call to "put our money where our mouth is."

On an early spring morning in 1820, the light of truth and revelation dispelled the gloom of apostasy and confusion. To a young boy who was to become the Prophet of the Restoration, God the Father gave the gracious and divine invitation to hear His Beloved Son. His words are as personal an invitation to each of us as they were to Joseph Smith, and they carry with them an obligation to act appropriately upon what we hear.

We see all about us examples of those who listen and then do, those who hear the Savior's voice and then respond compassionately, instinctively, and naturally to reach out to people in need, those who share their testimonies, their wisdom, and light from their lamps filled with eternal truths.

JST James 1:27

Pure religion and undefiled before God and the Father is this, To visit the fatherless and widows in their affliction, and to keep himself unspotted from the vices of the world.

The beauty of this scripture lies in its cause and effect lesson, which is so characteristic of much of scripture. *If* we busy ourselves with good and charitable works, with little random acts of kindness, *then* we very likely won't have time to become entangled in the vices of the world. This responsibility goes well beyond our monthly obligatory visits as home teachers and visiting teachers. It goes well beyond those who are easy to love and invites us to reach out to those who may not always behave well or wisely—be they family members, neighbors, ward members, or complete strangers.

"Do you want to be happy? . . . Lend your efforts to helping people. . . . Look to the Lord and live and work to lift and serve His sons and daughters. You will come to know a happiness that you have never known before if you will do that. . . . Heaven knows there are so very, very, very many people in the world who need help" (*TGBH*, 597).

"A man is called selfish not for pursuing his own good, but for neglecting his neighbor's" (Richard Whately).

James 2:17, 26

Even so faith, if it hath not works, is dead, being alone. . . . For as the body without the spirit is dead, so faith without works is dead also.

When we speak of faith, we are really speaking of faith in the Lord Jesus Christ, in His atoning sacrifice, and in the gift of His amazing grace: "Latter-day Saints believe . . . that salvation is a gift (D&C 6:13; 14:7), but we also emphasize that a gift must be received (D&C 88:33). Our receipt of the ordinances of salvation combined with our efforts to keep the commandments are extensions and manifestations of true faith" (*Coming to Know Christ*, 149).

The Savior taught that where there is faith, there are miracles. The greatest miracle of all is the Atonement, which our Savior wrought, and we manifest our faith in that great gift by our works: "We will be judged according to our works, *not according to the merits of our works* but to the extent that our works manifest to God who and what we have *become* through the transcendent powers of Christ. We are saved by grace alone, but grace is never alone. . . . The work of salvation of the human soul is a product of divine grace, coupled with true faith and its attendant actions" (Ibid., 149, 151).

James 3:18

And the fruit of righteousness is sown in peace of them that make peace.

The Savior is the Prince of Peace. In contrast to the prince of darkness, who has always delighted in heart-hardening disputations that lead to disastrous eternal consequences, the Savior seeks to turn our hearts one to another in love and desires to bestow an inner peace upon us that leaves no room for anger, pride, or contention.

We have only to listen to news reports to know contention is rampant in various parts of the world and fear has a firm grasp on the hearts of many. Our mandate as disciples of the Lord Jesus Christ is to seek for and cultivate in our personal lives, in our homes, and in all our relationships the peace that prevents prideful contentions.

The Savior reiterates His stance on those who seek and radiate His peace: "And blessed are *all* the peacemakers, for they shall be called the children of God" (3 Ne. 12:9; emphasis added). The word *all* lets us know that His family is not a private and exclusive club. We are all invited to join, but the membership rules are clear: "Thou shalt love the Lord thy God with all thy heart, with all thy might, mind, and strength" and "thy neighbor as thyself" (D&C 59:5–6).

James 4:10

Humble yourselves in the sight of the Lord, and he shall lift you up.

In a world where seeking preeminence at any cost is prevalent and where rising to the top often involves pushing someone down, this scripture is a breath of fresh air and a reminder that in the Lord's scheme of things, there is room at the top for everyone.

In fact, the Savior promises to give everyone a helping hand: "Be thou humble; and the Lord thy God shall lead thee by the hand, and give thee answer to thy prayers" (D&C 112:10). We are reminded of little children who, when going for a walk or crossing the street, trustingly allow a parent to hold their hand to keep them safe from harm. Occasionally, in a bid for independence, a child will try to pull his hand away from his parent, but grown-ups are quick to reclaim it, knowing it is in the child's best interest.

There can be no safer hand to hold than our Savior's, who sometimes has to reach out gently to remind us that it is in our best interest to stay connected to His protective hand as He lifts and leads us: "What doth the Lord require of thee, but to . . . walk humbly with thy God?" (Micah 6:8).

James 4:17

Therefore to him that knoweth to do good, and doeth it not, to him it is sin.

"One of the most serious human defects in all ages is pro-crastination, an unwillingness to accept personal responsi-bilities *now*. . . . There are even many members of the Church who are lax and careless and who continually procrastinate. They live the gospel casually but not devoutly. . . . They do no major crime but merely fail to do the things required— things like paying tithing, living the Word of Wisdom, hav-ing family prayers, fasting, attending meetings, serving.

"Perhaps they do not consider such omissions to be sins, yet these were the kinds of things of which the five foolish virgins in Jesus's parable were probably guilty. . . . The Lord will not translate one's good hopes and desires and intentions into works. Each of us must do that for himself" (*The Miracle of Forgiveness*, 8).

Alma refers to our time of preparation as a probationary state, "a time to prepare for that endless state . . . which is after the resurrection of the dead" (Alma 12:24). *Endless* is a long time to find ourselves in the wrong state but just right if we are where we really want to be—where the Lord wants us to be.

James 5:16

Confess your faults one to another, and pray one for another, that ye may be healed. The effectual fervent prayer of a righteous man availeth much.

Think of the power and privilege of praying for spiritual healing and relief for one another. It would be a shame to give up on someone just because we feel they have no redeeming qualities or because we doubt whether our prayers can make a difference. What if Alma had ceased praying for his wicked and wayward son? Could someone so far gone in sin and rebellion be redeemed? The answer, of course, is a matter of exquisite spiritual record (see Mosiah 27:8–29).

We read the tender words of the Savior to His Apostle Peter: "But I have prayed for thee, that thy faith fail not" (Luke 22:32). He does no less for any of His cherished children, whose "very hairs of [the] head are all numbered" (Matt. 10:30). Likewise, we must not discount the spiritual potential of our brothers and sisters.

C. S. Lewis said, "It is a serious thing to live in a society of possible gods and goddesses, to remember that the dullest and most uninteresting person you talk to may one day be a creature which . . . you would be strongly tempted to worship. . . . There are no ordinary people" (*The Joyful Christian* [New York: Simon and Schuster, 1996], 197).

James 5:20

He which converteth the sinner from the error of his way shall save a soul from death, and shall hide a multitude of sins.

Each of us has the responsibility to preach the gospel, for "it becometh every man who hath been warned to warn his neighbor" (D&C 88:81). It is our opportunity to actively participate in God's work and glory, extending the blessings of His gospel to our friends, neighbors, associates, and family members—and to the world at large. This means living so our examples invite instead of repel others.

The message of the gospel will fall on deaf ears if our behavior belies our words. The Apostle Paul admonishes, "Be thou an example of the believers, in word, in conversation, in charity, in spirit, in faith, in purity" (1 Tim. 4:12).

And the Savior's wise counsel to His beloved Apostle Peter is appropriate counsel for all: "When thou art converted, strengthen thy brethren" (Luke 22:32). It is a timely reminder for each of us that ours is a lifelong, ongoing, and sacred process of individual conversion in which the Savior is personally invested. "Take heed unto thyself, and unto the doctrine; continue in them: for in doing this thou shalt both save thyself, and them that hear thee" (1 Tim. 4:16).

1 Pet. 1:18–20

Ye were not redeemed with corruptible things, as silver and gold . . . But with the precious blood of Christ, as of a lamb without blemish and without spot. Who verily was foreordained before the foundation of the world.

The epistles of the Apostle Peter are packed with eternal truths. Of Peter's writings, the Prophet Joseph Smith said, "Peter penned the most sublime language of any of the apostles" (*TPJS*, 301), and President Spencer W. Kimball characterized Peter as "a man with vision, a man of revelations, a man fully trusted by the Lord Jesus Christ" ("Peter, My Brother," *BYU Speeches of the Year*, July 13, 1971). Who better to speak of the Savior's Atonement than this stalwart and personal witness of the unfolding hours of that transcending event that commenced in a Garden, continued on a cross, and culminated in the Garden Tomb?

"Peter . . . became a mighty witness of the risen Lord. He . . . dedicated . . . his life to testifying of the mission, the death, and the resurrection of Jesus Christ, the living Son of the living God" (*TGBH*, 533). His was an unshakable testimony of our Savior's premortal commitment to fully underwrite the hazards accompanying our mortal experience. Perfect and blameless, Christ willingly paid the full price for our salvation.

"His precious blood he freely spilt; / His life he freely gave, / A sinless sacrifice for guilt, / A dying world to save" ("How Great the Wisdom and the Love," *Hymns*, no. 195).

1 Pet. 1:15

But as he which hath called you is holy, so be ye holy in all manner of conversation.

There are times when we are tempted to take shortcuts around common courtesies, especially with strangers we might never see again. How often are we short-tempered with clerks who ring up the wrong price on an item? Are we quick to correct a perceived offense with a sharp retort (ever so cleverly phrased)? Then there is the highway, rich with opportunities for abusive thoughts, threatening language, rude gestures, and honking horns. After all, what goes on in our cars stays in our cars—doesn't it?

Even if we are fortunate enough to escape immediate retribution for such behavior, our Maker notes our thoughts, words, and actions and is saddened and disappointed by our failure to live by His example.

No matter the lateness of the hour, the difficulties of the day, or the seeming failure of people to behave decently, the Savior's example of courtesy and kindness was perfect. His tender love and consideration for others' feelings always took precedence over His personal concerns.

Well might we emulate our Savior's example by being "ready to pardon, gracious and merciful, slow to anger, and of great kindness" (Neh. 9:17), not only with strangers but with our acquaintances, neighbors, and families too.

1 Pet. 1:3–5

Blessed be the God and Father of our Lord Jesus Christ, which according to his abundant mercy hath begotten us again unto a lively hope by the resurrection of Jesus Christ from the dead, To an inheritance incorruptible . . . reserved in heaven for you, Who are kept by the power of God through faith unto salvation.

"Salvation could not come to the world without the mediation of Jesus Christ" (*TPJS*, 323). His mediation is a manifestation of His mercy, and His supreme mercy was manifested through His great atoning sacrifice, an infinite gift of love extended to every child of God. We must have faith that through His Atonement we can be made spiritually clean and whole. This is the quality of faith that motivates us to sincere repentance, which qualifies us to receive the cleansing power of the Atonement.

We have all witnessed in the media the miraculous rescues of people who jump from burning buildings into safety nets. In simplistic terms, the Atonement is our safety net, put in place by our loving and gracious Savior to save us from the Fall and from our personal falls from grace.

"If thou wilt do good, yea, and hold out faithful to the end, thou shalt be saved in the kingdom of God, which is the greatest of all the gifts of God; for there is no gift greater than the gift of salvation" (D&C 6:13).

1 Pet. 2:1–2

Wherefore laying aside all malice, and all guile, and hypocrisies, and envies, and all evil speakings, As newborn babes, desire the sincere milk of the word, that ye may grow thereby.

Who can resist the beauty and innocence of a newborn baby? "Trailing clouds of glory do [they] come / From God, who is [their] home: / Heaven lies about [them] in [their] infancy! (William Wordsworth, "Ode on Intimations of Immortality from Recollections of Early Childhood," in Edward Frost, ed., *Romantic and Victorian Poetry* [New York: Prentice-Hall, Inc., 1952], 97).

As newly baptized persons emerge from the waters of baptism, they are spiritually comparable to these newborn babes. It is a new beginning and a start on the path leading to eternal life. At that point, we are washed clean of petty faults and failings and, just like newborn babies, are ready to be nourished by simple gospel precepts, which warm and expand our spirits in preparation for the reception of greater light and knowledge.

This is the grand principle of progression in our gospel growth, and we cannot bypass the basics to move on to higher principles. We know the Savior grew from grace to grace, and it is no different for us. Paul reminds us that "every one that useth milk *is* unskilful in the word of righteousness: for he is a babe. But strong meat belongeth to them that are of full age" (Heb. 5:13–14).

1 Pet. 2:7

Unto you therefore which believe he is precious: but unto them which be disobedient, the stone which the builders disallowed, the same is made the head of the corner.

In a modern revelation, the Savior says, "I am the good shepherd, and the stone of Israel. He that buildeth upon this rock shall *never* fall" (D&C 50:44; emphasis added). Stones can either be perceived as building blocks or stumbling blocks. To the Jews, the Savior was viewed as a stumbling block—an annoyer, a nuisance, a bothersome burr under their Pharisaic saddles. They preferred the corrosive sandstone of slavish, constricting rules and regulations, the brittle bricks of self-righteousness that were good for nothing but to tear down and crush the spirit of the law.

Through Isaiah, the Lord prophesied, "Behold, I lay in Zion for a foundation a stone, a *tried* stone, a *precious* corner stone, a *sure* foundation" (Isa. 28:16; emphasis added). What marvelous imagery and symbolism! Christ is identifying Himself as this tried, sure, and precious foundation upon which all Saints must build. Cornerstones, of course, are basic foundational elements in the building process. If cornerstones are carefully selected and properly laid, the entire structure built upon them will stand the test of time. There can be no more perfect cornerstone than the Son of God, who stands not only the test of time but of all eternity.

1 Pet. 2:9

But ye are a chosen generation, a royal priesthood, an holy nation, a peculiar people; that ye should shew forth the praises of him who hath called you out of darkness into his marvellous light.

Some of us remember (and not too fondly) our public school experiences when team captains chose us to play on different sides for a particular sport. How painful it was for those of us who were chosen last and somewhat grudgingly. We could hear the flat tone of resignation as the captains realized they had no other choice. We were all that was left, and we certainly felt like leftovers!

The Savior has a whole different system for choosing His team. Peter refers to us as a chosen generation, those the Savior has "taken from the ends of the earth . . . chosen [them], and not cast [them] away" (Isa. 41:9). He chooses us, not as leftovers but as "the progeny of Jacob in all ages; the house of Israel both anciently, in the meridian of time, and now in these latter-days. . . . Those who join the Church thereby become the Lord's people. They are adopted into his family; they are set apart from the world; they become part of the nation and kingdom of Israel" (*DNTC*, Vol. III, 294–295). In other words, we are all valued and valuable players on the Lord's team.

1 Pet. 2:20

For what glory is it, if, when ye be buffeted for your faults, ye shall take it patiently? but if, when ye do well, and suffer for it, ye take it patiently, this is acceptable with God.

"Being human, we would expel from our lives physical pain and mental anguish and assure ourselves of continual ease and comfort, but if we were to close the doors upon sorrow and distress, we might be excluding our greatest friends and benefactors. Suffering can make saints of people as they learn patience, long-suffering, and self-mastery. The sufferings of our Savior were part of his education" (*Faith Precedes the Miracle*, 98).

While patience in adversity is often thought of as a passive trait, it actually requires great faith and trust in the Lord's watchful care. Elder Neal A. Maxwell defines *patience* as "a willingness, in a sense, to watch the unfolding purposes of God with a sense of wonder and awe, rather than pacing up and down within the cell of our circumstance" (*The Neal A. Maxwell Quote Book*, 241).

All things will be made right in the Lord's good time, and no matter how painful our difficulties seem now, they will be but a moment in the eternal view of things. "Whosoever shall put their trust in God shall be supported in their trials, and their troubles, and their afflictions, and shall be lifted up at the last day" (Alma 36:3).

1 Pet. 2:21–22

For even hereunto were ye called: because Christ also suffered for us, leaving us an example, that ye should follow his steps: Who did no sin, neither was guile found in his mouth.

The Savior invites us, entreats us, and pleads with us to follow Him. By His perfect example, "He marked the path and led the way" so we can, if we humbly repent and accept the greatest gift ever given to mankind, return to that place "where God's full presence shines," ("How Great the Wisdom and the Love," *Hymns*, no. 195). That is where the Savior waits to encircle us in the arms of His love.

A favorite teaching tool of parents is to remind their children that as they make their choices, they should ask themselves, "What would Jesus do?" This is an appropriate question for young and old alike. The Savior asked this very same question: "Therefore, what manner of men [and women, and children] ought ye to be?" (3 Ne. 27:27). And He doesn't leave us to wonder about the answer. He said, "Even as I am" (Ibid.).

We might consider this goal a tall order, but it is nothing like a fast-food order, which needs to be filled immediately. This is a life-long commitment that continues into eternity for us who, as diamonds in the rough, require constant polishing and shaping. But what splendid gems we can become through following the example and accepting the grace of our Savior.

1 Pet. 2:23

Who, when he was reviled, reviled not again; when he suffered, he threatened not; but committed himself to him that judgeth righteously.

These words bring to mind the pain-filled night and the day of indignities that began in the Garden of Gethsemane, where Christ's suffering caused great drops of blood to come from every pore. There were no recriminations or regrets for a promise He made premortally and fulfilled mortally, only His tender submission to His Father's will.

There followed in quick succession a traitor's kiss of betrayal and the Savior's quiet acquiescence as He was questioned, mocked, spit upon, slapped, and then taken before Pilate, a man who lacked the courage of his convictions because he had no convictions. Again, Jesus conducted Himself with the utmost dignity, answering questions without fear of consequences (see Luke 22–23).

On Calvary's cruel cross, the Savior relived the agonies of Gethsemane as well as the hideous horrors of crucifixion. He was taunted and tortured, but His only words were a plea for His Father's forgiveness for those who drove the nails, a request for a drink, quiet comfort for his malefactors, a loving concern for His mother's well-being, and finally, His words of completion: "Father, into thy hands I commend my spirit" (Luke 23:46). Only the Son of God could set such a perfect and righteous example of dignity, restraint, and obedience.

1 Pet. 2:25

For ye were as sheep going stray; but are now returned unto the Shepherd and Bishop of your souls.

"Out in the desert they wander, / Hungry and helpless and cold; / Off to the rescue he hastens, / Bringing them back to the fold" ("Dear to the Heart of the Shepherd," *Hymns*, no. 221).

"We must never forget that one of the Lord's most beloved titles is that of the Good Shepherd. When a sheep goes astray in search of greener grass and more pleasant grazing, seldom does that sheep make its way back by finding the shepherd. Rather, the Good Shepherd, the one who knows and loves his flock, who knows them one by one, leaves the ninety and nine and goes on a search-and-rescue mission in behalf of the one. The Good Shepherd does not stop loving the wandering sheep, nor does he conclude, 'Well, ninety-nine out of a hundred isn't bad. There's no use wasting time on one lousy sheep.' Because the shepherd has in fact paid a price to raise his sheep, to feed and protect them, to lead them, and to know them well . . . he will not leave them out in the desert to wander forever" (*Coming to Know Christ*, 26).

"Our Redeemer is [our] great and true shepherd, and [we are] numbered among his sheep" (Hel. 15:13).

1 Pet 3:7

Likewise, ye husbands, dwell with them according to the knowledge, giving honour unto the wife . . . being heirs together of the grace of life.

An integral clause in the plan of salvation provides for husbands and wives to be sealed together throughout eternity—a sacred union made possible through the Savior's saving grace. The Apostle Paul reiterated this lovely doctrine: "Neither is the man without the woman, neither the woman without the man, *in the Lord*" (1 Cor. 11:11; emphasis added).

President Gordon B. Hinckley shares his wisdom regarding the sacred nature of the relationship between husband and wife and our obligation to nurture it: "Under the gospel plan marriage is a companionship, with equality between the partners. We walk side by side with respect, appreciation, and love for one another. There can be nothing of inferiority or superiority between the husband and wife in the plan of the Lord" (*TGBH*, 322).

A poem by Robert Browning describes the beauty of pure, compassionate, and enduring love between a husband and wife:

Grow old along with me!
The best is yet to be,
The last of life, for which the first was made:
Our times are in his hand
Who saith: "A whole I planned,
Youth shows but half; trust God, see all, nor be afraid."
(*A Treasury of Poems*, 333)

1 Pet. 3:14

But and if ye suffer for righteousness' sake, happy are ye: and be not afraid . . . neither be troubled.

Some of our temporal and physical fears can be alleviated by installing security systems or buying insurance. However, we must rely on an entirely different security system to alleviate our spiritual fears. When we are assailed by undeserved criticisms or false accusations, we often feel helpless and abandoned, and our spirits long for healing and comfort. Sometimes we turn to friends or loved ones with our doubts and fears, hoping for solace and understanding but receiving instead hurried, impersonal, or distracted words, which may feel insincere and even judgmental. Where, then, can we turn for the safety and peace our spirits crave?

The Psalmist answers this question beautifully: "The Lord is my light and my salvation; whom shall I fear? the Lord is the strength of my life; of whom shall I be afraid?" (Ps. 27:1). The Savior's comfort is unfailing. His is the eye that looks into our hearts, the ear that listens compassionately; the hand that wipes away our tears, the encircling arm that soothes and comforts us.

"Lift up your hearts in praise to God; / Let your rejoicings never cease. / Though tribulations rage abroad, / Christ says, 'In me ye shall have peace'" ("Though Deepening Trials," *Hymns*, no. 122).

1 Pet. 4:12–13

Beloved, think it not strange concerning the fiery trial which is to try you, as though some strange thing happened unto you: But rejoice, inasmuch as ye are partakers of Christ's sufferings; that, when his glory shall be revealed, ye may be glad also with exceeding joy.

Of our mortal sojourn, the Lord said, "We will prove them herewith" (Abr. 3:25). We know that part of that proving process involves trials that move us out of our comfort zones. The proof of our spiritual stamina lies in whether we emerge vanquished or victorious.

C. S. Lewis compared these trials to remodeling a house: "Imagine yourself as a living house. God comes in to rebuild that house. At first, perhaps, you can understand what he is doing. He is getting the drains right and stopping the leaks in the roof and so on: you knew that those jobs needed doing and so you are not surprised. But presently he starts knocking the house about in a way that hurts abominably and does not seem to make sense. What on earth is He up to? The explanation is that He is building quite a different house from the one you thought of—throwing out a new wing here, putting on an extra floor there, running up towers, making courtyards. You thought you were going to be made into a decent little cottage; but He is building a palace. He intends to come and live in it Himself" (*Mere Christianity*, 176).

1 Pet. 5:5

Yea, all of you be subject one to another, and be clothed with humility: for God resisteth the proud, and giveth grace to the humble.

The promise of God's amazing grace is a prize we are privileged to claim as we humbly submit to His will. King Benjamin describes little children as being "submissive, meek, humble, patient, [and] full of love" (Mosiah 3:19). This is an impressive list of qualities worthy of closer examination and emulation. We admire the humility of little children, who bask in the praise of others instead of boasting about their own accomplishments. As we read in Proverbs 27:2, "Let another man praise thee, and not thine own mouth."

There is no need for us to remind the Lord (or anyone else) of our goodness and accomplishments; rather, we should be quietly and obediently engaged in good works. As always, we can look to the Savior for His wondrous example. Nowhere in the scriptures do we find evidence of the Savior patting Himself on the back for a job well done. In all things, He gave honor and glory to the Father.

"[Jesus] rejoices in our genuine goodness and achievement, but any assessment of where we stand in relation to Him tells us that we do not stand at all! We kneel! (*The Neal A. Maxwell Quote Book*, 166).

1 Pet. 5:7

Casting all your care upon him; for he careth for you.

Not all friendships have staying power. Due to various circumstances, sometimes we lose touch, or sadly, we lose interest or let grievances estrange us. However, there is one friend who will never leave us or be too busy to listen or too involved with other friends to pay attention to our needs. He cares *about* us, and He cares *for* us. He is the perfect example of the proverb that says, "A friend loveth at all times" (Prov. 17:17).

He is the One whose love for us (His friends) is so great that He laid down his life for us (see John 15:13). He is the One who invites us to cast our burdens upon Him, promising to sustain us and keep us safe (see Ps. 55:22). He is the one from whom all good things cometh (see Moro. 7:24). He is the one who was "wounded in the house of [His] friends" (D&C 45:52). He is "Jesus that was crucified . . . the Son of God" (Ibid.), our dearest friend for time and all eternity.

Jesus is our loving friend.
He is always near.
He will hear us when we pray;
Ev'ry child is dear.
("Jesus is Our Loving Friend," *CSB*, 58)

Romans 15:13

Now the God of hope fill you with all joy and peace in believing, that ye may abound in hope, through the power of the Holy Ghost.

President Dieter F. Uchtdorf teaches us that hope is the undergirding virtue upon which faith and charity depend. Our faith may be momentarily weakened by sin or the vicissitudes of life, our charity may be challenged by our personal shortcomings, but our hope will strengthen and purify our efforts to cultivate those two virtues (see "The Infinite Power of Hope," *Ensign*, Nov. 2008).

Moroni helps remind us that through Christ's Resurrection, we have hope for an unconditional promise of immortality, and through His Atonement, we have the hope for exaltation (see Moro. 7:41). The Atonement is the source of hope in the gospel; it is the "perfect brightness of hope" of which Nephi speaks (see 2 Ne. 31:20). It is the very foundation upon which we build our faith.

We are all familiar with the saying "Hope springs eternal," and it could not be truer. Hope is our mainstay in mortality and our spiritual springboard to eternity. Victor Hugo wrote that "hope is the word which God has written on the brow of every man." It is the God-given attribute that prioritizes our expectations and reminds us that its full and glorious name is Jesus Christ (see 1 Tim. 1:1).

2 Pet. 1:10

Wherefore the rather, brethren, give diligence to make your calling and election sure: for if ye do these things, ye shall never fall.

"To have one's calling and election made sure is to be sealed up unto eternal life; it is to have the unconditional guarantee of exaltation in the highest heaven of the celestial world; it is to receive the assurance of godhood: it is, in effect, to have the day of judgment advanced, so that an inheritance of all the glory and honor of the Father's kingdom is assured prior to the day when the faithful actually enter into the divine presence to sit with Christ in his throne, even as he is 'set down' with his 'Father in his throne' (Rev. 3:21)," (*DNTC*, Vol. III, 330–331).

"It is little wonder then that the Prophet Joseph Smith, particularly during the latter and crowning years of his mortal ministry, repeatedly exhorted the saints to press forward with that steadfastness in Christ which would enable them to make their calling and election sure. 'I am going on in my progress for eternal life,' he said of himself; and then in fervent pleading to all the saints, he exclaimed: 'Oh! I beseech you to go forward, go forward and make your calling and your election sure' (*TPJS*, 366)" (*DNTC*, Vol. III, 325).

2 Pet. 2:18–19

For when they speak great swelling words of vanity, they allure through the lusts of the flesh . . . those that were clean escaped from them who live in error. While they promise them liberty, they themselves are the servants of corruption: for of whom a man is overcome, of the same is he brought in bondage.

The Savior makes it clear that we "cannot serve two masters: for either [we] will hate the one, and love the other; or else [we] will hold to the one, and despise the other" (see Matt: 6:24). Paul echoes this message: "Know ye not, that to whom ye yield yourselves servants to obey, his servants ye are to whom ye obey; whether of sin unto death, or of obedience unto righteousness?" (Rom. 6:16).

Nephi provides a bold sketch of Satan's tactics for getting us to serve him: he rages "in the hearts of the children of men, and [stirs] them up to anger against that which is good"; "others will he . . . lull them away into carnal security"; "others he flattereth away, and telleth them there is no hell" and no devil, until he has enslaved them in "his awful chains" (2 Ne. 28:20–23).

"Yes, the devil is decidedly a person . . . clever and trained. With thousands of years of experience behind him he has become superbly efficient and increasingly determined. . . . It is a smart person . . . who will accept advice and counsel from experienced people who know the pitfalls, the crumbling walls, and the cracking dams which bring on destruction" (*The Miracle of Forgiveness*, 21–22).

2 Tim. 4:7

I have fought a good fight, I have finished my course, I have kept the faith.

These words, penned by a valiant and courageous Apostle, are exemplary and motivating. In spite of persecution, imprisonment, shipwreck, betrayal by foes, and abandonment by friends, Paul remained true to his faith, which so miraculously took root on the road to Damascus and flowered to full bloom on his missionary journeys that spanned the vast reaches of the Mediterranean regions. These few poignant words might well serve as a motto and goal for all faithful children of God.

Talk of finishing a race usually brings to mind runners. No matter the length of the course, running a race requires dedication, training, persistence, focus, courage, and discipline. So it is with spiritual races as well.

And what is the reward that all spiritual runners seek, whether they be courageous leaders of armies, faithful prophets or Apostles, mighty missionaries, mothers and fathers, or teachers of Sunbeams? It is to overcome the world and triumph over Satan and all his tools of discouragement and distraction designed to take us off course.

In short, the only ribbon spiritual runners are looking to receive is the Savior's approval: "Come unto me ye blessed, for behold, your works have been the works of righteousness upon the face of the earth" (Alma 5:16).

1 Jn. 1:5

This then is the message which we have heard of him, and declare unto you, that God is light, and in him is no darkness at all.

"And I, God, said: Let there be light; and there was light. *And I, God, saw the light; and that light was good. And I, God, divided the light from the darkness*" (Moses 2:3–4; emphasis added). And as Jesus Christ divided the light from the darkness in creating the heavens and the earth, just so He divides the light from the darkness in our spiritual lives: "He that followeth me shall not walk in darkness, but shall have the light of life" (John 8:12).

His is the light that penetrates *all* darkness for *all* of God's children; His merciful ministrations brought light to blind eyes, both physically and spiritually. His redeeming light penetrated and dispelled the darkness of a lonely Garden and the shame of a punishing cross, both of which symbolized the darkness of the sins of the world. And, on that first Easter morn, the glorious light of His Resurrection dazzled the world with its redeeming and reassuring brilliance.

"For God, who commanded the light to shine out of darkness, hath shined in our hearts, to *give* the light of the knowledge of the glory of God in the face of Jesus Christ" (2 Cor. 4:6).

1 Jn. 1:8

If we say that we have no sin, we deceive ourselves, and the truth is not in us.

Probably the three most significant words in this scripture are *we deceive ourselves*, because we certainly do not deceive God. This condition is what many parents refer to as "the cookie jar syndrome," where we ask our children whether they have helped themselves to the cookies before dinner, and they soundly deny having done any such thing, even when telltale crumbs cling to their mouths and their hands still clutch their cookie contraband. A proverb describes it as someone who has eaten, wiped their mouth, and declared that they have done nothing wrong (see Prov. 30:20).

When we look at the sins of others, we think our vision is 20/20, and we wonder why they don't see themselves for what they are and what they do—and do something about it! But when it comes to seeing our own shortcomings, we suddenly develop a debilitating myopia that blinds us and binds us: "We mortals . . . tend to tolerate our own little clusters of sin. We rationalize that we can dismiss these whenever we really want to. The trouble is that these 'squatters,' too, come to have 'rights.' By means of their persistent presence, they take over more than we ever intended" (*The Neal A. Maxwell Quote Book*, 320).

1 Jn. 1:9

If we confess our sins, he is faithful and just to forgive us our sins, and to cleanse us from all unrighteousness.

Paper towels are great for wiping up worrisome spills, and they leave behind no unsightly residue. How much more wondrous is the blotting power of the Savior's Atonement. We treasure the prayer of the Prophet Joseph Smith in the Kirtland Temple: "O Jehovah, have mercy upon this people, and as all men sin, forgive the transgressions of thy people, and let them be *blotted out forever*" (D&C 109:34; emphasis added). How comforting are the words of the Savior, who tells us, "I, even I, am he that blotteth out thy transgressions *for mine own sake, and will not remember thy sins*" (Isa. 43:25; emphasis added).

When the Savior says "for mine own sake," it is His reassurance that He has—always and forever—a personal investment in our salvation and that we are His work and His glory (see Moses 1:39). His words are comforting when He reminds us, "None of his sins that he hath committed shall be mentioned unto him" (Ezek. 33:16). The file of past offenses is sealed, and there are no ever-so-faint but unsightly stains, no "Remember when you . . . " comments, no belittling, embarrassing, or knowing nudges of condemnation. "Though [our] sins be as scarlet, they shall be as white as snow" (Isa. 1:18).

1 Jn. 2:2

And he is the propitiation for our sins: and not for ours only, but also for the sins of the whole world.

The Savior regards *all* of God's children as His friends, and he willingly suffered "the pains of every living creature, both men, women, and children, who belong to the family of Adam" (2 Ne. 9:21) so all might have eternal life.

Though He suffered for the repentant and the unrepentant alike, He makes it clear that only those who repent and come unto Him are eligible for exaltation: "For behold, I, God, have suffered these things for all, that they might not suffer if they would repent; But if they would not repent they must suffer even as I" (D&C 19:16–17).

His desire is that all of us *will* repent. He takes no satisfaction in excluding anyone from the full blessings of His Atonement. The kingdom of God is large enough to accommodate all who desire a residence therein. There will never be a No Vacancy sign posted, nor will the price of admission fluctuate. The only One who could truly afford the cost has already paid this *full* purchase price, and His gracious hospitality is extended to one and all who will repent and come unto Him.

1 Jn. 2:10

He that loveth his brother abideth in the light, and there is none occasion of stumbling in him.

We increase in righteousness as we increase in love for one another. And as we increase in love for one another, we increase in love for God and His Beloved Son.

The following poem by James Henry Leigh Hunt reminds us of the correlation between love of our fellowmen and love of God:

Abou Ben Adhem (may his tribe increase!) /Awoke one night from a deep dream of peace,

And saw, within the moonlight of his room, / Making it rich, and like a lily in bloom,

An angel writing in a book of gold:— / Exceeding peace made Ben Adhem bold,

And to the Presence in the room he said / "What writest thou?—The vision raised its head,

And with a look made of all sweet accord, /Answered, "The names of those who love the Lord."

"And is mine One?" said Abou. "Nay not so,' / Replied the angel. Abou spoke more low,

But cheerily still, and said, "I pray thee, then, / Write me as one that loves his fellow men."

The angel wrote, and vanished. The next night / It came again with a great wakening light,

And showed the names of those whom love of God had blessed,

And lo! Ben Adhem's name led all the rest.

1 Jn. 2:28

And now, little children, abide in him; that, when he shall appear, we may have confidence, and not be ashamed before him at his coming.

In what or whom can we safely place our confidence? The answer, of course, is straightforward and simple: "Trust in the LORD with all thine heart; and lean not unto thine own understanding. In all thy ways acknowledge him, and he shall direct thy paths" (Prov. 3:5–6).

An investment of confidence in the Lord yields high spiritual returns. Helaman tells us that "the Lord in his great infinite goodness doth bless and prosper those who put their trust in him" (Hel. 12:1). The Lord promises that "he who doeth the works of righteousness shall receive his reward, even *peace in this world*, and *eternal life in the world to come*" (D&C 59:23; emphasis added).

Trusting in the Lord with all our hearts means having confidence in His word and His works. We are cautioned to acknowledge the Lord as the source of *all* of our knowledge and avoid the pitfall of becoming overly self-confident in our own accomplishments, either secular or sacred.

As we increase our confidence in the Lord, He extends another gracious promise to us: our well-placed confidence in Him will earn us the right to stand (or kneel) in His presence without shame. "Then shall [our] confidence wax strong in the presence of God" (D&C 121:45).

1 Jn. 2:15, 17

Love not the world, neither the things that are in the world. If any man love the world, the love of the Father is not in him. . . . And the world passeth away, and the lust thereof: but he that doeth the will of God abideth for ever.

The world with all its bounteous goodness was created for our blessing and use: "The fulness of the earth is yours . . . . Yea, all things which come of the earth . . . are made for the benefit and the use of man" (D&C 59:16, 18). But the Lord warns us about the dangers of using the things of the world for unwise purposes that can estrange us from the love of God: "And it pleaseth God that he hath given all these things unto man; for unto this end were they made *to be used, with judgment, not to excess, neither by extortion*" (D&C 59:20; emphasis added).

"For what is a man advantaged, if he gain the whole world, and lose himself, or be cast away?" (Luke 9:25). We have only to look at the pride cycles in the Book of Mormon to remind ourselves of how this dangerous possibility becomes a reality, in our day as well as in theirs. Putting all our eggs in the basket of here and now is spiritually precarious, "for the fashion of this world passeth away" (1 Cor. 7:31), "but the word of the Lord endureth for ever" (1 Pet. 1:25).

1 Jn. 3:1

Behold, what manner of love the Father hath bestowed upon us, that we should be called the sons of God.

When Enoch saw the God of heaven weep because of His wayward children, he beheld firsthand the love of a tender, compassionate God, thus discounting any mistaken notions that He is a cold and dispassionate Deity. Enoch marveled that a God who was "holy, and from all eternity to all eternity" was not only just but also "merciful and kind forever," and Enoch was touched and humbled by the Lord's poignant reply: "Behold these thy brethren; they are the workmanship of mine own hands" (Moses 7:29–32). For all of God's children, the Savior would willingly lay down His life to offer them a way back to that God who gave them life.

Through the power of the Atonement, we are promised the gift of eternal life if we believe in Jesus Christ and *keep His commandments*, thereby accepting God's great gift of love to us. This manifestation of infinite love confirms the Savior's declaration that "the worth of souls is great in the sight of God" (D&C 18:10). By giving us the gift of His Only Begotten Son, God prepared the way whereby we could be welcomed back into His presence, where our heavenly Hosts await that glorious reunion, ready to enfold us in the arms of Their love.

1 Jn. 3:2–3

Beloved, now are we the sons of God, and it doth not yet appear what we shall be: but we know that, when he shall appear, we shall be like him; for we shall see him as he is. And every man that hath this hope in him purifieth himself, even as he is pure.

"Here John speaks of . . . a special love bestowed upon those who keep [God's] commandments and are adopted into his family as joint-heirs with his natural Son. Their reward is to be like Christ . . . and to reign in glory with the gods forever" (*DNTC*, Vol. III, 384).

The prophet Moroni exhorts us to "come unto Christ, and be perfected in him, and deny [ourselves] of all ungodliness" (Moro. 10:32). This means putting off the natural man or woman and putting ourselves in God's hands.

C. S. Lewis describes it this way: "The more we get what we call 'ourselves' out of the way and let Him take over, the more truly ourselves we become. . . . Give up yourself, and you will find your real self. Lose your life and you will save it. Submit to death, death of your ambitions and favorite wishes every day and death of your whole body in the end: submit with every fibre of your being, and you will find eternal life. Keep back nothing. . . . Look for yourself , and you will find only hatred, loneliness, despair, rage, ruin, and decay. But look for Christ and you will find Him, and with Him everything else thrown in" (*Mere Christianity*, 190, 191).

1 Jn. 3:8

For this purpose the Son of God was manifested, that he might destroy the works of the devil.

In all dispensations, there has been opposition to the Lord's work and purposes. The avowed purpose of Satan and his minions is to frustrate the work of the Lord—to "breathe out wrath and strifes against . . . the covenant people of the Lord who are of the house of Israel" (Morm. 8:21). They seek to destroy the work of the Lord so that He "will not remember his covenant which he hath made unto the house of Israel" (Ibid.).

Despite temporary victories in their unholy attempts to destroy and nullify God's purposes and His people, Satan and his hosts will ultimately prove wholly unsuccessful in their efforts. The Lord's purposes cannot be derailed, "for the eternal purposes of the Lord shall roll on, until all his promises shall be fulfilled" (Morm. 8:22).

The words *eternal* and *roll on* are particularly meaningful in this scripture. We are assured that God never changes His mind or His plans or His promises and that there is an impetus that cannot be stopped by *any* means or force and certainly not by Satan. God is most assuredly our "mighty fortress," "a tower of strength ne'er failing," who "overcometh all" ("A Mighty Fortress Is Our God," *Hymns*, no. 68).

1 Jn. 3:18

My little children, let us not love in word, neither in tongue; but in deed and in truth.

Nearing the end of His powerful and sacred Sermon on the Mount, the Savior spoke these words: "Not every one that saith unto me, Lord, Lord, shall enter into the kingdom of heaven; but he that doeth the will of my Father which is in heaven" (Matt. 7:21).

Is it possible that sometimes we say to the Lord, "I love you, but—please don't ask me to accept *that* calling, visit *that* family, or keep *that* particular commandment." The Savior is our perfect example of love in deed and in truth. He did not say, "I love you, but it would be too hard for me to die for you." Manifesting His greater love, He laid down His life for us, whom He calls His friends (see John 15:13).

If we love Him, we must ensure that our heart service matches our lip service: "Lip service alone does not save; it is not confessing that Jesus is the Lord . . . that opens heaven's door; belief without works has no saving power" (Bruce R. McConkie, *The Mortal Messiah*, 2:172). If we do not do His will, the Savior will "profess unto [us], I never knew you [because you never knew me]" (Matt. 7:23).

1 Jn. 4:8

He that loveth not knoweth not God, for God is love.

"God is the embodiment and personification of every good grace and godly attribute" (*DNTC*, Vol. III, 398). This cannot be said of anyone or anything else we might love. Surely then, it should be easy for us to love God. "We need God. We must have God in our lives if we are to survive. Our souls should seek after God's living word and his liberating love" (*Coming to Know Christ*, 10).

Unlike some forms of love, God's love can bear the closest scrutiny, and it weathers our worst storms. It is a love bestowed freely and benevolently; no one is excluded, nor is anyone ever dropped from God's list of who He loves in favor of someone else. "Remember the worth of souls is great in the sight of God" (D&C 18:10).

Jacob joyously invites us to "feast upon his love" (Jacob 3:2). "To feast upon the love of God is to partake freely of the powers of the Savior's atonement and the blessings of his gospel . . . to glory in the salvation which is his; and to eat of that bread of life and drink of those living waters which are the food and drink of saved beings" (*DCBM*, Vol. 2, 26).

1 Jn. 4:10

Herein is love, not that we loved God, but that he loved us,
and sent his Son to be the propitiation for our sins.

"For God so loved the world, that he gave his only begotten Son, that whosoever believeth in him should not perish, but have everlasting life" (John 3:16). This love is almost incomprehensible, but also undeniable. It is a love that reaches back into our premortal existence: "Yea, I have loved thee with an everlasting love" (Jer. 31:3). This everlasting love motivated God's grand plan of salvation, whereby all His children who kept their first estate were privileged to come to earth, exercise agency, and, through the merciful principle of repentance and the grace of His Son's atoning sacrifice, return to that God who gave us life because He loves us.

"On the whole, God's love for us is a much safer subject to think about than our love for Him. . . . But the great thing to remember is that, though our feelings come and go, His love for us does not. It is not wearied by our sins, or our indifference; and, therefore, it is quite relentless in its determination that we shall be cured of those sins, at whatever cost to us, at whatever cost to Him" (*Mere Christianity*, 117–118).

1 Jn. 4:19

We love him, because he first loved us.

A commandment, given thousands of years ago to a prophet, is an ensign for all times and all people: "Thou shalt love the LORD thy God with *all* thine heart, and with *all* thy soul, and with *all* thy might" (Deut. 6:5; emphasis added). The power of love is unparalleled in its ability to bring us closer to the Savior and our Heavenly Father, but only if other loves do not dilute that love.

If love of God is uppermost in our minds and hearts, there will be no room for any other gods. President Dieter F. Uchtdorf reinforces this concept through his wise insight that what we seek is determined by what we love, that what we think and do is determined by what we seek, and that who we become is determined by what we think and do (see "The Love of God," *Ensign*, Nov. 2009, 22).

As with any commandment, God our Father and His Only Begotten Son provide the perfect patterns. As President Uchtdorf so beautifully reminds us, Their love for us is constant and eternal and has its origins in our premortal existence; therefore, our inclination and ability to love Them is part of our spiritual genetics (Ibid.).

JST 1 Jn. 4:12

No man hath seen God at any time, except them who believe.

Many scriptural accounts testify of believers who have seen God. Among others, Adam and Eve walked and talked with God. Moses "saw God face to face" (Moses 1:2). Abraham also records that he "talked with the Lord, face to face" (Abr. 3:11). And the Lord showed Himself to the brother of Jared, whose faith is legendary.

In the Book of Mormon, we read of others who were privileged to see God. Nephi and his brother Jacob enjoyed that honor, and we rejoice with the repentant Lamanite king Lamoni regarding his fervent testimony: "For as sure as thou livest, behold, I have seen my Redeemer" (Alma 19:13).

In our own dispensation, Joseph Smith saw and spoke with God the Father and His Son Jesus Christ in the Sacred Grove.

In each instance, the faith of those who saw God was remarkable and was remarkably rewarded. To all of His faithful children, the Lord makes this promise, which will be fulfilled either in time or in eternity: "Verily, thus saith the Lord: It shall come to pass that every soul who forsaketh his sins and cometh unto me, and calleth on my name, and obeyeth my voice, and keepeth my commandments, shall see my face and know that I am" (D&C 93:1).

1 Jn. 4:18

There is no fear in love: but perfect love casteth out fear: because fear hath torment. He that feareth is not made perfect in love.

The Savior uttered these profoundly comforting words to one of the rulers of the synagogue, who had petitioned the Savior to heal his grievously ill daughter and who subsequently received word that this precious child had died before Jesus reached her: "Be not afraid, only believe" (Mark 5:36). These are words for every faithful Latter-day Saint to live by.

"Our Lord's message is one of love and joy and the hope of eternal life. Fear plays no part in it. There is no dread or disquiet in the souls of the saints; they are free from apprehension and anxiety with reference to the course of events in this world and their eternal destiny in the world to come" (*DNTC*, Vol. III, 400).

"For God hath not given us the spirit of fear; but of *power*, and of *love*, and of a *sound mind*" (2 Tim. 1:7; emphasis added). President Gordon B. Hinckley reminds us, "These principles are the great antidotes to the fears that rob us of our strength and sometimes knock us down to defeat. They give us power. What power? The power of the gospel, the power of truth, the power of faith, the power of the priesthood" (*TGBH*, 221).

1 Jn. 4:20

If a man say, I love God, and hateth his brother, he is a liar: for he that loveth not his brother whom he hath seen, how can he love God whom he hath not seen?

The family tree of mankind has its roots in eternal soil, and when pruned and nourished with love, it spreads its branches of brotherhood over the whole earth. When neglected, its branches droop and shrivel, clinging close to the self-serving trunk and producing none of the fertile fruit of Christ's commandment to love "as I have loved you" (see John 13:34, 15:12).

Concerning brotherly love, William James offers this insight: "Human beings are born into this little span of life of which the best thing is its friendships and intimacies . . . and yet they leave [them] without cultivation, to grow as they will by the roadside, expecting them to 'keep' by force of mere inertia."

These oft-quoted words echo the same sentiment:

No man is an island, entire of itself; / every man is a piece of the continent, / a part of the main; / . . . any man's death diminishes me, because / I am involved in mankind; / and therefore never send to know for whom the bell tolls; / it tolls for thee. (John Donne, from *"Devotions XVII," Treasury of Poems*, 221).

"Therefore, my son, see that you are merciful unto your brethren; deal justly, judge righteously, and do good continually; and if ye do all these things then shall ye receive your reward; yea, ye shall have mercy restored unto you again" (Alma 41:14).

2 Jn. 1:6

And this is love, that we walk after his commandments. This is the commandment, That, as ye have heard from the beginning, ye should walk in it.

John's use of the word *beginning* here has thought-provoking connotations as we recall the opening words of his gospel epistle: "In the *beginning* was the Word . . . and the Word was God" (John 1:1; emphasis added). Jesus often refers to Himself as Alpha, or the *beginning*: "I am Alpha . . . Christ the Lord" (D&C 19:1). So the message from the beginning— or the Beginning—is love: love for God, "Thou shalt love the Lord thy God" (Deut. 6:5); love for one another, "This is my commandment, That ye love one another, as I have loved you" (John 15:12); and love that motivates obedience, "If you love me, keep my commandments" (John 14:15).

As we walk after the Lord's commandments, His love for us is manifested both in mortality and immortality: "He who doeth the works of righteousness shall receive his reward, even peace in this world, and eternal life in the world to come" (D&C 59:23).

The lovely words of a favorite hymn embody this message:

> For thrones, dominions, kingdoms, pow'rs,
> And glory great and bliss are ours,
> If we, throughout eternity,
> Obey his words, "Come, follow me."
> ("Come, Follow Me," *Hymns*, no. 116).

2 Jn. 1:9

Whosoever transgresseth, and abideth not in the doctrine of Christ;
hath not God. He that abideth in the doctrine of Christ, he
hath both the Father and the Son.

If we are disobedient, we lose the blessings our Father and Savior have promised us. But if we are obedient, we will be privileged to enjoy an association with both the Father and the Son. Fellowship with the Father and the Son means an inheritance of celestial glory: "God has in reserve a time, or period appointed in His own bosom, when He will bring all His subjects, who have *obeyed His voice* and *kept His commandments*, into His celestial rest. This rest is of such perfection and glory, that man has need of a preparation before he can, according to the laws of that kingdom, enter it and enjoy its blessings. This being the fact, God has given certain laws to the human family, which, if observed, are sufficient to prepare them to inherit this rest" (*TPJS*, 54; emphasis added).

When we stop to think of the joy of inheriting such a glorious fellowship, it is no wonder the Prophet Joseph Smith stated that "happiness is the object and design of our existence; and will be the end thereof, if we pursue the path that leads to it; and this path is virtue, uprightness, faithfulness, holiness, and keeping all the commandments of God" (*TPJS*, 255–256).

1 Jn. 5:3

For this is the love of God, that we keep his commandments: and his commandments are not grievous.

We learn to love someone only when we come to know that person; love universally declared must become love individual and intimate. But it is far easier to say "I love everyone" than it is to particularize that love to specific individuals and really get to know them.

The same principle applies to our love of God. The Savior said, "And this is life eternal, that they might *know thee the only true God, and Jesus Christ*, whom thou hast sent" (John 17:3; emphasis added). God the Father and Jesus Christ are specific and individual Beings. As we come to know God and Jesus Christ, we learn that Their commandments are not burdens; they are the safe stepping stones to eternal life, integral parts of the plan of salvation. Our knowing the Father and the Son becomes love that motivates the willing submission of our hearts to them—the very essence of obedience and the means of our sanctification.

Helaman describes this process beautifully: "They did fast and pray oft, and did wax stronger and stronger in their humility, and firmer and firmer in the faith of Christ . . . even to the purifying and the sanctification of their hearts, which sanctification cometh *because of their yielding their hearts unto God*" (Helaman 3:35; emphasis added).

1 Jn. 5:14–15

And this is the confidence that we have in him, that, if we ask any thing according to his will, he heareth us: And if we know that he hear us, whatsoever we ask, we know that we have the petitions that we desired of him.

A close friend is someone with whom we can safely share the feelings of our hearts—our joys and sorrows and even our secrets. We are confident they will not betray our trust, and in most cases, our confidence is well placed. Sometimes, however, friendships falter, our trust is betrayed, and the feelings we privately shared are rejected and judged and even publicized.

Not so with God. Our confidence is *always* well placed when we approach Him in prayer with grateful, contrite hearts and appropriate, heartfelt petitions and confessions. The words of George Eliot describe the nature of such an intimate interchange: "Oh, the comfort, the inexpressible comfort of feeling safe with a person: having neither to weigh thoughts nor measure words, but to pour them out. Just as they are—chaff and grain together, knowing that a faithful hand will take and sift them, keep what is worth keeping, and then with the breath of kindness, blow the rest away."

God carefully considers our petitions, and according to our needs and His will—which is always in our best interest—"He will fulfill the desire of them that fear him: he also will hear their cry, and will save them" (Ps. 145:19).

JST 1 Jn. 5:18

We know that whosoever is born of God continueth not in sin; but he that is begotten of God and keepeth himself, that wicked one overcometh him not.

Herein lies the essence of true and honest repentance, and the promise of God's forgiveness. President Spencer W. Kimball gives the following insightful analogy: "When a physical body is filthy, the process of cleansing is a thorough bath, the brushing of teeth, the shampooing of hair, the cleaning of fingernails, and the donning of fresh, clean clothing. When a home is renovated, roofs are mended or replaced, walls washed or painted, floors swept and scrubbed, furniture repaired and dusted, curtains laundered and metals polished. When a defiled man is born again, his habits are changed, his thoughts cleansed, his attitudes regenerated and elevated, his activities put in total order, and everything about him that was dirty, degenerate or reprobate is washed and made clean" (*The Miracle of Forgiveness*, 352).

He then continues with these remarkable and reassuring words: "The effect of the cleansing is beautiful. These troubled souls have found peace. These soiled robes have been cleansed to spotlessness. These people formerly defiled, having been cleansed through their repentance—their washing, their purging, their whitening—are made worthy for constant temple service and to be found before the throne of God associating with divine royalty" (Ibid., 353).

1 Jn. 5:21

Little children, keep yourselves from idols.

These brief closing words from the First Epistle of the Apostle John, "whom Jesus loved" (see John 13:23), give us a glimpse into his exceptional personality and spirit. Little children are precious, and our hearts may immediately soften with warm feelings of love and tenderness when we think of them or are privileged to be in their presence. What a loving compliment, then, does this man of God pay us as he addresses us as such. Though his injunction is strong and to the point, he nevertheless demonstrates his kind and caring nature. After all, this is the gentle man to whom the Savior entrusted the care of His beloved mother.

John's love for Jesus Christ precludes any other loves that would encroach upon that sacred territory, and he exhorts rather than invites us to exhibit that same kind of fidelity. Notice that he does not say, "It would probably be wise if you . . . ." or "Maybe you should think about . . . ." This was a man who loved the Lord with all of his heart, might, mind, and strength and had no other gods before Him, and who found joy, peace, and safety in so doing. His motto of moderation and adoration is worthy of our emulation.

3 Jn. 1:4

I have no greater joy than to hear that my children walk in truth.

As parents, we share a sacred partnership with the Lord, a partnership in which we covenant to do all in our power to teach and guide our children in His ways.

"Children are like trees. When they are young, their lives can be shaped . . . usually with ever so little effort. Said the writer of Proverbs: 'Train up a child in the way he should go: and when he is old, he will not depart from it' (Prov. 22:6). That training finds its roots in the home" (*TGBH*, 421).

Immediate success is not always guaranteed. Sometimes we have to rely on that part of the proverb that says our children will return to what they have been taught when they are old. Again, President Hinckley counsels, "They may do, in the years that come, some things that you would not want them to do, but be patient, be patient. You have not failed as long as you have tried" (Ibid., 422). There are times when our very best efforts as parents may be far from perfect. But because the Lord loves us and *is* a perfect Parent, His Atonement will make all the difference.

3 Jn. 1:11

Beloved, follow not that which is evil, but that which is good. He that doeth good is of God: but he that doeth evil hath not seen God.

The sophisticated and subtle forces of evil are alive and well, both in and out of the Church. They are the wolves in sheep's clothing, and they sprinkle just enough morsels of truth (even of scripture, if necessary) into their facade of falsehoods to give us spiritual unsurity.

Moroni provides us with the sure formula for determining the difference between safe and counterfeit entrees: "And the way to judge is as plain, that ye may know with a perfect knowledge, as the *daylight* is from the *dark night*" (Moro. 7:15; emphasis added). What an inspired choice of words for Moroni's message, which reminds us that we are enlightened by the Spirit of Christ, whereas no such light emanates from Satan.

And here is the simple but foolproof test: "Every thing which inviteth to do good . . . is sent forth by the power and gift of Christ; *wherefore ye may know with a perfect knowledge it is of God.* But whatsoever thing persuadeth men to do evil . . . then *ye may know with a perfect knowledge it is of the devil* . . . for he persuadeth no man to do good, *no, not one*" (Ibid., 16–17; emphasis added).

Jude 1:6

And the angels which kept not their first estate, but left their own habitation, he hath reserved in everlasting chains under darkness unto the judgment of the great day.

Jude is the brother of James, the half-brother of Jesus. Both James and Jude identify themselves as servants of the Lord Jesus Christ, but "with an appropriate sense of reverential awe, neither claimed in their epistles to be brothers of the Lord" (*DNTC*, Vol. III, 416).

Jude is the only Bible writer who speaks of our premortal existence as *the first estate*—knowledge vital to understanding the plan of salvation. Abraham also expounds on this doctrine: "And they who keep their *second estate* shall have glory added upon their heads for ever and ever" (Abr. 3:26; emphasis added).

Regarding this doctrine, the Prophet Joseph Smith teaches us this: "At the first organization in heaven we were all present, and saw the Savior chosen and appointed and the plan of salvation made, and we sanctioned it. We came to this earth that we might have a body and present it pure before God in the celestial kingdom. The great principle of happiness consists in having a body. The devil has no body, and herein is his punishment" (*TPJS*, 181), which the Lord declares is eternal: "And now, behold, . . . never at any time have I declared . . . that they should return, for where I am they cannot come" (D&C 29:29).

Rev. 3:20

Behold, I stand at the door, and knock: if any man hear my voice, and open the door, I will come in to him, and will sup with him, and he with me.

It is imperative that we prepare carefully for when Christ visits. He stands ready at the door; however, the knob is on our side. Will we tentatively ask Him to come back a little later? Can He give us just a couple of days to put our house in order? Shall we tell Him our spiritual checks are in the mail? Or will we eagerly receive and accept His warm offer of shared hospitality? He tenderly entreats us to come unto Him: "Behold, he sendeth an invitation unto all men, for the arms of mercy are extended towards them, and he saith: Repent, and I will receive you" (Alma 5:33). All He requires of us in this sacred gesture of friendship is our obedience.

"Who among us will be safely encircled in [His] arms of love? Are there a chosen few reserved for this honor? Alma lets it be known that there is no exclusionary policy. . . . 'Behold, mine arm of mercy is extended towards you, and whosoever will come, him will I receive' (3 Ne. 9:14). Such an invitation was not for a brief moment alone, but for our entire probationary period" (*The Infinite Atonement*, 28).

Col. 2:2

That their hearts might be comforted, being knit together in love. . . .

When we examine closely a beautifully knit sweater, we may be impressed with the unity and symmetry of design and the brilliant blending of yarns. However, it takes just one little snag to start an unraveling process that ruins the overall effect and functionality. And so it is with contention; it can start out as a little snag, but if left unchecked, it soon works its way into our hearts and unravels our loving relationships. Then these become unsightly adornments for our spiritual wardrobes.

Satan is clever as he sows his seeds of contention, which thwart our personal progress in the gospel of Jesus Christ. He carefully tailors his dastardly darts to prey upon our personal weaknesses, and he delights in using something as petty as an offhanded remark to encourage us to take offense. And he positively gloats over heated doctrinal disputes: "Disputation and anger, even in the noblest of causes, is displeasing to the Lord, cuts us off from the Spirit of the Lord, and undermines the very purposes we are seeking to fulfill" (*DCBM*, Vol. 4, 58).

May we reject the myopic view of others' failings and choose instead the perfect knitting together of hearts that leads us to love one another.

Rev. 3:15–16

I know thy works, that thou art neither cold nor hot. . . . So then because thou art lukewarm, and neither cold nor hot, I will spue thee out of my mouth.

There is nothing more disagreeable or disappointing than anticipating either a cold or hot drink and finding with the first sip that it is simply tepid. According to this scripture, it is equally disappointing to the Lord when our spiritual efforts and attitudes are just lukewarm. The Prophet Joseph Smith called this *a sleeping Christianity*, a condition we must avoid "to enjoy the smiles of our Savior in these last days" (*TPJS*, 14). We need to be vigilant against the deadly disease of spiritual indifference.

Elder M. Russell Ballard cautions us that we may need to give ourselves a spiritual shake to be proactive in our commitment to the Lord and intensely dedicated in our service to Him (see "How Is it with Us?" *Ensign*, May 2000).

It is not enough to be a card-carrying member of The Church of Jesus Christ of Latter-day Saints; we must be vigilant about which aspects of our efforts we need to renew and which areas of our commitment need to be reviewed. We need to be up and doing—eagerly enrolling in refresher courses that keep us current in our eligibility for membership in God's kingdom.

Rev 5:11–12

I beheld, and I heard the voice of many angels round . . . and the number of them was ten thousand times ten thousand, . . . Saying with a loud voice, Worthy is the Lamb that was slain to receive power, and riches, and wisdom, and strength, and honour, and glory, and blessing.

What glorious imagery is found in these verses as we envision the majesty of this hymn of praise—sung by millions of grateful souls—to Jesus Christ, the Author and Finisher of our salvation.

"These verses are deeply profound. They make the grand announcement that . . . finite and erring souls, may, through accepting the gospel of Jesus Christ by covenant and ordinance, and through spiritual transformation and dedicated discipleship, receive the highest honor and glory and title that one can receive within the holy priesthood of God. Having obtained the fulness of the blessings of the priesthood (which certainly would include the covenants and ordinances of the temple)" (Robert L. Millet, *Making Sense of the Book of Revelation* [Salt Lake City: Deseret Book, 2011], 24).

The words of a familiar hymn come to mind:

Glory to God on high! / Let heav'n and earth reply. / Praise ye his name. / His love and grace adore, / Who all our sorrows bore. / Sing aloud evermore: / Worthy the Lamb! . . . / Let all the hosts above / Join in one song of love, / Praising his name. / To him ascribed be / Honor and majesty / Thru all eternity: / Worthy the Lamb! ("Glory to God on High," *Hymns*, no. 67)

Rev. 6:9

And when he had opened the fifth seal, I saw under the altar the souls of them that were slain for the word of God, and for the testimony which they held.

"In the gospel sense, martyrdom is the voluntary acceptance of death at the hands of wicked men rather than to forsake Christ and his holy gospel. It is the supreme earthly sacrifice in which man certifies to his absolute faith and to the desires for righteousness and for eternal life which are in his heart. Martyrs of religion are found in every age in which there have been both righteous and wicked people on the earth. Christ himself was a martyr who voluntarily laid down his life" (*DNTC*, Vol. III, 483).

The list of martyrs both ancient and modern is impressive, sacred, and solemn. It includes Abinadi, many of the Savior's original Twelve, Stephen, and Paul. It also includes the Prophet Joseph Smith and his brother Hyrum, of whom Elder John Taylor wrote this powerful and poignant tribute: "Their *innocent blood*, with the innocent blood of all the martyrs under the altar that John saw, will cry unto the Lord of Hosts till he avenges that blood on the earth" (D&C 135:7).

The Savior Himself pays high tribute to the martyrdom of Joseph Smith: "It was needful that he should seal his testimony with his blood, that he might be honored and the wicked might be condemned" (D&C 136:39).

Rev. 22:14

Blessed are they that do his commandments, that they may have right to the tree of life, and may enter in through the gates into the city.

When we buy an appliance or a vehicle, it usually comes with a warranty that guarantees remuneration, replacement, or repairs if that merchandise fails to operate as promised. However, this guarantee is null and void if we neglect or abuse the terms of the warranty. And so it is with the warranty the Savior gives to each of us. "I, the Lord, am bound when ye do what I say; but when ye do not what I say, ye have no promise" (D&C 82:10).

The tree of life is the "love of God, which sheddeth itself abroad in the hearts of the children of men" (1 Ne. 11:22) and which manifested itself in Christ's Atonement. Our right to this tree depends on our willingness to keep God's commandments (and not just those closest to our comfort zones). The fruit of the tree is "most precious and most desirable . . . and it is the greatest of all the gifts of God" (1 Ne. 15:36), which gift is eternal life (see D&C 14:7).

"We believe that through the Atonement of Christ, *all mankind may be saved, by obedience* to the laws and ordinances of the Gospel" (A of F 1:3). This is a glorious promise and an infallible warranty!

Rev. 7:9–10

I beheld, and, lo, a great multitude . . . of all nations, and kindreds, and people, and tongues, stood before the throne, and before the Lamb, clothed with white robes, and palms in their hands; And cried with a loud voice, saying, Salvation to our God which sitteth upon the throne, and unto the Lamb.

The depiction of Jesus's triumphal entry into Jerusalem just days prior to His Crucifixion is triumphant: "On the next day much people that were come to the feast, when they heard that Jesus was coming to Jerusalem, Took branches of palm trees, and went forth to meet him, and cried, Hosanna: Blessed is the King of Israel that cometh in the name of the Lord" (John 12:12–13).

It is marvelous to visualize this scene of joyous and unrestrained worship as Christ's faithful followers, waving aloft their symbols of joy and triumph, acknowledged His status as their Lord and spiritual King, whose throne at that moment was a young donkey. They had no comprehension of what was to follow—or its eternal significance—in the few remaining fateful days of Jesus's mortal ministry.

By contrast, picture the vision unfolded to John as he beheld a vast, diverse multitude waving those same symbolic palms of triumph and praising God and the Savior upon Their most royal and eternal thrones. It is a vision that testifies of the Savior's victorious completion of His mission of mercy and of His status as the Lamb of God and the Savior of *all mankind*.

Rev. 7:13–15

What are these which are arrayed in white robes? . . . These are they which came out of great tribulation, and have washed their robes, and made them white in the blood of the Lamb. Therefore are they before the throne of God, and serve him day and night in his temple.

These people had been less than perfect, whose robes had become soiled through sin and weakness but who had become clean and pure through sincere and complete repentance and the blood of the Savior's Atonement. The fact that they are worthy to be in God's presence and serve in His temple indicates their purity of heart, a complete abandonment of sin to the point where sin has become abhorrent.

Alma speaks of just such a condition: "Therefore . . . their garments were washed white through the blood of the Lamb. Now they . . . being pure and spotless before God, could not look upon sin save it were with abhorrence; and there were many . . . who were made pure and entered into the rest of the Lord their God" (Alma 13:11–12). This is a comforting and encouraging doctrine, as is the doctrine that we too can become pure in heart and perfected, which is taught in John's vision of the righteous: "Verily, thus saith the Lord: It shall come to pass that every soul who forsaketh his sins and cometh unto me, and calleth on my name, and obeyeth my voice, and keepeth my commandments, shall see my face and know that I am" (D&C 93:1).

Rev. 12:7–9

There was war in heaven: Michael and his angels fought against the dragon; and the dragon fought and his angels, And prevailed not. . . . The great dragon was cast out, that old serpent, called the Devil, and Satan, which deceiveth the whole world: he was cast out into the earth.

In the war in heaven, that premortal showdown between good and evil, Satan came before God, "saying—Behold, here am I, send me, I will be thy son, and I will redeem all mankind, that *one soul shall not be lost*, and surely I will do it; wherefore, *give me thine* honor" (Moses 4:1; emphasis added). And like every forgery, this phony offer was detected for just what it was—a self-serving grab for personal glory.

Jesus responded with a proposal that exposed Satan's insidious counterfeit offer: "Father, thy will be done, and the glory be thine forever" (Ibid., v. 2). It all boiled down to this: "Jesus said there would be certain souls that would not be saved; and the devil said he could save them all, and laid his plans before the grand council, who gave their vote in favor of Jesus Christ" (*TPJS*, 357). Sadly, a third part of our spirit brothers and sisters bought into Satan's cheap, shabby deal, "and they were thrust down, and thus came the devil and his angels" (D&C 29:37).

We are here *now*, so we know where we stood *then*, and we must *never* let down our guard or reject our Savior as we anticipate a glorious *hereafter*.

Rev. 14:6

And I saw another angel fly in the midst of heaven, having the everlasting gospel to preach unto them that dwell on the earth, and to every nation, and kindred, and tongue, and people.

When angels fly in the midst of heaven, mankind can always expect the advent of wondrous events. Angels and their good tidings are a matter of scriptural record. Consider the angel who guided Nephi through his wondrous vision in which he saw the Virgin Mary and her baby (see 1 Ne. 11–14); the angel Gabriel, who visited Mary to announce her impending motherhood and who visited Joseph to reassure him of Mary's pure and sacred mission (see Luke 1:26–27; Matt. 1:20); and the angels who hovered over shepherds' fields and brought good tidings of great joy, not just to those humble shepherds but to all people (see Luke 2:9–10), as they announced the birth of the Savior of the world.

In Revelation 14:6, the angel referred to is Moroni "as well as every heavenly visitor with a message or authority, every Elias, a *composite angel*, who came to restore the ancient order of things. It is Moroni, Michael, Peter, James, John, John the Baptist, Gabriel, Raphael, Moses, Elias, Elijah, and all others with important keys and instructions reserved for the dispensation of the fulness of times" (*Making Sense of the Book of Revelation*, 45). And once again, just as in Bethlehem, the mission and message of these angels is of eternal significance for *all people.*

Rev. 21:6

And he said unto me, It is done. I am Alpha and Omega, the beginning and the end. I will give unto him that is athirst of the fountain of the water of life freely.

Scripturally, water is used to symbolize Christ's saving grace, and He urges us to freely partake. His water is spiritually satisfying, with the miraculous generating power of eternal life: "Whosoever drinketh of the water that I shall give him shall never thirst; but the water that I shall give him shall be in him a well of water springing up into everlasting life" (John 4:14).

His water is plentiful and available to everyone; no one will be denied: "If any man thirst, let him come unto me, and drink" (John 7:37).

His water is cleansing: "Then will I sprinkle clean water upon you, and ye shall be clean: from all your filthiness . . . will I cleanse you" (Ezek. 36:25).

His water is refreshing: "And the Lord shall . . . satisfy thy soul in drought . . . and thou shalt be like a watered garden, and like a spring of water, whose waters fail not" (Isa. 58:11).

His water is the well of salvation: "Therefore with joy shall ye draw water out of the wells of salvation" (Isa. 12:3).

His water is peaceful and restorative: "He leadeth me beside the still waters. He restoreth my soul" (Ps. 23:2–3).

Who can possibly resist His gracious, eternally thirst-quenching invitation?

Rev. 19:8

And to her was granted that she should be arrayed in fine linen, clean and white: for the fine linen is the righteousness of saints.

From ancient times until the present, the phrase "robes of righteousness" has been symbolically equated with the personal righteousness of Saints. Isaiah speaks of the rejoicing of the righteous as they don such robes: "I will greatly rejoice in the LORD, my soul shall be joyful in my God; for he hath clothed me with the garments of salvation, he hath covered me with the robe of righteousness" (Isa. 61:10).

In this same spirit, Nephi speaks of the joy of those who keep the Lord's commandments: "And the righteous shall have a perfect knowledge of their . . . righteousness, being clothed with purity, yea, even with the robe of righteousness" (2 Ne. 9:14).

Alma provides the key to understanding how our robes become clean, righteous, white, and pure: "For there can no man be saved except his garments are washed white . . . through the blood of him of whom it has been spoken by our fathers, who should come to redeem his people from their sins" (Alma 5:21).

All righteousness is inextricably linked to the Savior's great atoning sacrifice; it is through His merits that our robes of righteousness are purchased. As we repent and come unto Him, the Savior graciously presents us with our gowns of eternal life.

Rev. 21:4

And God shall wipe away all tears from their eyes; and there shall be no more death, neither sorrow, nor crying, neither shall there be any more pain: for the former things are passed away.

The Savior's healing power is infinite and complete, and His compassion for all of us who suffer or sorrow in any way is incomparable. One person's source of sorrow is not necessarily like any others', but it is real and personal, and the Lord has intimately known and felt it. In those agonizing and pain-filled hours in Gethsemane, He knew and experienced *every* sin and sadness *all* of His children would feel.

During His earthly ministry, both in the Old World and in the New, the Savior healed and comforted those who were crippled in body, mind, and spirit. That healing and comforting power is available to all who will reach out to Him: "Mourners who believe the gospel and who gain an understanding of the part grief, sorrow, and death play in this mortal probation, shall—in this life and through that knowledge—gain comfort and peace from the Spirit; then, eventually, perfect comfort shall be theirs in that glorious day [a millennial day] when 'God shall wipe away all tears.' (Rev. 7:17)" (*DNTC*, Vol. I, 215).

Rev. 7:2–3

And I saw another angel ascending from the east, having the seal of the living God: and he cried with a loud voice to the four angels, to whom it was given to hurt the earth and the sea, Saying, Hurt not the earth, neither the sea, nor the trees, till we have sealed the servants of our God in their foreheads.

The Prophet Joseph Smith explains the blessings of this sealing power: "When a seal is put upon the father and the mother, it secures their posterity, so that they cannot be lost, but will be saved by virtue of the covenant of their father and mother" (*TPJS*, 321).

Elder Orson F. Whitney explains, "The Prophet Joseph Smith declared—and he never taught a more comforting doctrine—that the eternal sealings of faithful parents and the divine promises made to them . . . would save not only themselves, but likewise their posterity. Though some of the sheep may wander, the eye of the Shepherd is upon them, and sooner or later they will feel the tentacles of Divine Providence . . . drawing them back to the fold. Either in this life or in the life to come, they will return. They will have to . . . suffer for their sins; and they may tread a thorny path; but if it leads them at last . . . to a loving and forgiving father's heart and home, the painful experience will not have been in vain. Pray for your careless and disobedient children; hold on to them with your faith. Hope on, trust on, till you see the salvation of God" (*Conference Report*, April 1929, 110).

Rev. 7:12

Blessing, and glory, and wisdom, and thanksgiving, and honour, and power, and might, be unto our God for ever and ever. Amen.

These words of loving and poetic praise bring to mind Ammon's unrestrained praise for the tender mercies of the Almighty: "Blessed be the name of our God; let us sing to his praise, yea, let us give thanks to his holy name, for he doth work righteousness forever. . . . [B]ehold, my joy is full, yea, my heart is brim with joy, and I will rejoice in my God" (Alma 26: 8, 11).

Do we find reasons to rejoice in our God? Do we weep with gratitude as we contemplate the priceless gift of the Atonement? Do we pause to gaze in wonder at the beauties of His creations? Do we feel a fullness of joy as we search, ponder, and pray over the scriptures? Do our hearts brim with joy as we count and name our blessings? Do we long to sing God's praises?

> The shepherds sing; and shall I silent be?
> My God, no hymn for thee?
> My soul's a shepherd too; a flock it feeds
> Of thoughts, and words, and deeds.
> The pasture is Thy Word; the streams, Thy Grace
> Enriching all the place
> Shepherd and flock shall sing,
> And all my powers
> Out-sing the daylight hours.
> (George Herbert, 1593–1633)

Rev. 22:17

And the Spirit and the bride say, Come. And let him that heareth say, Come. And let him that is athirst come. And whosoever will, let him take the water of life freely.

This imagery is familiar as we recall the Savior's declarations that He is the bread and water of life—even eternal life. His invitation is universal: "Behold, he sendeth an invitation unto *all* men, for the arms of mercy are extended towards them, and he saith: Repent, and I will receive you. Yea, he saith: Come unto me and . . . ye shall eat and drink of the bread and the waters of life freely" (Alma 5:33–34; emphasis added).

He stands with open arms, ready to receive all who will repent. Elder Tad R. Callister writes that the Savior's invitation is all-inclusive, and it is not a one-time offer. The Savior waits with open arms to encircle all of His children for all of our lives: "Behold, mine arm of mercy is extended towards you, and whosoever will come, him will I receive" (3 Ne. 9:14; see *The Infinite Atonement*, 28).

Regarding the Lord's invitation to come unto Him, Elder Jeffrey R. Holland assures us that God's divine embrace is available to all who seek it. No matter what adversities we may experience, His Atonement guarantees us safety and peace (see *Trusting Jesus* [Salt Lake City: Deseret Book, 2001], 66).

John 6:67–69

Then said Jesus unto the twelve, Will ye also go away? Then Simon Peter answered him, Lord, to whom shall we go? thou hast the words of eternal life. And we believe and are sure that thou art that Christ, the Son of the living God.

When we look back at the Savior's earthly ministry, we may marvel that so few understood His message or believed that He was the Son of God. True, many lives were changed, but there were also those who listened and followed for a time, but when the doctrine hit too uncomfortably close to home or when the price for betrayal far outweighed fidelity and friendship, they turned aside to alternate paths and did not embrace the full and abundant life the Savior offers.

Does the Savior change *our* whole life? Is our way of life and our code of conduct a witness that we are His friends and faithful followers "at all times and in all places" (Mosiah 18:9)? When we feel the sting of adversity, do we turn our backs on Him, feeling abandoned and forgotten? When His commandments interfere or conflict with our desires or seem uncomfortably prescriptive, do we walk no more with Him?

The Savior's poignant question to the Twelve "Will ye also go away?" is one we might well ask ourselves. May our response be as firm and positive as Peter's, and may our every action stand as a witness of His divinity and our gratitude for His saving grace.